Empowering Black Boys
to Challenge Rape Culture

Empowering Black Boys to Challenge Rape Culture

GORDON BRAXTON

OXFORD
UNIVERSITY PRESS

Oxford University Press is a department of the University of Oxford. It furthers the University's objective of excellence in research, scholarship, and education by publishing worldwide. Oxford is a registered trade mark of Oxford University Press in the UK and certain other countries.

Published in the United States of America by Oxford University Press
198 Madison Avenue, New York, NY 10016, United States of America.

Library of Congress Cataloging-in-Publication Data
Names: Braxton, Gordon, author.
Title: Empowering Black boys to challenge rape culture / Gordon Braxton.
Description: New York, NY : Oxford University Press, [2022] |
Includes bibliographical references and index.
Identifiers: LCCN 2021033807 (print) | LCCN 2021033808 (ebook) |
ISBN 9780197571675 (hardback) | ISBN 9780197571699 (epub) |
ISBN 9780197571705 (online)
Subjects: LCSH: Sexual ethics—United States. | African American
young men—Sexual behavior. | Sexual abuse victims—United States. |
African American women—Violence against.
Classification: LCC HQ32 .B73 2022 (print) | LCC HQ32 (ebook) |
DDC 305.242/108996073—dc23
LC record available at https://lccn.loc.gov/2021033807
LC ebook record available at https://lccn.loc.gov/2021033808

DOI: 10.1093/oso/9780197571675.001.0001

9 8 7 6 5 4 3 2 1

Printed by LSC communications, United States of America

CONTENTS

ACKNOWLEDGMENTS

To the long list of women who invested in me and inspired me to write this book. It includes but is by no means limited to Katie Koestner, Susan Marine, Lori Robinson, Tonya Prince, Sarah Rankin, Claire Kaplan, Salamishah Tillet, and Heather Wilson Henderson.

To Bob Franklin, Brad Perry, Ben Atherton-Zeman, Rus Ervin Funk, Craig Norberg-Bohm, Chad Waxman, Jody Plauche, Men Can Stop Rape, and all of the men challenging sexual violence who reminded me that I was not alone.

To Taressa Stovall, Latoya Smith, and Dana Bliss for believing in my project and showing me how to turn a dream into a reality.

To John Foubert and the men of One in Four for starting me on the path. Continue to go forth and make a difference.

The lives of the boys who you know will almost certainly be touched by sexual violence. Boys may come to know this violence as they respond to a daughter, friend, sister, or spouse who has survived it. They may come to know it as they interact with other boys and men who have perpetrated it. They will likely come to know it as the media and their colleagues pass on lessons about it. They may even come to survive it or perpetrate it themselves. So why do we not talk to them about sexual violence when they will surely see its influence as they look back on their journeys into manhood?

Whether we are unequipped, afraid, or unaware of the urgency of the problem, we spend little to no time empowering boys to raise their voices against sexual violence. That leaves them in the hands of a world that minimizes and normalizes it. I did not learn to raise my voice until concerned teachers pulled me aside and asked me to help. You too can extend an invitation to the boys in your life. In a better world, they will know the following:

1. They will recognize that they personally know survivors of sexual violence even though these survivors may not disclose themselves.
2. They will learn that how they react to these survivors could have a huge impact on their well-being.
3. They will recognize that they also know perpetrators. Violent men are rarely masked outcasts, and how boys react to them

may go a long way in determining how these men perceive their actions.

4. They will understand that ensuring that they do not perpetuate violence themselves requires more than just understanding that "no means no."

5. They will accept that not being personally violent does not excuse them from caring about a brand of violence that affects hundreds of thousands.

6. They will recognize that they are free to break from the "manly" choices preselected for them. For starters, they will know that it is acceptable to be upset by violence even though society does not always give boys and men permission to admit this.

7. They will see that breaking from traditional expectations of men can bring its own rewards.

8. They will realize that others may come to stand with them when they decide to stand against violence. When they do, they will be joining a global community of concerned women and men who seek to eradicate sexual violence.

9. They will see that there are many ways that they can use their voices to help. To name a few, they can interrupt comments and attitudes that diminish the seriousness of sexual violence, treat survivors with dignity, develop strategies for ensuring consent in their own lives, and challenge their peers to do the same.

10. They will understand that it may take time and practice to become effective at sharing their voices.

11. They will believe that rape and sexual assault do not have to exist and that boys and men can play a critical role in ending them.

I once presented to the senior class of a prestigious all-boys school in New York City. I was talking to them about how we could prevent sexual assault, and one young man in the back of the room stood up and exclaimed how it was pointless for men to discuss such things since it all boiled down to women choosing to be responsible. I geared up to push back because I believed that men and boys have a role to play in preventing violence but settled down after seeing one of the young man's peers respond. He raised his hand rather tentatively but was far from bashful once I gave him the floor. He told the audience about how he had a friend who had experienced a terrible assault and how he wished that he could have done more to help her. His peers followed his lead and a steady stream of young men rose to voice how they could help. The direction of the conversation changed entirely because one young man had the courage to speak up. Even the student who initially sparked the conversation with his comment about women needing to take responsibility walked up to me after the program and told me that he had spoken clumsily. He wanted to help. If we get past the stereotypes of young men and give them a space to speak, we might be surprised at the leadership potential waiting to be channeled.

I am so thankful that somebody once asked me to help. That invitation changed the course of my life in ways that I am still learning.

I do not think that there is too much that stands out about me were you to pass me on the street. Get to know me and you will find out that I was raised in Virginia and have lived in the Philadelphia, Boston, Los Angeles, and Washington, D.C., areas since graduating from college. My mother very much wanted a little girl but instead ended up with three knucklehead boys, of which I am the oldest.

But ask me how I spend my time and things will start to get interesting. I have spent the last two decades of my life speaking about sexual violence prevention in some fashion or another. It started when I was introduced to the field as an undergraduate student, found that I had a passion for it, and made it a personal mission to speak up. Following college, I accepted an invitation from a prominent speaker on survivor advocacy. She was looking for a man of color to accompany her on a speaking tour of public schools. I joined her and went on to speak to secondary schools, colleges, military units, and community-based organizations. From there, I became a prevention specialist at Harvard University, where I was able to address sexual violence from a student affairs perspective. At the same time, I worked alongside statewide and national coalitions, which allowed me to better understand the effects of public policy on the perpetration of violence. Throughout it all, I had the great opportunity to hear from thousands of young men. I have a more conventional office job these days but still regularly find myself in conversation with coworkers and acquaintances regarding some aspect of sexual violence in the news or in somebody's personal life.

I was not always this concerned about sexual violence and would have found this topic to be off limits 20 years ago. Sexual violence was not something that I thought about, and it certainly was not something to be discussed. Even though I was blessed to have many adults in my life who cared about me, I cannot recall a single adult saying anything meaningful to me about sexual violence before I entered college. Our culture does not consider talking to boys about rape to be a vital life lesson. Any education I did receive on the subject came from conversations in the school cafeteria, references in pop culture, and news media discussing the alleged actions of celebrities and politicians.

I am not alone in this. Many boys will mature well into adulthood without having a constructive conversation about the presence of rape and sexual assault in the world. This does not mean that they do not want to talk. In my experience, boys always have something to say and questions to ask when given the chance to share. They are waiting for an opportunity to unleash their fears, flesh out their viewpoints, and confront their anxieties about the violence that they know exists in the world and the policies surrounding it. They recognize that sexual violence is relevant to their lives, but so few adults ever take the time to give them a space to process complicated concepts and develop their values. We avoid this responsibility because we might see sexual violence as rare—as something that is relegated to the nightly news and does not warrant any further discussion. Others of us are well aware of the scope of sexual violence but do not realize that there is anything to be done about it. And still others know that there is work to be done but are unprepared to have tough conversations with boys.

We must recognize sexual violence as preventable behavior that a rising generation of boys can play a role in eliminating. Talking to girls about how to avoid violent men comes to us naturally enough, but history has clearly shown that placing the burden of prevention solely on them is inadequate. A more holistic approach involving the other half of the global population is needed to combat violence on a cultural scale.

Sending unprepared boys into the world is not an option. We live in a nation where many boys will come to know victims, will know others who victimize, will be victimized themselves, or will knowingly or unknowingly commit acts of violence of their own. Few caretakers of boys want to think of their children as belonging to any of these groups, but the numbers guarantee that most boys will find themselves in at least one of them as they mature into adults. The Centers for Disease Control and Prevention estimates that 18.3% of women and 1.4% of men in the United States experience an attempted rape or a completed rape in their lifetimes.[1] And there are plenty of sources with higher estimates. We leave boys on their own to face this reality. No wonder many are baffled when faced with helping a survivor who confides in them or confronting a friend who brags about taking advantage of someone sexually.

As a result of our inattention to them, most boys grow into men with understandings of rape that are so insufficient that they unknowingly pose a danger to themselves and others. They blindly accept the ideals of masculinity that are pushed on them, only to end up behaving, thinking, and speaking in ways that harm themselves and others. This can all take place without any ill intentions or conscious realization of what is going on.

No boy is immune from sexual violence touching his life. Even should he beat the odds and go through life without the companionship of someone who has survived or perpetrated sexual violence, he will still interact daily with a culture that produces and normalizes copious amounts of violence. *How serious is sexual violence? How should we treat those who survive it? How should we treat those accused of perpetrating it? How should we respond to those who we know to have perpetrated it? Can it be prevented, and how?* We daily cast our votes on these questions in the jokes that we tell privately, the conversations that we have at the water cooler, and the media that we choose to consume. Children and young adults are no different. If anything, they face unique challenges as they come of age in an increasingly hypersexual environment where evolving technologies are testing the boundaries of privacy and personal space. Peers, music, movies, social media, and pornography have countless things to tell youth about sex and the violence that arises in its context. Boys need to be taught that they are capable of talking back.

This book will give you some perspective so that you are better prepared to initiate and navigate essential conversations to prepare boys for a violent world. I have spent the better part of the last two decades doing just that. I share my observations and thoughts with you in hopes that you will find the confidence to connect with the boys in your lives. The majority of this book is organized around key ideas that boys should learn. They are the lessons that I wish someone had shared with me when I was growing up. I have distilled useable tips where possible. Some are derived from research literature, some from my experience, and others directly from the mouths of boys.

Chapter highlights are provided in order to remind readers of key takeaways. I also utilize additional appendices in order to provide further resources for those who desire backup for conversations with boys. Those resources include websites, other books, and some points of discussion that you may want in your back pocket.

Some chapters are also accompanied by brief interviews that I conducted with veterans of necessary conversations with boys and men in order to provide perspective beyond my own. They are reminders that you are not alone. There is a global community working to end sexual violence that will someday hopefully include the boys who you know.

I submit all of this with a particular audience in mind—the caretakers of, and most often the mothers of, Black boys. This has been the audience that has reacted the most passionately upon learning about my efforts to educate young men about sexual violence. I have met mothers struggling to understand their sons as sexual beings, and parents searching for resources to assist their sons in an ongoing war against youth cultures that promote disrespecting others, and women in particular. But I encourage fathers and male educators to step up as well—to lead by example and to expand their own ways of thinking alongside their boys.

I target Black boys not because I buy into myths that they are particularly violent or predatory, but because I feel an urgency to expand the limited resources for boys and men of color. I distinctly remember being a young initiate into antiviolence work and struggling to find the voices of other men who looked like me. I want to explicitly tackle the unique fears that Black boys share. Focusing on them is also in line with the wishes expressed to me by many of the parents, mentors, and caretakers who encouraged me to write this book. Many of them stated that the racial identifications of their children (either their self-identifications or the identifications that society imposed on them) were central to their understanding of how to prepare these children for the world. I am still confident that aspects of this book will relate to those who care for boys of all races, since American boys tend to be subjected to some recurring pressures regardless of their background.

I have admittedly found the focus on Black boys to be a daunting challenge because Black communities are by no means homogenous. Boys who self-identify as Black do not have universal experiences and values.

Understand that everything in this book may not pertain to the young men who you have in mind, but I do hope that you can find some materials that reflect the young men who you know.

I want to highlight another admitted gap in my coverage. I have largely focused on heteronormative youth experiences. I have relied on my own perspectives as a heterosexual male, and the majority of my educational work has been with boys who identify as the same. I hope that others continue to expand the diversity in antiviolence literature just as I am trying to do and speak to boys who may see their experiences as materially different from the cisgender and heterosexual perspectives that dominate this book.

Lastly, I disclose that I am not a child development expert or a child psychologist. I am not even a parent as of this writing. I am an antiviolence educator; but, at the end of the day, I am just a guy who thinks that we can do better. Think of me as an embedded reporter, broadcasting from the front lines of a conflict for the hearts and minds of America's boys.

The narrative that follows is ultimately a commentary about the state of manhood in our culture, and I submit it for anybody who might get something out of it. If you are invested in raising boys who are equipped to navigate a world where sexual assault is rampant but overlooked, then this book is for you. It covers issues that extend to every imaginable community of men. Every person who makes a conscious effort to oppose sexual violence, regardless of race, gender, sexual orientation, or any other demographic factor, makes a choice to step outside of the norms of a culture that makes it far easier to ignore and excuse violence. I submit this contribution as one further reminder that it is not you who has lost your moral compass, but the world. I write so that the voices carrying this reminder will be more numerous and more diverse. If our voices continue to grow and diversify, one day we will find that we no longer stand against a culture. One day we could be the ones controlling it. One thing is for certain: If that kind of social revolution is going to become a reality, it is going to require a generation of boys who are strong enough to share their voices.

Recognizing a Public Health Crisis

In my senior year of college, some like-minded men and I went on a tour of the southeastern United States during our spring break. We visited several institutions in order to teach audiences how men can help sexual assault survivors who disclose victimization to them—a message in service of a broader mission to reduce the troubling rates of sexual violence on our campus and elsewhere. Our first stop was a university in the Atlanta area, where we met with some of the school's faculty and staff.

The audience thanked us after we presented, gave us some feedback, and discussed what it might take to get a similar group of undergraduate men working against sexual violence on their own campus. As we made our way out of the room, a woman whom I figured to be African American pulled me aside while my co-presenters headed off to figure out how to spend the rest of our afternoon. She disclosed that she had survived a horrific rape—the details of which no decent person could possibly defend. She then mentioned that there had been no criminal conviction for the incident. I was shocked. She had described an experience that no competent jury would possibly excuse but told me that she had never even pressed charges.

From what limited training I had on victim advocacy at the time, I knew it was common for survivors of rape to avoid criminal adjudication. I also knew that there were certain lines of questioning that one should generally avoid when listening to someone disclose victimization, such as prying questions that might imply judgment on a victim's decisions. The words that came out of my mouth in response were ill formed, and I regretted them as soon as they came out. They simply reflected the first thing that came to my mind after hearing of the actions of a criminally violent man who was presumably still going about his business. I asked, "Why didn't you press charges?"

She produced another shock with her answer. She said, "I never pressed charges because I wanted to protect you." This woman had been a complete stranger to me only an hour earlier. I frantically searched my memory in order to place how she knew me. My confusion must have been apparent. She clarified her statement without any prompting on my part and said, "I didn't press charges because I couldn't bear to see another Black man in jail."

It was the first, but definitely not the last, time that I would hear those words: "I didn't want to further assault the Black male image." "I didn't want to tear the community apart." "I didn't want to provide ammunition to racists taking aim at a successful Black man." Whatever the language might be, the burden of Black women "taking one for the team" eventually became all too familiar to me.

That was one of my first glimpses into the network of Black women who choose to bury their personal victimization for perceived communal good. I suspect that we would find these silent sisterhoods among most minority groups—all of them fueled by a belief that their community needs to be protected. One survivor who was raped by a stranger when she was 10 years old shared her experience in Dr. Charlotte Pierce-Baker's *Surviving the Silence* and described the need to keep things behind closed doors as follows:

> But now that I think about it, I wouldn't call the police because [sic] I wouldn't want to ruin his life. Him going to prison and being another statistic to me is almost as great an evil as what happened. I love black people. Even when we're sick.[1]

I doubt that Black women adhere to the practice of covering up men's offenses as often as they did in the past, but the practice survives nonetheless. Some of the women who shared their stories with me were advised to remain silent by friends or family, but others reached the conclusion to do so entirely on their own. They simply believed it was the right thing to do.

Some people hear of women making decisions to remain silent and view them as misguided. They argue that these choices only serve to shield violent men who should rightfully be exposed. As I am not a survivor of sexual violence, it is impossible for me to truly know how I would react if I were victimized, so I do not see it as my place to criticize survivors for whatever responses they find most helpful. But I hope we can all at least agree that it is troubling that many women are forced to expend energy and spirit deciding how to respond to violence inflicted on them. The fact that so many women are forced to ponder difficult choices between healing themselves and healing their communities demands action. There is a debt to be repaid.

Many who have shared their experiences with me over the years did indeed speak up publicly on some level. Some viewed holding their attackers accountable as a vital piece of their personal recovery. Others interpreted their duty to community to mean that they were to speak up so that others were not placed in similar danger. Some were simply seeking a community who could relate to their experience. Many of these women were people who I deeply respected long before I knew they were survivors of violence. Knowing this brought a special kind of inspiration for me as I was in awe of the fact that these women carried memories of an intimate betrayal but still chose to shine as mothers, professionals, students, and citizens. I still saw a debt to be repaid.

I wondered then what I was supposed to do in return. If there is a reciprocal practice stitched into the souls of Black men, I never learned it. How could I have when I cannot recall a single conversation with my family, teachers, or coaches about sexual violence prior to my 20s? Now, having had the opportunity to speak with many Black boys about sexual violence, I know that I am not an anomaly. No effort has ever emerged from Black men to match the continued sacrifices of Black women.

Staunch defenders of Black men disagree. They cite repayment in the Black men who contribute positively to their communities, take care of their families, and never raise a hand to their partners. Those defenders would be correct in noting that the vast majority of men have never raped, beaten, or abused a woman, but they would be wrong in arguing that this is sufficient. To say that we have done our duty merely by not acting on the most repulsive of urges is a poor standard. We can do better.

God forbid that we should apply similar logic to other areas of our lives. We do not think that we have done our best in school when we do not attack our teachers for assigning too much homework, and we do not think we have fulfilled our civic duties because we do not beat up the politician whom we detest. I do not know why we believe that we have dutifully responded to incessant reports of sexual violence by saying that we are not personally violent.

As it stands, boys are allowed to grow into manhood without seriously considering how they should respond to the presence of sexual violence in the world. They have been trained to sit quietly on the sidelines of a crisis in which an estimated quarter of the women in America go through life with memory of being assaulted by a man in some fashion.[2] We have trained them to respond to accounts of violence with ridicule and disinterest unless someone close to them is crying on their shoulder or pleading his innocence.

* * *

Much of my professional career has been spent working alongside educators and activists who daily think on sexual violence and how to respond to it. I have since left behind formal work in violence prevention and moved into a more conventional career. I am now constantly reminded that most people do not intentionally think about rape and sexual assault unless they have personally experienced violence or are close to someone who has. Thus, it is worth taking some time to review and define the problem.

Let us start by coming up with a common definition of sexual violence. That is easier said than done because every state defines rape and sexual assault a bit differently in their statutes. They do not even use consistent terms to label them. For anybody looking to review the legal definitions used by a particular state, I recommend a great resource put together by the Rape, Abuse, and Incest National Network (RAINN) that catalogs state definitions (https://www.rainn.org/public-policy/laws-in-your-state). In addition to states providing a range of definitions, there are many other institutions in the business of defining sexual violence, such as schools and workplaces. Nonetheless, there are some common components of definitions that we can identify.

Generally speaking, rape is defined as vaginal, anal, and oral penetration enacted against a person's will. This includes penetration with a digit or object. Sexual assault is any sexual contact enacted against a person's will. As sexual assault is all touching of a sexual nature that is done against a person's will, you can see that rape is a more specific form of sexual assault. Acts are typically defined as against a person's will if they are accompanied by force, threats, or intimidation.

Policymakers are increasingly moving toward consent-based definitions of sexual violence. That is, they identify acts as violent if a participating party does not consent to them. Obviously, consent that is arrived at via coercion or intimidation should be understood by other parties as no consent at all. Please also note that intent and awareness from a perpetrator do not matter so much under consent-based definitions. A perpetrator could unknowingly commit a violent act by wrongly presuming that a partner has given consent. In Chapter 7, I highlight common misunderstandings of consent held by boys. Boys who lack a firm grasp of what consent means hold the potential to commit violence that disrupts their lives and the lives of others. Many of them rule out the possibility of violence if a partner is not physically resisting and screaming "no," but they need to understand consent as the presence of a "yes" rather than the absence of a "no."

Most state laws and school policies go on to identify situations in which people are incapable of providing consent to sexual activity. For example, statutory rape laws indicate when a party is too young to consent to sexual activity with another person. An older party is required to understand that a younger party is incapable of providing consent even if that younger party is willing to engage in sexual activity. The age difference required for a party to be unable to consent also varies from state to state (the aforementioned RAINN website also covers the ages at which people can consent). The other primary areas in which a person would be unable to consent are when a person has a permanent mental incapacity or is temporarily incapacitated and thus unable to communicate. Temporary incapacitation could result from a medical condition or the use of drugs or alcohol.

For the purposes of this book, I consider *rape* to be vaginal, oral, or anal penetration of a sexual nature with a person who cannot consent or chooses not to consent. When I refer to *sexual assault*, I mean any and all touching of a sexual nature with a person who cannot consent or chooses not to consent. I collectively refer to both rape and sexual assault under the umbrella term of *sexual violence*.

Now that we have established working definitions, let us get a sense of how often sexual violence occurs. Most studies researching incidence rates conclude that a quarter or more of women have been raped or sexually assaulted.* Researchers at dozens of academic institutions and community-based organizations have turned up similar figures and measure the annual incidence of this violence in the hundreds of thousands. This means that if you were to sample four of your female friends or relatives at random, at least one of them carries or will carry a story of sexual victimization if statistics hold true.

If you are skeptical of the output of academic institutions, we could also look to the campus sexual assault study published by the National Institute of Justice, which returned similar numbers. The study found that 15.9% of undergraduate women reported experiencing an attempted or completed sexual assault before entering college and another 19% reported experiencing an attempted or completed sexual assault since entering college. There are, of course, some who experienced an assault both before and after college, so the aggregate number of women reporting an attempted or completed sexual assault was 28.5%.[3]

---

* I do recognize that framing sexual violence in terms of the number of people who have been assaulted obscures focus from those who perpetrate it. I am building to placing accountability where it belongs.

A sizeable portion of prevalence research features college students, given our access to these populations, but there is also the National Crime Victimization Survey administered by the U.S. Department of Justice for those looking for a broader snapshot. There is some criticism that the methodology of the survey leads to sexual violence being vastly underreported, but we can at least take it as a floor for how much violence takes place. There were an estimated annual 734,630 rapes or sexual assaults in the most recent iteration of the survey.[4] While these numbers fall short of what we see estimated by some other sources, they are still considerable. It is still the case that boys will likely encounter survivors, even by conservative estimates.

Decades of work from academic institutions, community organizations, and criminal justice agencies have given us an overwhelming body of research. We can safely conclude that sexual assault is a common experience for girls and women. This research does not generally include less severe forms of violence such as a man "copping a feel" under the guise of playing around or flirting. We would come up with some truly astronomical rates if we were to capture all of the unwanted touching that women endure.

Studies that take race into account often come up with even higher victimization rates for Black women. The foundational National Violence Against Women Survey conducted in 2000 concluded that 17.7% of White women and 19.8% of non-White women reported that they had experienced a completed or attempted rape in their lifetime.[5] The Bureau of Justice Statistics has placed the rate of intimate partner victimization for Black women as much as 35% higher than that of White women.[6] *Intimate partner violence* refers to all violence inflicted by a current or former spouse, boyfriend, girlfriend, or partner. That includes murder, rape, sexual assault, robbery, simple assault, and aggravated assault.

Before leaving statistics behind, I should note that sexual violence is an unmistakably gendered crime in that men represent the overwhelming majority of perpetrators (as they do for all forms of violence). This is fact, and no credible statistical source paints a different picture. Believe it or not, this is not a particularly controversial idea for most boys. They understand just fine that violence is largely a male arena by virtue of their own experiences. *So what is in the training of boys that makes us more violent than the sisters and female friends who are raised alongside us?* This is one of many tough questions that we have to explore if we are to raise boys who will help turn around the sad statistics that I mentioned.

* * *

I need to cover one final definition now that we have some common definitions in our toolbox. *Rape culture* is a term that I find helpful and adopt in this book. The term has been around since at least the 1970s, and here I use it to encapsulate the far-ranging behaviors and attitudes that normalize, trivialize, and condone sexual violence.

Rape culture can be difficult to see because most of us were raised in environments where it was the status quo. If you are uncertain as to how to demonstrate rape culture to the boys in your life, consider that many of them already accept that there are brands of violence that are fostered by cultural supports. We saw this very clearly in the summer of 2020 when many of them connected with the protests for racial justice energized by the death of George Floyd after a police officer placed a knee on his neck for over 7 minutes. Let us consider some of the questions asked afterwards as communities wrestled with how to prevent more deaths.

Some delved into locker-room cultures that fostered hostility against the communities that police officers are to serve. Some criticized law enforcement training curricula for not focusing enough on techniques of de-escalation and community outreach. Some wondered if we should be celebrating television shows and movies that portray excessive force by officers as an acceptable means to an end. Some considered if law enforcement had too broad of a role in the first place and was simply being called on for tasks that it was unsuited to handle. Notice that all of the lines of inquiry that I just mentioned have one thing in common—they are not directed at the individual officers who were named as defendants in George Floyd's death; rather, they are aimed at systemic and cultural processes.

Sexual violence very much functions in a similar context. Simply put, it is not the work of a few "bad apples" but of a far-reaching culture. Ultimate accountability rests with the perpetrators, but the rest of us play a role as well. Here are some commonly cited examples of behaviors that facilitate and/or excuse sexual violence:

- Pressuring young men to "score"
- Expecting "real" men to be sexually aggressive
- Catcalling and other behaviors that view women as sex objects more so than as people
- Making statements such as "bros before hoes" in connection to violence that presume a party that is deserving of support
- Dismissing all reports of sexual violence as false reports

Many see no connection between everyday behaviors such as these and actual violence, but remember that even conservative estimators measure the annual incidence of sexual assault in the hundreds of thousands. This is too high a rate for us to dismiss this violence as socially deviant behavior. It is normative behavior that our culture reinforces on some level.

If you are still having difficulty detecting rape culture, then I ask you to think on a real-world report of sexual violence. Consider a past report that you have in your memory, or choose whatever case is dominating headlines at the time that you are reading this. You can choose a case involving a famous celebrity or one that just received local attention. It almost does not matter which one you choose; I am confident that you will identify many of the same responses from the public. With your case in mind, think about if you heard any of the following ideas:

1. *We expect "real" violence to come with definitive physical evidence.* Many people insist on seeing rock-solid evidence before believing that an alleged perpetrator could potentially be at fault. Let us return to our consent-based definitions of sexual violence to see one of the problems with this mindset. Remember that sexual assault is sexual activity done without a person's consent.

Consent (or the absence of consent) cannot always be uncovered via physical evidence. Sure, criminal justice personnel can find physical evidence that corroborates an account of what occurred, like bruises, bodily fluids, or ripped clothing (and they often do), but many people have an unrealistic depiction of the criminal justice system's ability to obtain this evidence. And even if they have it, it may not tell the full story. Just as consensual activity can leave behind bruising and tearing, nonconsensual activity can fail to leave behind any evidence of force.

2. *We expect "real" violence to be resisted and avoided by victims.* People tend to ask questions of alleged victims such as "Did she fight?" or "Did she scream?" In order to see the problem with demanding this kind of resistance, again we have to return to our consent-based definitions of sexual assault. Physical resistance and verbal resistance clearly indicate that consent is not present, but their absence does not necessarily mean that consent is present. The actions of an alleged victim are largely independent from the question of whether or not a person has obtained consent before engaging in sexual activity. Whatever actions they have taken prior to an alleged assault are also irrelevant (e.g., wearing a particular outfit, voluntarily going to a hotel room, consenting to some amount of intimate contact, consenting to past sexual activity). The only question that matters is whether or not an alleged victim consented to *all* of the sexual activity in question. Let us also not forget that, like with any form of trauma, people can freeze or shut down physically, verbally, or mentally upon experiencing violence. This would make it difficult for some to react in the moment or even fully process that they are experiencing a violent act.

3. *We expect "real" victims to behave in certain ways.* It is not just the actions that alleged victims take before and during an incident that come under scrutiny; many criticize the behaviors that they take afterwards as well. For example, people might look at claims that an alleged victim has been intimate with another

person after an incident and conclude that this means that he or she could not have been a victim because "real" victims do not behave like that. Or they might draw this conclusion from observing a person wait for years before reporting an incident. There are indeed some common reactions to sexual assault, and many great volumes have been written on the subject. However, it is still the case that there is no universal response to sexual assault. Human beings are complex, and their reactions to trauma are varied and inconsistent—not to mention that many of the decisions that people cite as proof that an assault did not occur are actually very plausible reactions to an assault. For example, a survivor of violence may seek the intimate company of somebody that he or she trusts after experiencing an incident in which trust was violated. Or a survivor may be looking to regain control after it was taken from him or her. Likewise, a survivor could take months or even years to formally report an incident because he or she does not feel prepared to face outside scrutiny of a painful experience.

4. *We expect "real" perpetrators to have no redeeming qualities.* It is quite common to hear people defend an alleged perpetrator by claiming that he is a "good guy" without a known history of violence. The belief that most perpetrators are social deviants whose violent qualities are apparent to society is just not supported by research. Many of these men are otherwise able to function in society just fine. We cannot look to behaviors in other contexts to definitively ascertain if a violent act occurred.

If there is a common thread to all of the aforementioned beliefs, it is that they distract from the issue of whether or not all parties consented to all sexual activity in question. They minimize the importance of ensuring consent in a world in which policymakers and adjudicators are increasingly (and I think rightly) identifying consent as the most important factor in determining fault. How an alleged victim fought back, how an alleged victim behaved afterwards, what kind of physical evidence was left behind, and whether or not an alleged perpetrator was a "good guy" are all secondary to the presence of consent.

The four aforementioned beliefs come from an understandable place, but they have the effect of condoning behaviors that harm others. These beliefs collectively limit what we consider to be "real" violence. If we consider violence to be legitimate only when victims fight back against perpetrators who are previously known to be violent, when victims act as is stereotypically expected of them, and when they have the cuts and bruises to prove that they put up a fight, then we implicitly teach boys that all other behavior is nonviolent. Boys raised under these narrow definitions can be genuinely confused as to how they can be in the wrong if they consider themselves to be good people and are not faced with a sexual partner who is physically resisting them. They may also come to view survivors who do not behave as expected as undeserving of empathy. The statistics that I gave earlier in this chapter reveal that this is exactly what many of them do.

If there is a silver lining to the way that culture indoctrinates young men into minimizing sexual violence, it is that learned behaviors are preventable. All social behaviors that are not fed by cultural acceptance eventually fade into obscurity. That includes what clothes are in style, the slang that we use, and whether or not we choose to pursue sexual activity without obtaining consent. The responsibility of preventing sexual violence should therefore not be heaped on handfuls of educators and advocates sprinkled throughout the country. Nor should we isolate it as women's work or as the obligation of concerned survivors of rape. This is community work.

* * *

Many parents and guardians of girls are proactive about preparing them for a violent world. Teaching violence awareness is readily incorporated into the ways we raise our girls. When they are small, we might teach them the warning signs of predators or instill in them the confidence to speak up about unwanted touching. As they venture into adulthood, we continue to advise them on self-protective behaviors. We teach them not to lead men on, insist that they check in with us when they go out on dates, and tell them to watch how much they drink when out for the evening. Many women experience a lifetime of training on violence prevention (or, rather, risk reduction, but we will discuss this later).

Conversely, many guardians of boys have told me that it never crossed their minds to talk to their boys about sexual assault. Others limited their conversations with their boys to teaching them how to avoid sexual predators when they were young. They then promptly abandoned the subject once they believed their boys were old enough to protect themselves. Now the only time sexual violence might come up is in warning them to watch out for deceitful women who are out to get them. Those who did keep the conversations going often admitted that they did so with only a fraction of the energy that they spent talking to their girls about the same things. Sexual violence awareness is just not a natural part of the curriculum for the training of boys.

It is true that boys are less likely to be victimized than girls. We nonetheless do them a disservice by not pulling them aside for important conversations, as sexual violence is still likely to touch their lives. Here are five reasons why boys should learn about sexual violence:

1. *Boys are victimized.* The most obvious reason why boys need to be at the table is that many boys will be victimized. The same studies that have exposed high victimization rates of women often show that men have their own troubling rates of victimization throughout their lifetimes. For example, the aforementioned National Crime Victimization Survey determined that 9% of all recorded victims of rape or sexual assault were males.[7] Violence against men and boys often goes under the radar as compared to violence against women, but its frequency is astounding when viewed in isolation. As you might imagine, a significant amount of violence against men occurs when they are young. Children who experience sexual violence understandably report feeling confusion, guilt, and shame. We cannot expect them to accurately identify violence and report it

without preparation. Furthermore, feelings of embarrassment do not disappear as boys mature into men, as there simply is not much precedent for men to share their experiences with sexual victimization. Resources dedicated to addressing barriers to men reporting are growing, though.

2. *Boys know survivors.* Up until now, I have discussed sexual violence in a pretty sterile fashion. I have captured it in statistics while largely ignoring the humans behind those statistics. However, each person who survives it is more than a number to be tallied. The survivors of sexual violence are friends, relatives, partners, and spouses who may one day disclose to a boy you know. Ideally, boys will have given some consideration to the nature of sexual violence before such a disclosure and will be prepared to help. The process of recovering from sexual assault is beyond the scope of this book, but there are many eye-opening accounts out there that provide insight into recovery. One common theme in recovery is that the reactions of those to whom survivors disclose matter. People are naturally uplifted by reactions of belief and support rather than skepticism and judgment.[8] Boys should be educated in such a way that their default reaction to hearing of an assault is not to judge the victim or to tell her what she did wrong. When I first started in anti-violence work, I was surprised by how many female friends and relatives disclosed to me. I thought female survivors of male-perpetrated violence might not want to disclose to a man, but I now believe that people largely turn to those they trust, and that may include men. The boys you know will become trusted confidants to women close to them. This means that they may one day have the chance to help someone by treating a story of a violent encounter with the seriousness and respect that it deserves.

3. *Boys know perpetrators.* The majority of sexual assaults are committed by people known to the victim. They are committed by acquaintances, friends, dates, boyfriends, and spouses more

so than strangers.[9] If boys will come to know survivors, it then stands to reason that they will also come to know perpetrators. Perpetrators of violence will be included among their friends and family members. They do not generally come with flashing warning signs, but it is not unheard of for men to have some awareness of the sexual practices of those with whom they hang out. As such, boys can play a part in how their peers come to view the acceptability of their actions. Their reaction to a shared story—whether that story is told braggingly or portrayed as routine—could make someone reconsider their behaviors. In this respect, boys will have opportunities to actually prevent future violence. They should be prepared to do so, but this takes practice and is especially difficult for younger men who might be uncomfortable with voicing beliefs that go against their peer culture.

4. *Boys are capable of violence.* Preparing girls to detect and resist violent men assumes that there will always be violent men for women to avoid. That is likely true, but that does not mean that we do not have the ability to dramatically reduce the number of offenders. We do not like to think that boys we know are potential perpetrators, but all violent men were once boys learning the ways of the world. We play a role in helping them to understand appropriate behavior. When you talk to them, virtually all boys understand and agree that raping someone with overt force is indefensible. But many are far less adept at identifying violence in scenarios that fall outside of stereotypical ideas of rape. These breaks in understanding and empathy make boys capable of committing or condoning violence themselves. When we do take the time to talk to boys about sexual responsibility, it is usually restricted to self-protective activities like avoiding sexually transmitted infections, avoiding unwanted pregnancies, and even avoiding false accusations of sexual violence. A more holistic approach would include strategies to ensure that they avoid harming others as well. Boys trained in

this fashion will come to see consent not as something to be assumed, but as something that they should guarantee before initiating sexual activity.

5. *Boys interact with a violent culture.* Preparing boys is not simply about equipping them for negative encounters. It is about empowering them to be positive and proactive leaders who can shape culture rather than simply react to it. Even if boys should manage to live their lives without ever being a primary or secondary party to sexual violence, they will not make it into adulthood without hearing the world's opinions on this violence. News media, entertainment media, peers, and adults all have plenty to say about sexual violence and how we should respond to it. Their positions may or may not be conducive toward eliminating violence and treating survivors with dignity, so it is important that boys are exposed to multiple viewpoints and grounded in positions of their own. The dialogue between boys and the broader culture need not be a one-way conversation. Boys have a say as well.

It took a formal invitation for me to realize that there were actions that I could take as a man to combat sexual violence, but the boys in your life need not wait. Besides needing men in order to create a critical mass to challenge rape culture (we are half of the population, after all), there are several reasons why men are specifically needed in the movement to end sexual violence. One is that men commit the majority of sexual violence. There are countless studies and statistics to support the claim that men are primarily responsible for societal violence, but most of us know very well that this is the case without the benefit of research. Upon hearing that a violent act has taken place (a fight, a mugging, a shooting, etc.), most people will assume that men are behind it. As members of the offending community, boys then have an obligation to review their attitudes and behaviors in order to evaluate if they are part of the problem.

This leads us to a second reason why men are vital to anti–sexual violence work: Men listen to other men. Peer-oriented approaches where young people take on the task of educating other youth are widely employed at academic institutions and community organizations throughout the country. These programs are generally supported by older staff and faculty, but it is youth who are standing in front of their peers and holding difficult conversations. A cynic might say that peer education is popular because it is cheaper for institutions to send in students rather than to pay staff, but these approaches have broad support in the violence prevention community and associated research literature, with many peer education programs demonstrating at least short-term impact on the attitudes of audiences.[10] People receive messages differently depending on who delivers them, and there is evidence to support the practice of using people of backgrounds similar to the audiences that you are trying to reach. Hypothesized rationales as to why peers are effective include belief that messages must be as relevant as possible in order to be most effective, belief that audiences react better to positive messages than negative messages, belief that audiences need to be involved in championing solutions that they can personally enact, and belief that modeling behavior is one of the key processes by which behaviors are learned.

The most relevant peers for young men are quite often other young men. A male peer may be able to break through with a problematic young man in a way that a coach, teacher, or parent cannot. The effectiveness of men reaching other men does not mean that women are incapable of reaching men. I am partially a product of women's intervention myself and know very well that women can be effective recruiters of men. It is just that it is a little harder for men to dismiss other men as brainwashed products of a feminist agenda—something that men are prone to do with female educators. The power in having a male peer call you to task is not easily replicated.

As it stands now, boys routinely find themselves in situations for which they have little to no preparation. As they progress into and through adulthood, they may survive sexual violence, they may befriend violent men, they may come to know and love survivors, and they may even inflict violence themselves. We tend not to think of our boys in these ways, so we do not bother to train them on how to react when violence occurs or how to shift the culture in order to prevent it from occurring in the first place.

I read Hill Harper's acclaimed *Letters to a Young Brother* and found it to be a positive work of affirmation that encourages African American boys to seek out who they want to be rather than accept the limits of the peer cultures around them. Harper even includes a chapter called "Sex Matters" that rightly reassures boys that their masculinity is not linked to their sexual conquests. It warns young men about having sex before they are ready and engaging in irresponsible sexual activities that could lead to sexually transmitted infections or unwanted pregnancy. While reading, I hoped it would also go on to say how unconsciously going through the rituals of sex can harm a partner, or that it would further its theme of resisting peer culture and remind boys that they can have a role in influencing peers who justify sexual assault in certain contexts. But these messages did not show up. This was emblematic of a gaping hole in our training of boys. Even when we take great interest in their development, it does not always cross our minds to empower them to be the agents of change against rape culture that they have the potential to become.

Whenever a boy encounters an instance of rape culture—someone mocking a rape victim on social media, listening to song lyrics promoting violence against women, etc.—he is faced with a choice: He must decide whether to represent himself as an agent of change or as a follower. Granted, boys cannot fight every battle that presents itself, nor can we demand that boys put themselves in harm's way in all situations. But conversation in advance of these battles goes a long way toward them generating the strength to step up. Identifying and reacting to opportunities to speak up takes practice, and habits formed at a young age are especially powerful.

I wrote much of this book against the backdrop of the COVID-19 epidemic and the nation's response to it. The appropriate response to the epidemic is very much a divisive topic, so I will leave chiming in on that for the subject matter experts, but I hope that we can at least agree on one key takeaway: that it is extremely difficult to address a public health concern unless you have all relevant parties collaborating on and implementing shared solutions. We all need to be moving in the same direction for the best results.

Sexual violence is very much a public health concern once you consider the sizeable number of people affected by it and the vast reserves of energy that communities spend recovering from it. And just like COVID-19, the solutions are similar in that we have to isolate and stop the transmission of harmful ideas and behaviors. We have come a long way toward addressing the crisis, mostly thanks to the tireless work of women who pioneered anti-violence work. However, the record of progress is marked with relapses and resistance. It is pretty clear that it is going to take a larger effort if we are to ever push sexual violence to the margins of society. It is going to take the men and boys whom you know.

HOW DO YOU CREATE SPACE FOR MALE VOICES? A CONVERSATION WITH REGGIE WALKER

Reggie Walker is a former NFL player and team captain whose childhood experiences with mental, physical, and sexual abuse shaped his work as a passionate survivor advocate. He is a renowned TEDx speaker and a board member for 1in6, an organization that addresses the lack of resources on negative childhood sexual experience affecting men.

Q: Chris Rock had a routine in the late 90s where he talked about "molester Uncle Johnny." While we're much better at recognizing and talking about the scope and impact of child sexual abuse, most of the casual commentary on the topic shows up in jokes, particularly regarding the abuse of boys. Would you agree with this sentiment? And what is it going to take to achieve a step forward in this area?

A: I fully agree. I think it's going to take people that have had this happen to them to speak up about it a lot more. I became comfortable talking about it during my fourth or fifth year in the NFL. I was comfortable enough to just tell people, "This happened to me." The thing that shocked me the most is that every single one of the guys I spoke to said that the same thing happened to them, whether it was physical abuse, mental abuse, or sexual abuse. Then I would ask them when they first told someone and they would always answer that this was the first time. It did not matter who I was talking to—White, Black, it didn't matter what their race was. That was scary to me because I had spent time talking about it in therapy and I'm thinking about these guys who haven't talked about it or dealt with it. Then you see people transition out of professional sports and they have issue upon issue and people wonder why. A good portion of people were playing football for the same reason that I was. It was a coping mechanism for dealing with the internal conflict that every single one of us was going through. You could go out there and be the most violent person you could think of, leave it all out there, and never actually deal with your demons.

Q: As you work to examine male cultures and training, what have you learned that can help readers motivate the young men in their lives to speak up and share their thoughts, questions, and experiences?

A: I would definitely want people to understand that if they want to get their sons to open up, they have to create a welcoming space that is based in empathy, and not judgment. What stops people more times than not is they say something and then a person judges it. Just listen. You don't even necessarily need to respond. They just need to get this out. That's the first step. If you really want to help, you need to develop that listening muscle.

Q: In my book, I'm asking young men to walk into potentially hostile spaces and share their voices, but that's not easy to do. You have spent time in what many would consider to be among the most hyper-masculine environments out there and the environments that most need to hear anti-violent messaging: locker rooms for Division I college athletics and the National Football League. What does it take to move the needle in those environments?

A: When you're in these environments, you are supposed to be one of two guys. You're going to be this choir boy. And then in other situations, you are supposed to be the exact opposite guy. You have no feelings, no emotions, and no heart. The big thing in these environments is that everybody—the coaches, the athletic directors, the general managers, the support staff—needs to understand that the guys are somewhere in the middle. You need to create an environment where guys understand that these are just sides of them and not who they fully are. But it's not encouraged. Individualism is not encouraged. It's not encouraged because things in that environment are built like a machine and players are just parts in the machine. You want these parts of a machine to act accordingly.

We don't have enough people in these environments who understand emotional intelligence. We need people that understand that these big, strong guys have feelings. When we're dealing with human beings, they have thoughts, feelings, and emotions. I've talked to so many guys that are so used to being either "super good" or "super bad" that they cannot find equilibrium. It doesn't feel natural. That's why we see so many documented problems when people transition out of these environments. I've had friends commit suicide, end up homeless, or spend time in treatment centers as I did because people are more concerned with getting the cogs in the machine to work instead of understanding the cogs for who they are.

CHAPTER 1: TEACHING BOYS THAT THEIR VOICES ARE NEEDED

- Chances are that sexual violence will touch boys during their lifetimes. They may:
  - Learn of a friend, relative, or partner who has experienced violence,
  - Come to know men who have inflicted violence, or
  - Experience violence themselves (either as a victim or perpetrator).

- As of now, many boys are unequipped to respond to sexual violence because they have never had any constructive conversations on the matter. The most immediate lesson that boys should learn is that their voices are needed. Many boys only imagine sexual violence as the acts of sadistic strangers in alleys. This leaves them with little to do to prevent violence. Once they understand that the majority of violence is rooted in normalized behaviors and perpetrated by men who are known to victims, then they will see that they have a role to play in preventing violence. High rates of sexual violence are undoubtedly supported by cultural practices that minimize the impact of this violence.

- There are two key reasons why boys are needed to stand against violence: Men commit the majority of violence, and men listen to other men. They will have contact with violent men and thus have chances to interrupt the ongoing trends of violence in America.

- One of the biggest mistakes that you can make in educating boys about sexual violence is assuming that they have no desire to help simply because they are boys. As men, many of us are silent simply because we do not realize that our help is needed. A random invitation got me into anti-violence work, and I have remained active ever since. Contrary to popular belief, boys generally have a lot to say about sexual violence when asked. They might question the behavior of their peers, have investment in a celebrity accused of violence, know survivors of violence, have anxiety about the policies governing sexual behavior, or have concerns about stereotypes of men. In all cases, there is an emotional connection that serves as an opportunity to recruit boys to stand against violence.

Defining Manhood for Ourselves

As stated in Chapter 1, men are responsible for the majority of all violence. You might then wonder why men are more violent than their female counterparts on average. The answer to this question is not a simple one and would require input from sociology, biology, and psychology, but the answer that I would like us to consider is that men are simply trained to be more violent.

To understand why this might be, we first have to establish that there is a male training in the first place. Some of the dominant theories as to how those born as males come to adopt similar traits boil down to boys simply pursuing those traits that are rewarded. Caretakers of even extremely young children may reward and discourage certain habits in males while rewarding and discouraging different habits in females. An example of this would be discouraging crying in boys because we expect them to be tougher than girls. Caretakers go about rewarding and discouraging traits both knowingly and unknowingly. This training continues through early childhood as boys learn to stay away from certain interests and activities that will have others calling them "sissies," "fags," "pussies," and "girls." In his book *You Throw Like a Girl: The Blind Spot of Masculinity*, NFL veteran Don McPherson comments that "we do not raise boys to be men, we raise them not to be women—or gay men."[1] Much of the training of boys is intent on steering them away from behaviors thought to represent groups other than "real" men. This likely never stops as grown men are not immune to friends, loved ones, and rivals alike reminding them when they are not acting like a man.

I do not think that any of this is terribly controversial to most readers. Most people readily understand that boys are taught lessons growing up that are dramatically different than those taught to girls. Boys know this in their bones as well. There is an activity widely credited as having been pioneered by the Oakland Men's Project known as the "Man Box" or "Act Like a Man Box." It is a pretty common tool used by those teaching on gender identity and violence prevention, and I have used it myself. I have seen many variations of it, but the primary point is to list the attributes of men according to society. Many educators even literally draw a box and place all of the attributes inside it. This helps to illustrate that men are confined to the limits of the box.

When I have used the man box activity with male audiences, I always ask members of the audience to identify the qualities that belong in the box. They never have any difficulty with this and they quickly rattle off a list that might include adjectives such as "stoic," "strong," "athletic," "tough," and "in control." They might even mention specific activities such as providing for others and being popular with women. I rarely hear any disagreement about what belongs in the box. Somebody will shout something out and the rest of the group simply knows that he got it right. The lack of diversity in responses is also noteworthy. You hear the same words thrown out whether you are working with an urban public school or a rural private school, with little exception.

Tony Porter, co-founder of A Call to Men, which provides training on healthy manhood, leaned on the man box terminology in his book *Breaking Out of the "Man Box": The Next Generation of Manhood.* In it, he defines the man box as the "collective socialization of manhood" and discusses how it pressures men to operate on "remote control—doing things the way we always have, the way they were taught to us."[2]

I have a personal story that demonstrates men operating on "remote control." I was placed into a medically induced coma for about a month during the tail end of my high school career due to an undiagnosed complication. I emerged weighing less than 100 pounds and lacking the muscle strength to even sit up in a chair. This was all less than 2 months before I was expected to set foot into a college classroom for the first time.

Friends have picked my brain for the most pressing thoughts I had leading up to college in the wake of this life-threatening event. Some speculate that being so close to death led to me having more appreciation for life. These people give me far too much credit. The most salient concern running through my head at the time was a pressing need to put on weight. I dreaded introducing myself to a new set of peers as a frail and wiry first-year student. At a time when I should have been figuring out financial aid and selecting an appropriate course schedule, I was instead fixated on my appearance. My first semester at college was characterized by obsessive late-evening meals, trips to the weight room, and many strange behaviors that I thought would make me appear larger, like tucking in my shirts and wearing clothing with horizontal stripes.

This was all done in the name of manhood. I figured that I had no chance of acquiring new friends, attracting interest from women, and establishing credibility in the social battlefield of youth as long as I felt like a stick figure. I felt far too distant from the "real" man I thought I needed to be in order to survive. Of course, I had no input in determining what this real man looked like. But I lost a semester of college to my pursuit of this ideal, focusing on superficial weight gain when I should have been striving for more holistic betterment.

The societal expectations of men are so well established that marketers absolutely rely on them. It is interesting to me just how many commercials play on some expectation of manhood, even when the products being advertised are not targeted specifically at men. I recall one television commercial where a mobile phone company featured a Black father and son. The father communicated how proud he was of his son for graduating from college. Both men said they were going to miss one another and eventually said they loved one another. The father and son expressed all of this via a series of grunts, head nods, and short phrases. The "dialogue" was interpreted via captions at the bottom of the screen. The commercial was a playful rendition of the societal expectation that men seldom give or receive affection, especially in regards to other men. However, the expectations we place on men are not always as harmless in real life.

* * *

If I stop to listen, I find that a good portion of the dialogue among boys and men concerns who is "real" and who is not. The criteria for being "real" vary across time and the particulars of our upbringings, but all men are nonetheless expected to adhere to the rules and learn the consequences for not doing so. Mockery and ostracism are the most popular methods of enforcing the rules of manhood, but physical enforcement is not unheard of.

In January 2003, a burgundy Cadillac Escalade rolled up to the 1800 block of Philadelphia's Wingohocking Avenue. The driver was rapper Beanie Sigel, best known as a former label-mate to popular rappers Jay-Z and Kanye West. The Philadelphia native took aim at a woman standing within earshot of his car and reportedly shouted, "What's up, hoe?" from the vehicle's window.

A man who was holding a conversation with the woman responded by saying, "Why do you have to disrespect her?" This caused the Escalade to come to a halt and all 260 pounds of the man known as the "Broad Street Bully" made its way toward the man who dared to speak back.

"Do you know who I am?" Sigel asked.

The man replied, "Yeah. Beanie Sigel."

As the story goes, Sigel stared down the man for a moment. He then turned as if to leave only to whirl around and strike the man twice in the face. The other man later reported to police complete with a bruised face and a broken orbital bone. In triumph of the moment, Sigel stood over the man and said, "Beanie Sigel. That's right. Beanie Sigel." He then returned to his Escalade and went on his way.[3]

Whether or not the incident happened exactly as described, this is the version of the story that stuck with the people around me. I doubt that too many people intently discussed the incident outside of Philadelphia because the assault charges Sigel acquired as a result of the incident are quite possibly the least sensational in a litany of legal troubles, but it was news locally. I lived in Philadelphia during this time and was able to observe a real-time case study on Black male authenticity.

The barbershop in West Philadelphia that I frequented at the time was the venue for some animated discussion about Sigel's antics. The near-unanimous consensus was that Sigel was the more "authentic" of the two men. Sigel was the one "keeping it real." This was an interesting thought. The authentic man was not the man who objected to the commonplace disrespect that many men direct toward women. The authentic man was not the man brave enough to confront a world-famous celebrity. No, this distinction was awarded to Sigel—the man who exercised his casual right to demean a woman and then aggressively asserted this right when challenged.

It is entirely possible that I hang around a bad crowd, but I think that what I found that summer was and still is representative of the realities for many men and boys. Displays of masculinity based on physical dominance, material wealth, and female subjugation remain the easiest paths to authenticity. Boys and men are not free to express the totality of their feelings and insights. We are trained to be cowards and followers. Our environment hands us a predetermined (though ever-changing) set of behaviors and emotions that it allows us to possess. "Real" men are perpetually confident, stoic, and powerful. Sexual conquest comes naturally to them and they find little reason to express emotions outside of excitement, lust, and anger. Our environments even go so far as to tell us exactly what kinds of music we can like, what kinds of hobbies we can enjoy, and what sports we can play. In response, most of us roll over in submission. Few of us ever speak against the rigidity of this male template, yet many of us own an ironic audacity to consider acquiescence to be a female trait. We spend a considerable portion of our lives trying to prove that we are "real" men in full possession of all of the clout that we think comes with that title.

We do not come into the world like this. We enter with the capacity to find a true self that has its own unique blend of needs, joys, and sensibilities. As children, we delight in discovering this true self only to later find that it is easier to give in to the cookie-cutter manhood already prepared for us and avoid the wrath of our family, our peers, and the women whom we aim to impress. We go through life unable to exercise genuine moral or social initiative unless the cultures around us give us permission to break out in a new direction. Soon we have invested so much into the defense of our prepackaged identities that we no longer recognize the voices of the layered human beings that we were meant to be. We begin to believe that the voice that we adopted for survival is our own.

There are consequences to roughly half of this nation's population adopting the same tired archetypes. We lose tremendous pieces of ourselves when we bend to conform to the preapproved images heaped upon us. We willingly restrict our own freedom as to who we might be—feigning interest in things that are "manly" but ultimately unfulfilling to us and discouraging any activity that evokes anything outside of our preapproved list of emotions. We close ourselves off from relationships with men and women that do not conform to what we think is expected of us, even when we know full well that those relationships will better us as people or that we would simply enjoy them. We thus voluntarily submit to being finite persons who intentionally utilize only a portion of the emotions and talents bestowed unto us. We even ignore our own pain and trauma so as not to be seen as weak or vulnerable. We get so used to disguising our pain that we blunt our ability to even acknowledge it. It is little wonder that men lead the way in mortality rates and lag behind women in addressing their physical and mental health.[4]

If our pursuits of manhood damaged only ourselves, that would be one thing. But other men, women, and children have to interact with the unthinking and unfeeling husks into which we transform ourselves. Having had the opportunity to engage in conversation with men who I believe to have perpetrated sexual violence, I do not believe all of them to be sadistic individuals who fulfilled an intentional desire to harm women. Many of them are men blindly going through the motions of being a man and giving about as much conscious analysis to their socially assigned behaviors as they do to pondering why the sky is blue. Thankfully, some of us do indeed look up to the sky and start asking questions.

We do not always think of male-perpetrated sexual violence as having a source, but it must, just the same as any other widespread practice. Some of the more popular theories as to why men are violent include those that are biological in nature. These theories commonly hold that men rape on account of biological factors such as increased levels of testosterone in male bodies. Or they might point to evolutionary traits that encourage males to overcome resistance from potential mates and therefore further the continuation of the human species. I have admittedly never cared too much for these explanations because they often minimize the anti-violent faculties that our biology has blessed us with, such as the abilities to reason, empathize, and appeal to higher values. Other theories about male violence are psychological in nature and hold that male-perpetrated violence is a manifestation of past psychological trauma. There are also sociological theories asserting that sexual violence is largely learned behavior. I have always gravitated toward these theories because I can easily recall the pressures that were placed on me to be sexually active as a teenager and well into adulthood. This pressure was fueled by an intense posturing that "real" men are constantly up for sexual conquest and do not allow such trivial things as conscience and reason to dissuade them from this goal. This indoctrination is so unrelenting that I do not find it at all surprising that some of us subscribe to it so blindly that we lose the ability to accurately read when sexual pursuits are unwanted. Or, more accurately, we never develop this ability in the first place.

I also gravitate toward sociological explanations because they offer the most hope. If something is taught, then it can be unlearned or never learned in the first place. This perspective provides us with something to do—namely to go about the business of disrupting the problematic education of boys. This disruption takes mentors willing to remind boys that they are beholden to priorities greater than their pursuit of sex and that these priorities should not bend when doors are closed, alcohol is flowing, or peers' expectations are pressing. This takes women and men willing to take anti-violent messages into dens where traditional manhood is used to running unchecked and its carriers will be branded as "pussies" and traitors for rocking the boat. If young men grew up consistently hearing countercultural messages from mentors they respected, they will take it for granted that there are times when men should choose to shut down their sexual pursuits. They will understand that their opportunity to do so does not decrease when a woman has earlier flirted with them or is wearing a revealing outfit. They will understand that the decisions of others have nothing at all to do with their own capacity to make good decisions.

Some might still say, "What's so wrong with training boys to be men?" and I do not think that they would be wrong in asserting that there is nothing inherently problematic about a male socialization. Nor should anybody have to apologize for being born in to a particular sex that brings on a set of cultural expectations. Yet arguing that there is nothing wrong with the particular brand of manhood pushed on us is a vote for the status quo, and we must remind ourselves of what the status quo represents.

The status quo is one in which American prisons are packed with men sentenced for violent offenses, and few of us outside of prison can claim to have never had a violent encounter in our lives. The vast majority of male violence is inflicted on other men, but it is still perpetrated against women at such rates that at least a quarter of the female population has survived male violence.[5] The status quo is one in which most men are content to leave the challenge of ending sexual violence to women and law enforcement despite the outrageous numbers. Business as usual is indefensible.

* * *

Sticking to a script for manhood that I did not write nearly cost me my life. I already explained how an experience in a coma in high school led me to chase manhood, but manhood also explains how I ended up in the coma in the first place. I had a stretch toward the end of high school when I was tremendously sick. Every day, I would drag myself to school, return home, and lie down. Then I would wake up and repeat the process the next morning. This routine continued for several days before my mother dragged me to the emergency room. The doctors then believed that my condition was life-threatening and induced unconsciousness. This is one of the earliest lessons I can recall about just how dangerous the blind pursuit of masculine ideals can be. I was gravely ill but never asked anyone for help or considered making a trip to a physician on my own. I was not so much making a conscious decision to waste away. Asking for help just was not in my training. It was an option that my frame of reference for manhood did not include.

When men are given space and time to truly reflect on how they were raised as men, they themselves readily identify aspects of manhood that are worth changing. Read a biography or watch an interview featuring an older male and there is a good chance that you will hear him speak to how some aspect of his childhood failed to teach him empathy for others, how to recognize his emotions, how to communicate with others, or something of the sort. These men will specifically link this failure to the fact that they were boys being taught how to be "real" men. I hear the same things when given the opportunity to work with young men behind closed doors. Sure, there are plenty of men who are unapologetic about all things male, but they do not speak for all men.

I hope the boys in your life are more equipped than I was, but I have spoken with enough boys to know that I am far from alone in the way that I grew up. When boys are given a chance to honestly examine manhood, many agree that there are some aspects of manhood that are worth evaluating. Here are some common complaints that I hear from boys. These are some of the things that many boys harbor resentment about but feel that they will be ridiculed for if they do not go along with the crowd:

- Boys pretend to be interested in activities that do not actually interest them.
- Boys feel that they do not have the right to challenge the sexual decision-making of other boys and men.
- Boys avoid discussing experiences that cause them pain, anxiety, embarrassment, or discomfort. They also avoid even revealing that they have such emotions.
- Boys are obligated to confront anybody who disrespects them in any fashion.
- Boys are to welcome sexual advances from all attractive women at all times.

A common theme across these complaints is a manipulation of emotions. Boys spend a great deal of time suppressing and disguising emotion. Constantly dealing with warped emotions might explain why girls are consistently cited as having greater emotional intelligence than their male counterparts, even at very young ages.

Listening to boys' own admissions of their limitations underscores why most need training before they can effectively challenge rape culture. They have to possess some ability to detect and act against unhealthy practices rather than writing off those practices as "just the way things are." They have to see that there is room for change. Boys and men can be so critical of the expectations of manhood and so aware of its costs behind closed doors, yet we collectively show little willingness to fight back publicly. Being that men have historically controlled the vast majority of resources and power, you would think that we would have long ago torn down rigid notions that dictate how we are supposed to think and act.

In *The Will to Change: Men, Masculinity, and Love*, noted activist bell hooks speaks to the capacity of men to give up aspects of manhood once we recognize the cracks:

Male violence in general has intensified not because feminist gains offer women greater freedom but rather because men who en-dorse patriarchy have discovered along the way that the patriarchal promise of power and dominion is not easy to fulfill, and in those rare cases where it is fulfilled, men find themselves emotionally be-reft. The patriarchal manhood that was supposed to satisfy does not. And by the time this awareness emerges, most patriarchal men are isolated and alienated; they cannot go back and reclaim a past hap-piness or joy, nor can they go forward. To go forward they would need to repudiate the patriarchal thinking that their identity has been based on.[6]

hooks reminds us that both men and women stand to gain from men evaluating the gender roles assigned to us. My appeals for you to encourage boys to take up anti-violence work to this point have primarily centered around boys having concern for others beyond themselves; however, there is reason for boys to get involved for their own sake. Challenging rape culture requires boys to interrogate behaviors and attitudes that contribute to violence. That interrogation may bleed into other aspects of manhood, as it did for me. I have many times witnessed the joy that comes when boys discover the freedom to figure out things for themselves.

Anti-violence work is a prime catalyst for assisting boys in learning how they are hurting themselves. Do not lose sight of discussion of manhood as one of the tools in your toolbox as you invite boys to stand against violence. Some boys will not be in a place to challenge the ideals that they have been celebrating since early childhood, but those who are will have fuel to keep going on their own.

* * *

I have to make a few admissions before I close out this chapter. The first is that I am fortunate enough to be in a situation where pushing back against the codes of manhood is not likely to bring me any physical harm. This is a luxury that not all boys possess and adopting these codes is very much a survival mechanism for some. As you approach boys, some have more freedom to push back than others, so I take this as yet another reminder that those of us who do have the freedom need to step up.

The second admission is that I have knowingly glossed over quite a bit in this chapter. People have written entire volumes on gender identity and gender construction, and I only scratch the surface here. There are also many readers who would find that my breaking the world down into two sexes who receive a corresponding gender socialization to be a vast oversimplification that ignores people such as those who are intersex and transgender. If you want to go beyond the crash course that I have offered here, there is now a lot of literature out there on the matter. Just as well, there are many individuals out there who have stories to tell. With this said, the oversimplified presentation of gender roles that I present here is one that reflects many of the boys with whom I have worked. They would tell you that they were born as a man and have been trained all of their lives on how to be a good one. The fact that they do not think about things on a more sophisticated level is kind of the point.

I tend to march to the beat of my own drum these days. I try to pursue things that truly interest me even if they are not on the list of expected activities for "real" men. I read before going to sleep every night and admit that this reading may include comic books. My primary source of cardio is playing in an indoor soccer league where I am quite often the only African American on the field. You are likely to find me playing some strategy game on my computer if you catch me relaxing. Or you might find me playing a game that is not digital at all, as I find great enjoyment in throwing dice, cards, and miniatures around a table. Oh, and I spend time writing about manhood and sexual violence prevention.

But I still remember the days when I marched in line and did my best to keep up with everything that I thought was expected of me. Earlier, I said that boys are trained to be cowards and followers, but I do not know the boys in your life. I can only definitively speak for myself. I vividly remember studying the rappers I watched on TV as a preteen for cues as to how I should walk. I tried to copy their clothing, I studied their mannerisms, and I even remember staring at a particular CD cover for hours so that I might perfectly copy a particular hairstyle.

My time as a follower was a natural part of growing up. But in retrospect I wish I had spent less time trying to pick up ways of living that I observed in others and more time thinking about who it was that I wanted to be. Many boys have received the same training that I did. The mass training of followers explains why it is possible to find yourself in a situation where the topic of male-on-female rape comes up among a group of men and you hear no diversity of opinion. You may very well only hear about the irresponsibility of women. Men will be described as helpless vessels incapable of deciphering a sexual partner's discomfort unless she is physically resisting. We are described purely as creatures of circumstance and impulse whose hands are tied when faced with the prospect of sex with a warm body whose consent can be envisioned in the slightest. We have no ability to fully utilize the judgment and empathy with which we were blessed as members of the human species.

Fortunately, I have had enough private conversations with boys to know that the notion of men as helpless bystanders in the face of violence is not always the voice of their true selves, but rather the voice of the caricatures they are trained to be. Given time and patience, nearly every audience of boys and young men I have ever worked with has eventually opened up and revealed more diversity of thought than what appeared on the surface. You will hear the party lines break and boys speak to greater purposes in life—purposes that render fleeting sexual gratification as meaningless. You will hear boys admit to the pressures to fill roles. You will hear boys speak about how their masking of insecurities hurts themselves and one another. You will hear boys admit they have a role to play in preventing sexual violence, either by improving their own behaviors or challenging the attitudes and behaviors of the people around them.

Boys do not have to waste time hiding behind someone else's definition of manhood as I did. Keep in mind that breaking free does not necessarily require boys to toss out everything that they value about manhood. Ask boys to identify the characteristics of "real" men and they will usually point to traits such as strength and toughness. These are traits that can certainly lead to problems if boys blindly adhere to them, but boys can also accomplish much good if they are strong and tough in the face of a peer culture that preaches conformity.

Boys are not always aware of the power they wield in determining the men they will become. Constantly telling them that "boys will be boys" leads them to mistakenly accept aspects of what we traditionally call manhood as immutable forces of nature rather than behavioral choices. We must do a better job of encouraging boys to develop the strength to stand apart. This includes the sexual arena, where many of us view the burgeoning sexuality of boys as a profound mystery to be avoided or something that will just take care of itself. But boys are bombarded with the message that "keeping it real" means sticking to a status quo that says that they should pursue any and all opportunities for sex. Decades of data on sexual violence demonstrates that we have not done enough to prepare boys to consistently act with integrity in those moments.

CHAPTER 2: HELPING BOYS TO EXPLORE MANHOOD FOR THEMSELVES

- Patience and trust almost always uncover diversity in boys' opinions. They generally display concern about commonly accepted ideals of manhood that lead to them harming themselves and others. Many will admit that social pressures often push them into actions that produce internal conflict. More commonly, they will cite inaction as the outcome of these pressures and cite moments when they withheld their voices because they were afraid.

- Boys often view themselves as independent and strong despite chasing masculine ideals that actually result in them pursuing the exact same interests, activities, and mannerisms as the peer group or role models they aspire to emulate. Pointing this irony out to boys may have a positive effect on some of them. Boys who go against the grain often display more courage than those who exhibit all of the traditional markers of "real" manhood.

- There is power in boys identifying the social pressures that lead them away from their authentic selves. I did not give serious thought to all of the ways that I pretended to be something that I was not until I was part of a regular conversation about the roots of male violence. Then I could see that many pressures pushed me away from the man I wanted to be and I began to recognize how I was manipulated into chasing ideals determined by others. This ultimately empowered me to pursue my own passions and interests. You can invite the boys you know to take a similar journey. Naming the pressures in their lives may have a freeing effect on them.

- I only scratched the surface of explaining the processes that account for gender formation. There are many theories on this matter. Processes by which children learn gender by imitating what they observe and by learning what behaviors are rewarded generally fall under the heading of social learning theory if you want to learn more. A really good summary of the dominant theories on gender formation can be found in *Gendered Lives: Communication, Gender, and Culture* by Julia T. Wood and Natalie Fixmer-Oraiz.[7]

- I also only scratched the surface in explaining how male socialization contributes to violence. Again, there are entire books dedicated to this subject; I list a few of them in Appendix I.

Starting the Conversation

If you have made it this far, then I assume that you agree that we need young men involved in the fight against sexual violence and the cultures that support it. Your first question might then be at what age should you begin talking to the young men in your life. At what point should we flip the switch from warning them about "stranger danger" to considering them as beings who might someday facilitate violence themselves? At what point should we consider them as agents who can confront the dangers of the world rather than solely shielding them from those dangers? Being that my background is on the prevention side of things, the answer for me is "before something negative happens." When I get opportunities to interact with college-aged men, they quite often already have a fair share of stories on which to draw. One study that utilized data of youth aged 14 to 18 in schools in Quebec found that 14.64% of them reported at least one episode of sexual violence by a romantic partner in the past 12 months.[1] A study conducted by the Black Women's Blueprint that utilized a variety of sources in order to identify survivors, including reports on social media and in-person disclosures, estimated that 70% of participating survivors had experienced a sexual assault before the age of 18.[2] This means that we would ideally get to boys at least by adolescence. Many educators agree as you can find many online resources with helpful tips for teaching the principles of consent to boys even below the age of 10.

You will get little help from public education officials on when to start your outreach as state policies vary widely as to when sex education should begin, what it should cover, or even if it should be provided in schools at all. Several of the states that do mandate sex education limit the messaging to avoiding premarital sex rather than discussing what children should do once they do become sexually active. Ultimately, you will have to decide the age at which your boys can handle the conversation. Just keep in mind that young men need not be sexually active in order to be primed for discussion. Trust me on this. They still have thoughts, anxieties, and questions even if they do not have a personal reference point for the behaviors being discussed. And do not forget that culture change is the name of the game anyway. Everybody has input into appropriate community values regardless of their own personal experiences.

* * *

If you are ready to dive in to holding overdue conversations with boys, I want to share my personal story with you. I will share how I came to the life-changing decision to lend my voice to anti-violence work in the hopes that it might provide you with some insight to help you reach the boys in your life.

I lived the first 20 years of my life without giving any real thought to rape culture and my role in fighting it. I was not opposed to fighting it. It is just that, like many boys and men, I was not aware that there was any work to be done. My shift away from this viewpoint began when I received a letter during my third year of college. It was from a student group on campus that wanted me to interview to become a member of their organization. The group educated men about sexual assault. Not only did they present to male audiences, but their entire membership was male. I had never heard of such a thing. I did not think I was capable of raping someone. I did not think any of my friends were rapists either. To me, rape was subject matter that was limited to the evening news alongside sketches of perpetrators. It was the police's job to handle and not mine. I had no idea what the topic had to do with me.

Several days later, I reread the letter to make sure it was really intended for me. Sure enough, "Gordon Braxton" was clearly printed on it. It was apparent that the strange proposal sitting on my desk was not going to answer itself, so I reread the letter in earnest. It was from a group called One in Four. The group took its name from a widely cited statistic that one in four college women report surviving rape or attempted rape since their 14th birthday. To combat this epidemic, this group was teaching male audiences how to help a survivor should a friend disclose an experience to them. They were doing this in service of working toward a day in which rape did not exist. It sounded like a commendable goal and I was looking to diversify my extracurricular activities, but it admittedly still sounded intimidating to go around talking about something as unconventional as rape. All of the men who I knew just did not talk about such things. However, the letter only requested an interview. There was no binding obligation, and so I replied with my intent to interview.

Three members of the group interviewed me a few weeks later. One of the interviewers was on the wrestling team, the second proudly belonged to a fraternity, and the third was a member of the campus ROTC program. They spoke about their chosen mission both passionately and nonchalantly. They seemed oblivious to the fact that the rest of the world agreed that men do not concern themselves with "women's issues" like rape. As a man who had not spent five minutes of his life seriously thinking about sexual violence, the example they set meant a lot to me. This was the first space that I had to really think about sexual violence and my relationship to it. I started to realize that I did have some things to say about it. The interviewers must have sensed my burgeoning interest, and they extended an invitation to join them.

I soon completed a multiweek training and was sent out into the world in the hopes that I might do some good. It still remained to be seen how long I would remain invested in this new cause. I had a habit of throwing my energy toward causes and hobbies only to have my commitment fizzle—and this new pursuit was one that would draw regular charges of betraying my race and gender on top of that.

However, my new cause seemed determined to keep ahold of me, and it intervened by sending a lengthy line of survivors of sexual violence into my life. I did not really know what I was getting into, but it stood to reason that family and friends who had experienced rape or sexual assault might seek me out after I revealed that I cared about the issue. The stream of survivors who made their presence known to me was so diverse and so far-reaching that you would have thought that these women had all met behind closed doors in order to concoct a plan to keep the issue of sexual violence on my front burner. Whatever their reasons, the previously silent network of survivors broke ranks for me, and I very quickly became the bearer of secrets belonging to others.

A fellow classmate was the first woman who I recall sharing her story with me. She was also African American. I did not know her very well but had a general impression of her as a perpetually joyful person. She was the kind of person whose mere pleasantness would make it impossible for anyone to think of harming her—or so I thought. One day I told her about my new role as a peer educator, and, without hesitation, she told me that a member of the school's football team had assaulted her. She explained that she never sought a judicial response because she did not want to be dragged through what she thought would surely be a public case. Soon after, another friend surprised me by explaining why her contact information had been unlisted in the school directory since our first year at school. She was afraid that a male student who was on leave after assaulting her would locate her. I later heard from a close friend who said her ex-boyfriend once assaulted her after she passed out at her own birthday party. Several other women shared stories of being abused by an older relative or acquaintance of the family when they were children.

The stories kept rolling in from relatives and friends alike. The stories shared with me were by no means limited to sexual violence. I unexpectedly began hearing stories of emotional and physical abuse suffered at the hands of boyfriends, dates, and partners as well. Once, a relative's girlfriend asked if I would intervene when her man "started beating on me again." I thought I had signed up to take on only sexual violence, but I soon found that many women drew connections between men raping them and men controlling or beating them.

It was in these early days of being bombarded with stories of men at their worst that I developed an immunity to an accusation that is commonly hurled at all people who speak against sexual violence: that we embolden women who falsely accuse men of assault out of greed, regret, or spite.

One of the common aspects running through all of the stories that were shared with me was that their authors had faced a serious disruption to their lives while the lives of the involved men barely skipped a beat. I heard stories from women of all races accusing men of all races of all kinds of hurtful and illegal behavior. Yet very few of these stories resulted in substantial consequences for the perpetrators. Not one of these men suffered a blow to his academic, professional, or athletic career. Not one of these accused men received jail time or paid out a settlement in a civil court. One of my friends did succeed in getting her attacker moved to a different residential area on campus, but that was pretty much the extent of any judicial repercussions. The majority of these stories remained secrets because their keepers feared that more harm than good would come out of formally reporting.

I have met many people who have tried to challenge my anti-violence perspectives by telling me stories about a woman who lied in order to get a man in trouble. If so many women had not thought enough of me to tell me of the things they kept locked away, then my sole affiliation with sexual violence might also be in smoking out false accusations and identifying malicious women as the real problem. Perhaps I would be the one to constantly remind those around me of how easy it is for women to "cry rape" or to constantly remind women of the serious consequences that their charges could have on a man's life.

I know that wrongful accusations most certainly exist. I also fully believe that mere accusations of sexual violence carry the power to wound a man's standing whether they are truthful or not. However, if I were to allow these realities to explain all accounts of sexual violence, then I would not only be oversimplifying the world, but I would also be neglecting all of the friends who shared their experiences with violence to me. I know that the women who fabricate stories are altogether separate from the truths of my friends and thousands of other women who have suffered violence at the hands of men.

My friends' stories also shielded me against a second inescapable argument—the charge that the prevalence of men's violence against women has been grossly overstated by groups who seek to promote the image of women as victims. When people accuse me of being on the wrong side of things by pointing to the fallibility of sexual violence statistics, I do not defend my convictions by investigating the methodological rigor of studies that quantify violence (though I think that many are quite good). I need only to picture my friends and remind myself that it makes no difference what the actual numbers may be. There are too many victims regardless. Sexual violence happens far more often than it ought to, and that is reason enough to train boys to resist it.

* * *

I received confirmation that I was forever changed soon after graduating from college when I tuned in on July 18, 2003, to listen to NBA superstar Kobe Bryant hold a highly anticipated press conference at the Staples Center, home of the Los Angeles Lakers. In the same building where he had amazed audiences with his on-court heroics, Bryant voiced the words "I'm innocent" in response to allegations of sexual assault against a 19-year-old Colorado resident. I had previously predicted that the charges against Bryant would harmlessly blow over as they do for so many well-known celebrities, but the next few weeks saw Bryant's tribulations skyrocket into one of America's hottest topics. My fear that America had discovered Exhibit A for its ongoing belief that Black males are inherently aggressive provided much of my personal interest in the case. However, my reaction to it marked my official confirmation that I could not return to the ways of thinking I had before I was educated about sexual violence.

I recalled my feelings 12 years earlier when I observed another Black, male athlete who was widely considered to be the best in his sport also capture headlines for his alleged role in a rape—former heavyweight boxing champion Mike Tyson. I was only 11 years old at the time, but I nonetheless sensed that the situation was of some importance. I feared that the world would associate me with Tyson's indiscretions due to our shared skin color and also feared that he would not get a fair shake because of it. I raced to defend Tyson to my White classmates. I felt that something was at stake even if I could not quite articulate what it was.

My White peers tended to echo the popular belief that Tyson was mentally unstable. This allowed us to distance ourselves from him. We all seemed to agree that "Iron Mike" was in a class all by himself and not representative of any particular demographic.

Bryant, however, was a different story. He was the Italian-raised phenom popularly picked to assume the throne of America's most talented athlete at the time. The popular cry of Bryant's innocence due to his status as a "good guy" was tied to the widely held belief that he was one of Black America's better representatives. His possible fall from grace cautioned that even the most respectable Black man was inherently prone to violence. To make this more complicated, all of this was set against a White woman's accusation, recalling a not-so-distant past in which the supposed insatiable lust of Black men for White women was often sufficient to trigger a death sentence for Black men (I discuss historical myths of Black men as rapists in Chapter 5).

The stakes in the Bryant case were high, and many of my Black peers took to the offensive. They reminded folks of the grand coincidence that America's two biggest "blockbuster" trials of recent memory (those of O. J. Simpson and Bryant) just happened to involve Black athletes accused of assaulting White women. They pointed out the apparently racist dealings and atmosphere in the county in which Bryant was to stand trial. They contended that Bryant had no history of misconduct. They fought on Bryant's behalf so passionately that you would think they knew him personally. Most fiercely of all, they took to dismantling the credibility of the woman who brought the allegation against Bryant.

As for me, I was no longer the 11-year-old who only faintly grasped the importance of the Mike Tyson rape trial, nor was I the strategically clumsy 15-year-old who had argued with my White classmates while awaiting the verdict of O. J. Simpson's murder trial. I was freshly removed from a college experience where I spent a good deal of time sharpening arguments against institutional racism.

Then the unexpected happened, and I found myself giving Bryant's alleged victim a chance. The stories of my friends and family who had survived violence had sunk in too deeply for me to do otherwise. I was mindful of America's long history of persecuting Black men for sexual violence against White women, but I knew enough to know that none of the claims levied against Bryant's alleged victim ruled out the possibility that she had been assaulted. I also knew enough to know that responsibility for most violence fell on the shoulders of boyfriends, fathers, dates, and otherwise "normal" guys. Masked psychopaths lingering in alleys account for only a small percentage of sexual violence (about 34% of acts of sexual violence are committed by strangers, according to the National Crime Victimization Survey).[3]

I do not know exactly how many accusations of being a sellout it took before it became clear that my career as a universal defender of Black men accused of violence had run its course. Those around me had a set of beliefs that they held about the case, and I constantly found myself entertaining alternative perspectives. When people argued that Bryant was innocent because his alleged victim knew full well what she was getting into by entering his hotel room, I considered that people always retain the right to withdraw consent. When people argued that Bryant's alleged victim could not possibly be a genuine sexual assault survivor since she reportedly had sex with another man after the alleged assault, I warned that there was no universal response to rape. And when people argued that Bryant could get any woman he wanted and thus would never need to rape anyone, I noted that their applied logic might also suggest that Bryant's overwhelming appeal might make him ill equipped to handle rejection.

Most of all, I considered that we were discussing an alleged sexual assault that featured an alleged victim who reported soon after the incident in question, a district attorney who was publicly confident that investigating the incident in question was a worthy use of his resources, and an alleged perpetrator who was at least contrite on some level. *If America did not feel that all of this was enough to warrant at least an investigation, then why even have the crime of rape on the books?* Surely, the alleged victim had enough in her corner to at least be given a chance. I was in no position to speak on Bryant's guilt or innocence but did feel confident that both parties had the right to be heard.

Bryant tragically passed while I was working on this book. I do not bring up his case in order to disparage his name or that of his family. Without knowing him or having firsthand knowledge of the incident in question, I am not making any particular claim on his guilt or innocence. I can only speak to the reactions that the criminal charges against him triggered in me and those around me. After so many survivors had taken the time and courage to share their stories with me, I had grown tired of overly simplistic readings of the world. The real world features many violent men. It also features many people who operate with conscious or unconscious prejudices toward men, and men of color in particular. It also features some percentage of women who would willingly raise a false accusation against a man. All of these things are true. In the real world, institutionalized racism is real, men's violence against women is rampant, and false allegations exist, but none of these things disprove the others. These concepts are not even mutually exclusive within the same incident, as it's more than conceivable that a guilty Black suspect can be handled in a racist manner.

I would certainly have more company had I remained in a world in which I saw all sexual assault complainants as deceitful tramps or all Black defendants as undeserving victims of a prejudiced criminal justice system. For a while, I kept a foot in that world, picking and choosing to whom I revealed my politics out of fear of losing the comfort of my former life. But I eventually had to let that approach go and truly honor the brave women who shared their stories with me. And I have been talking ever since.

* * *

In retrospect, there were some pretty clear factors that contributed to my transition from an indifferent man to somebody who chose to spend time advocating on behalf of victims. Let us go through them, as they might help you refine your approach to engage the boys and men who you know.

I WAS INVITED

The impact of an outright invitation to help cannot be understated. A few thousand years of observation has shown that men do not typically stumble into anti-violence work on their own. And even if men do feel compelled to help, they may not always know what to do with their energy. Challenging a rape culture does not always feel as tangible as more common civic activities such as registering people to vote or recycling (though it certainly can be). Consider not only inviting the boys who you know but also giving them something to do. The good news is that community and school-based organizations looking for contributions from men are as plentiful as ever.

PEOPLE BELIEVED IN ME

The peer education program that found me was clever in how it went about activating uninterested men. Not only did I receive an explicit invitation to help out, but that invitation was accompanied by a nomination from a member of the community. The fact that another individual believed in my ability to make a difference mattered greatly to me. I did not want to let down my nominee or the group of men who had hand-selected my voice from a campus of thousands.

If you were to walk onto a local college campus to see how they are dealing with sexual violence, there is a very good chance that you will find a peer education program similar to the one that found me. The sexual violence prevention community is increasingly entrusting young men with executing the solutions for violence perpetrated by other young men. The days of an outside group coming in to tell boys not to rape have largely given way to people who young men know and respect asking them to help.

The boys who you approach need to know that we are reaching out to them because we believe that they can help. They have an irreplaceable personality and a skill set that the global movement against violence would otherwise be missing.

I HAD COMMUNITY

In the next chapter, I review some common challenges faced by men who choose to speak against sexual violence. I was fortunate to have the benefit of an entire group of men who were facing the same challenges as I was. We could sync up on strategies and resources to overcome them. Or we could just find comfort in knowing that we were not facing them alone.

This was in addition to the community that I found in books and movies created by people with an anti-violent mission. There are now many content creators who touch on men's roles in ending violence. Some do so directly and others do so tangentially in their explorations of male socialization. Jackson Katz, Paul Kivel, bell hooks, John Stoltenberg, and Michael Eric Dyson were a few of my favorites when I first got into anti-violence work. I later discovered others such as Pearl Cleage, Don McPherson, Tony Porter, Beth Richie, Byron Hurt, Rus Ervin Funk, and Ted Bunch.

There is also a massive virtual community if boys cannot find an in-person community. Those looking for teaching and research aids can find a wealth of free resources available online. I highlight a few helpful sites in Appendix III, but there are many more beyond these. Social media has also allowed anti-violent youth to connect in ways that were not available when I got started.

I WAS TRAINED

I feel very strongly that men should undergo training of some kind if they are going to be serious about fighting rape culture. I may be biased because One in Four put me through an extensive multiweek training that broke the unspoken college rule of not scheduling anything early on Saturday mornings. However, I can now see that this training played a part in keeping me in the movement.

This goes beyond the simple fact that people are more likely to stick with those things in which they have invested. The movement to end sexual violence has a context of which newcomers should be aware. This is especially true for men as the movement has undoubtedly been pioneered by women. Men who step into it blindly run the risk of alienating those who are already there. These men who have negative interactions with others in the movement may fall away in turn.

There is also the fact that young men are not normally equipped with the kinds of skills and knowledge that they are going to need if they want to challenge the attitudes and behaviors of their peers. Most of the hostility that I received from peers in discussing sexual violence arose from me clumsily stepping into conversations. I got better with time. A space to practice and develop is invaluable.

I HEARD FROM SURVIVORS

I already mentioned the profound impact that survivors had on my development. Even before friends and family disclosed their personal experiences with me, One in Four's training for new members featured a brave volunteer who shared her story with us. The group understood the power of putting a face on a problem too often characterized by cold statistics. These stories also educate men on the very human decisions that survivors make before, during, and after assaults. This makes one more resilient to misinformation about survivor tendencies.

The decision to share a personal story with a young man is obviously a very personal one. I realize that hearing personally from a survivor is not an option for everybody, nor should you burden boys who are not prepared to handle stories of violence. Fortunately, awareness campaigns such as the #MeToo movement have done the world a service by bringing the voices of survivors to the masses. When young men are ready, the stories are out there to be found.

I CONNECTED WITH EXISTING SOCIAL JUSTICE BELIEFS

My entrance into anti-violence work may have come via an all-male organization, but every subsequent violence prevention role that I held was under the leadership of women. This exposed me to perspectives that I just did not hear growing up in a household with two brothers.

Because sexual violence is such an unmistakably gendered issue, many of those who comment on it do so from angles that arise out feminist theory, sociology, and gender studies. Getting involved in anti-violence work exposed me to a cohort of thinkers of which I was previously unaware. I was then surprised when much of what I was reading and hearing sounded familiar. I was able to draw connections between the work to end sexual violence and the work to end racial oppression that had already captured my imagination. Both efforts are full of arguments that society has not recognized the full humanity of its citizens, whether that be in regards to women or Black Americans. This made me want to learn more.

While boys may not have an existing passion for speaking against sexual violence, it is likely the case that they are already passionate about something. Those passions could serve as a bridge to receiving what anti-violence advocates are saying.

* * *

All of the aforementioned factors created the perfect storm where I was primed to think about how I could help, but you may not always encounter boys in such an accessible state. I know well of the defensiveness that men can carry, and I got better at addressing it over time. Sometimes these defenses are just excuses for men who want to remain comfortable in their status quo where they are not held accountable, but I do believe that they often come from understandable places of concern. I next review four of the most common defenses that I hear. I suspect that they are familiar to anybody who spends time speaking against sexual violence, and you would do well to be prepared for them.

"I'M NOT A RAPIST"

In the spring of 2007, I participated in a coalition that brought filmmaker Byron Hurt to the university where I worked. He was there to accompany a showing of his acclaimed film in which he, as an avid hip-hop fan, takes a hard look at masculinity, sexism, violence and homophobia as they are represented in his beloved music genre. I would serve as his primary host for the day and showed him around. The last stop before the screening was a dinner that he graciously agreed to share with several undergraduate students. Byron listened and responded to the students' thoughts on hip-hop as though it were the first time he had heard each thought, though I suspected that he had heard it all before.

I did my best to follow the excellent dialogue taking place, but my attention was quickly monopolized by a single comment. It came along with the following supporting lyrics from wildly successful artist and mogul Jay-Z:

> They call me this misogynist, but they don't call me the dude to take his dollars to give gifts at the projects.[4]

The lyrics came from Jay-Z's 2002 album *The Blueprint 2: The Gift & The Curse*, and I knew them well as the album was a large part of the soundtrack during my first year of post-college life. The student cited these lyrics in support of his assertion that Black men often receive unfair criticism for their harmful interactions with women despite their many positive contributions to the world.

I paused. *What did spending money to give gifts have to do with someone's stance toward misogyny? Could one not be both a misogynist and a financial contributor to worthy causes? And how did someone with the lyrical credibility of Jay-Z allow such a disconnect into a presumably literal and serious verse? And why did a table full of highly educated students find no fault with one man's attempt to explain away any crimes against women through unrelated financial donations?*

Intentionally or otherwise, Jay-Z had once again captured the tenor of many young men. We believe that we have made a sufficient contribution against rape culture simply by not forcibly raping women ourselves or by contributing to other causes that benefit women. Just ask a group of men what they have done in response to the outrageous levels of sexual violence in America and watch them react by citing that they are neither rapists nor wife beaters and that they have extensive track records contributing to community and family.

Men can be downright hostile when you ask them to help. And why shouldn't they be if they are not personally violent? Why should they be held accountable for the actions of other men including, those who they do not even know?

Sometimes it is worth pointing out the absurdly low bar that men have set for ourselves. Is not being a rapist really all it takes for us to be "good" men? Not assaulting others should be the baseline for the type of men that we want our boys to become, not the end goal.

Not to mention the extreme selfishness that underlies the "I'm not a rapist" defense. When I see people rallying against gun violence, I do not assume that they are doing so to atone for that time when they themselves shot somebody. When I see people giving to a food bank, I do not assume that they spend the rest of their time actively stealing food from households. Rather, I assume that many are working on behalf of loved ones or community health in general.

And never forget that we are approaching boys and men precisely because we think that they can help. Instead of blaming them for the problem, we are asking them to take part in the solution. So we ought to align perfectly with their contentions that they are "not rapists."

YOU SHOULD BE TALKING TO WOMEN

In Chapter 1, I explained why standing against violence is not "women's work," but boys have so few examples of men modeling otherwise. They may be genuinely confused as to why you are not talking to women if you are concerned about stopping sexual violence. After all, women are the ones who irresponsibly put themselves in danger by drinking too much, wearing revealing clothing, and not being mindful of their surroundings. And they need to learn to speak up if somebody is doing something to them that they do not like.

These kinds of ideas are examples of what is widely termed "victim blaming" as they place all of the responsibility on victims. Notice that the perpetrators are conceptualized as having no agency. They have no choices to make. They can only take advantage of the vulnerable people placed in front of them.

I just do not believe that this is the case. Even if a man is interacting with somebody who has made unequivocally bad decisions, he still has the ability to make a better decision of his own—a decision that reflects the man who he wants to be when his actions are reviewed the next day. Boys tend to acknowledge their own agency once you point out that they themselves are acting like they do not have any.

The irony of the idea that fighting sexual violence is "women's work" is that this violence says much more about men than it does about women. After all, we are responsible for the vast majority of the perpetration. It says much more about the ways that we train ourselves to see it as acceptable and the ways that we act like it is not our issue when confronted about it.

WHAT ABOUT FALSE ACCUSATIONS?

When a young Will Smith rapped about how "girls ain't nothing but trouble," his first example was naturally about a woman who yells rape after feeling slighted and gets him in trouble with the police.[5] The fear of women weaponizing claims that somebody has assaulted them is front and center for many young men—perhaps even more so for many Black men who are already wary of overreaches by law enforcement. I have found it nearly impossible to talk to men about sexual violence without the specter of false accusations showing up. You might hear, "What about all of the women who falsely accuse men of rape? The courts and the public are going to side with them even if they just make up a story." And this is all it takes for men to shut down from hearing any more about the hundreds of thousands of women and men who have survived sexual violence.

It would be disingenuous to argue that false reports never happen, and to say such a thing is likely to ruin your credibility with men. It is just that false reports soak up a disproportionate amount of attention from men. Know that nearly every study that looks into the matter finds extremely low rates of false reporting. For example, the National Sexual Violence Resource Center performed a review of studies that examined false reporting and concluded that the prevalence of false reporting is between 2% and 10%.[6] With this said, I have never found it particularly effective to focus on these statistics. I think that young men will still envision themselves and their friends as the targets of a malicious accusation even if they are extremely rare. They would likely voice concerns even if the statistics said that only one out of every thousand cases is a false report. I can understand that.

But while I can relate to this impulse, our intense fear of false accusations has turned many of us away from challenging violence that also deserves our resistance. I say this because these two things are not mutually exclusive. There are epidemic levels of violence in America. And some people make false claims for perceived personal gain. Both are true and neither should be ignored.

Often when I talk to somebody about the latest allegation in the headlines, they respond with a story about a man whose life was ruined by a false accusation, as if one person's experience invalidates a very real epidemic of violence. Sexual violence is far too complex to be summed up by believing that every person who comes forth with an allegation is either telling the truth or maliciously lying. The much messier truth lies in between these extremes. We live in a nuanced world where some routinely violent men are held unaccountable and praised while some nonviolent men unjustly spend years behind bars or in infamy. We have to elevate our awareness and our conversation to match the complexity of the real world.

Those who complain about the potential for abuse of sexual assault allegations are not wrong. Some complainants exaggerate or outright falsify their claims. Juries and judges often bring their biases to work. And the court of public opinion often makes up its mind using incomplete information. But couldn't we say the same things about every crime? While our judicial processes are imperfect across the board, sexual violence is pretty much the only time that I hear people arguing that we should just get rid of the crime.

One could argue that sexual violence is especially vulnerable to false accusations because hard "evidence" is difficult to come by and allegations sometimes come down to one person's testimony against that of another. But demanding a flawless criminal justice system before we take allegations seriously is to ignore very real violence that takes place every day. People have the right to seek justice for acts committed against them even if we have not figured out how to perfectly process accusations, and we seem to understand this just fine with other crimes.

I have one final question for those who cannot get past the idea of false accusations. Let's say that you want to create a world where people who make false accusations are shunned. A world where people have to seriously consider the merits of a claim of victimization before they step forward. A world where claims are vigorously pulled apart and scrutinized. *Haven't we already achieved all of this?*

If you think that we live in a world where one can lightly bring forth an accusation, then you have not been paying attention. Legitimate survivors of atrocious behaviors routinely report fears of reprisal and scrutiny as keeping them from reporting. Survivors already have to think on the possible backlash before they come forward. We have already created a social dynamic that weeds out many of those who do not have a strong conviction that what they are saying is true.

There are few human institutions, if any, that people cannot abuse for personal gain. But we cannot allow the potential for abuse to prevent us from taking a stand against very real violence. Conventional wisdom says that we have to choose between challenging violence or false accusations, but this choice is as false as the accusations that so many people rail against.

MEN ARE UNDER SIEGE

The misplaced concern about false accusations is often just part of a bigger contention that men and manhood are under attack. Young men might feel as though society is punishing them because of their gender and that the rules of the game are stacked against them. As it concerns men as the targets of accusations, there is admittedly tension between balancing the rights of complainants and respondents. It is worth thinking about how we can believe victims while honoring due process.

Yet we also have to ask ourselves if the current attention on men and the cultures that surround them is not a rightful course correction to a history of men doing as they pleased without consequence. Let us consider some of the stories that arose out of the #MeToo movement. The phrase "Me Too" was initially utilized by activist Tarana Burke and inspired a viral campaign that released stories that exposed the scope and impact of sexual assault and sexual harassment in 2017. Many of them came from men who admitted that the behaviors pinned on them were once just "business as usual." The concept that a woman could be raped by somebody with whom she has a relationship was not even widely accepted until the tail end of the last century.

Another thing that those defending men should consider is that many of the rationales to shift the focus away from men are actually deeply prejudiced toward men. For example, consider the victim-blaming comments that I mentioned above. When we put all of the focus on women's choices that increase their risk, then we simultaneously treat men as robots that have no say in the matter. Believing that men are capable of empathy and sound decision-making is hardly laying siege to them. Believing that men are an essential part of solving sexual violence is to believe in the best of men.

* * *

I was fortunate to get into anti-violence work alongside a group of other men. I was able to stand in front of audiences alongside these men and observe the myriad of ways to respond to a difficult question or comment. Many of these men had backgrounds that were very different from my own, and they would respond in some ways that never occurred to me or in ways that I could never pull off. I came out with the conclusion that the best ways to respond to the concerns of men are generally those that are authentic and personal. I have given some of my thoughts on the most common defenses raised by men, but the best ways to address the young men in your life probably belong entirely to you.

It is not entirely a negative thing if young men possess entrenched defenses to thinking on their role in preventing sexual violence. It means that they are already passionate about aspects of the conversation that we want to have with them. Use that passion as a way in, correct whatever misinformation they possess, and then empower them to develop positions of their own. If you do not feel comfortable addressing misinformation, then take advantage of the many online resources covering statistics and conversational strategies (I highlight some of them in Appendix III).

You can lean on lessons learned once you overcome boys' initial defenses. We now have a few decades' worth of research and experience about violence prevention techniques for you to draw on as you talk to boys. Most of the educational programming aimed at prevention employed today falls into one of three major buckets—bystander intervention, social norms, or empathy-based. They commonly borrow from several of these buckets. Bystander intervention strategies seek to equip people with the tools and confidence to interrupt violent attitudes and behaviors. I describe them further in Chapter 8. Social norms strategies are those that seek to decrease unhealthy behaviors and attitudes by correcting misperceptions that those behaviors and attitudes are common (or, conversely, promote healthy behaviors and attitudes by communicating their favorability in a community). Empathy-based strategies posit that generating empathy for victims, or generating knowledge of the dynamics of sexual violence, will in turn decrease one's likelihood to perpetrate violence.

Measuring the efficacy of violence prevention programming is difficult because we often have to rely on measuring attitudes rather than measuring actual shifts in behavior. Taken altogether, you can see some key goals for your discussions with boys, though. You can help them think through the human impact of failing to prioritize consent in intimate encounters, if they agree with what the world tells them about this impact, and how they can help. Having such conversations not only develops them as change agents but forces them to evolve their own values, as was the case with me.

* * *

Many women continuously engage in any number of protective habits under the threat of male violence. They may plan their lives to avoid being alone in certain areas or at certain times, constantly check their surroundings, or even carry deterrents such as mace or a weapon. Their defensive postures are not just aimed at strangers. Many perform a set of actions designed to keep them safe from acquaintances as well, such as having somebody keep track of their whereabouts when on a date. The women who have experienced sexual violence have likely expended energy contemplating the emotional, judicial, and medical avenues that will provide them with the best sense of recovery and many more hours navigating the systems and people along those avenues. Many more women who have survived negative encounters with men have devoted incredible amounts of energy attempting to classify what happened to them or even to deciphering how much they are to blame. Men and boys who have survived sexual assault or abuse can likely relate to many of these experiences. The rest of us have probably never had so much as a conversation about how we relate to the men who our sisters, girlfriends, and female friends do their best to guard against; nor have we ever stopped to consider how much we look like those men ourselves. We could change the world if we could convince boys to exert even a fraction of the energy that girls and women give to thinking about sexual violence.

I hope that this chapter helped you feel a little more equipped as you figure out how to invite the young men who you know to think about things to which they have not historically devoted much thought. Asking men to take up work to which they have previously been hostile or apathetic is not an easy task. You might be pleasantly surprised by what you find, though. People often assume that young men are not interested in having conversations about sexual violence or have little to contribute. But I consistently find that young men have a lot to say on the matter behind closed doors. In fact, I can honestly say that I have never sat down with an audience of boys and found that they had nothing to say. They are often very grateful to have a space to speak on topics that matter deeply to them, even if they did not previously recognize that they mattered. This is not because of any great skill on my part. Boys simply find this topic to be relevant to their lives. They crave opportunities for serious dialogue on a topic too often ignored or mocked in their day-to-day lives. Boys want to discuss how to handle themselves in sexual encounters. Boys want to examine peer cultures with which they are not entirely comfortable. They want to examine aspects of traditional manhood that do not reflect who they want to be. When I sit down with a group of boys, it is often the first time that they have had the opportunity to have a sustained conversation on these things. This must change.

I do not claim to be a perfect messenger. I have certainly walked away from presentations feeling embarrassed that I did not accomplish anything. Perhaps I stepped into a community that had a history of which I was unaware. Perhaps the logistics were not suitable to communicate effectively to the audience. Perhaps I could have broken through if I had had just a little more time out of the audience's packed schedule. Or perhaps I was just ineffective in my delivery.

However, my track record in engaging close friends is much better. The men who have stayed in my life are almost universally receptive to hearing about how they can help. I even have several friends who were initially defensive when I first told them how I was spending my time who eventually returned to say that they saw where I was coming from and respected my position. I say this because I do not want you to forget one of the most valuable assets that you have as you engage boys who you know—time. You have the option to reengage at a later date if things do not go well at first. You can identify sources of defensiveness, tweak your approach, and try again. Or you might just catch your addressee at a better time or when he has had some time to reflect on what you said.

Once you do break through, boys have to learn to overcome the same defenses that they once held. Few people openly support rape and sexual assault, but many do defend particular brands of violence whether they are aware that they are doing so or not. I fully believe that the majority of boys and men who are given the freedom to truly express themselves will come to question certain aspects of the status quo. But, as this freedom is so rarely afforded, anti-violent perspectives can lead to conflict and isolation. Fortunately, you can prepare boys by equipping them with community, opportunity for practice, a broader context for their work, and your belief in them.

INFORMATION IS POWER: A CONVERSATION WITH TONYA PRINCE

Tonya GJ Prince is the editor and founder of WESurviveAbuse.com, a "culturally inclusive and diverse information hub for Survivors of both sexual and domestic violence." She has over three decades of professional experience working to end sexual and domestic violence. I have known her since she was the state outreach coordinator for Virginians Aligned Against Sexual Assault, and greatly respect her unapologetic mission to release the voices of survivors.

Q: You have spent years curating the voices of survivors of intimate violence. Understanding that survivors are not all the same, what have you learned that survivors would like those of us who haven't experienced such violence to know and feel?

A: I think that survivors would like for us who are "doing the work" to understand that they are strong, resilient, and knowledgeable. They have learned a lot of lessons from the tragedy that they had to overcome and they are more than capable of providing us with information and leading "the work."

Q: You have a son. How does your awareness of this topic influence how you prepared him for the world?

A: Unfortunately, sexual violence runs in my family. It's almost a tradition going back many generations. What I've learned being "the vocal one" is that when you are the person that takes the lead in declaring that this is happening, you also take on the job of educating the family. People aren't always going to do this work in a formal way but it's sometimes even more impactful to do it in your family.

So, my mother encouraged me to impart some lessons to my son. In talking with him—about body safety, "good touch, bad touch" and all of this kind of stuff—I know that he has had at least two close calls with abuse that he was able to evade because we've been talking about it since he was able to talk. Even if you don't have a girl, you still have a young child who predators are unfortunately after as well. Even though I educated him, I don't know that I was ever really prepared to see my son use the skills we discussed.

Q: What was it like to transition from seeing your son as a potential victim to being in relationships of his own?

A: We have talked frequently about safe and balanced relationships. Love is a great feeling but how do you love and let your partner feel safe and empowered? I taught him that if he's going to take on the responsibility of getting involved with someone else, then he takes on the responsibility to make that person feel a certain way.

Q: You celebrate survivors who share their stories. Some comedians and other public figures have criticized the practice of sharing testimonials publicly for fear of demonizing men that have not been convicted of a crime. Many parents and guardians of boys share this concern. What is the best way to support survivors while honoring due process?

A: It is challenging being Black and woman at the same time. On the one hand, I deal with an unfair criminal justice system and the demonizing of Black boys and men as well as the "adultification" of Black girls. I think about the abuse to prison pipeline for both boys and girls. At the same time, I'm dealing with threats against women. There's a hashtag going around right now called #blackfemicide because we're losing Black women hourly to gun violence in America. So trying to balance the two is always a challenge.

First and foremost, I try to advocate for the most vulnerable. For me, that's children and women and girls simply because they are most vulnerable to violence. I often say that if you have concerns about striking the right balance, then join us. If you want things to be better and if you want fewer boys getting caught up, then help us make them more knowledgeable just the same as we educate them about their rights during a police stop. Let's help them to know what their rights are during a relationship. Help them know the rights of their partners. I listen to interviews after the fact and so many boys and men accused of violence sound unaware that a relationship could put them in this position. That's what I don't want. I don't want them tripped up by a system that's designed to capture them. Take the lead in your family and make sure that boys and girls have the same information. Information is power and boys are often missing so much of what they need.

CHAPTER 3: STARTING THE CONVERSATION WITH BOYS

- In retrospect, I can recognize several factors that contributed to me accepting and sticking with anti-violence work:
  - I was invited to help and others believed in me.
  - I had community.
  - I had a space to train.
  - I heard from survivors.
  - I connected with existing social justice perspectives.

Take whatever lessons learned will help you reach the young men in your life. Remember that positive approaches generally work better than negative ones.

- You must be prepared to counter the most common defenses from boys. Four that I hear regularly are:
  - Men should be left alone if they are not personally violent.
  - Anti-violence work should be aimed at women.
  - The real fight is against false accusations.
  - Men are under siege in contemporary America.

Recognize that the fact that boys possess these defenses is not entirely negative, as you can use topics that boys are already passionate about to transition to other conversations, such as talking about how they might counter prevailing stereotypes of men.

- Of the aforementioned defenses, concern about false accusations is generally the most immediate and most entrenched that I encounter. You have to be prepared to face it if you are going to have honest conversations with young men. Your response to it should be targeted and personal, but here are some general thoughts that I have found helpful in breaking through defenses:
  - Sexual violence and false accusations are not mutually exclusive. Proving one does not disprove the other.
  - The potential for errors in the criminal justice system does not disprove the realities of sexual violence in the world any more than it disproves the realities of murder, robbery, or any other crime.
  - The United States already has a climate that scrutinizes the claims of alleged victims. Ironically, young men immediately raising concerns about false accusations when the topic of sexual violence arises is verification of that climate.

Facing the Complications of Being an Anti-violent Man

I kept up speaking to boys and men about sexual violence prevention long after my college experience faded to memory. I have since held formal positions on the topic, such as serving as a prevention specialist in a college health department and working as a public speaker with a speakers' bureau that focuses on student health. But most often, I just take time to talk informally to those around me about sexual violence.

Upon learning about my work and thinking it to be worthwhile, a lot of people told me to go on *The Oprah Winfrey Show* while the show was running. "You should go on *Oprah*," said the lost childhood friend upon reuniting. "You should go on *Oprah*," said the woman seated next to me on an airplane. "You should go on *Oprah*," said the family member who I run into once a year at Christmas. It was rarely another show—always *Oprah*. *Why would so many who learn of my stance on sexual violence reference the same show over and over again?*

I have some theories. I think that meeting a Black man openly engaged in ending sexual violence is such an unexpected occurrence that many can only respond by citing the most available reference point that they possess for a rarity like me—a billionaire Black woman who has taken well-known stances against sexual violence. One oddity conjures memory of another.

This is telling because working against sexual violence is not the only cause for which I have marched. I have at times mentored at-risk teenagers, worked street rallies against gun violence, and held race relations forums. Yet not once did those actions drive someone to suggest that I reach out to an international celebrity with whom I have no relationship. I explain this by the absence of Black men pursuing anti–sexual violence aims and the shock factor involved in meeting one. It has always been common for Black men to work to protect Black boys from the things most likely to harm them (street violence and police brutality, for example), but no such tradition exists for one of the most prominent threats to Black girls and women.

There is a growing body of men working against sexual violence, but we remain a rarity and the world does not always know what to do with us. Our numbers have certainly improved, thanks to decades of activism, but it remains unclear if we are raising a generation of boys who will be any more successful in taking a stand than prior generations. Ask a group of boys what can be done to prevent sexual violence and they will almost invariably begin by rattling off a list of activities to be primarily carried out by women—increasing female awareness of male intentions, teaching women self-defense, directing women not to get too drunk or to lead men on, and so on. The idea of boys and men taking action does not generally kick in without further interrogation.

Once you do manage to break through and successfully empower a young man to stand against violence, your job is not done. Sustained conversations are needed to prepare boys for the enormous task of fighting against a culture. Additionally, they may need your support because their lives might become more challenging in any number of ways. I can think of three specific complications that entered my life once I began speaking against sexual violence.

COMPLICATION #1: HEARING THE STORIES OF OTHERS

I continued to meet people who wanted to share their experiences with violence. I have come to hold on to dozens of stories that were entrusted to me and sometimes to me alone. As these were not my stories, it was not my place to act on them without permission. Keeping stories of violence bottled up can carry stress of its own.

COMPLICATION #2: PERSONAL ACCOUNTABILITY

Once I was enlisted to speak out against sexism and its correlated violence, I had to pay that much more attention to my own behaviors and do my best to practice what I preached. As I began to recognize that blame for sexual violence rested not only on its primary perpetrators but also on the culture that excused it, this raised questions as to how much I personally contributed to the problem. I had to constantly evaluate behaviors, thoughts, and speech that I previously viewed as harmless.

Men with anti-violent aims are not exempt from enacting problematic attitudes and behaviors. Our faults and offenses do not disappear simply because we march in a rally, volunteer at a rape crisis center, or write a book on men's violence against women. If anything, doing these things exposes our imperfections so much more as our loved ones, our associates, and we ourselves become quicker to latch on to inconsistencies between our words and our deeds. I admit to sometimes longing for simpler days when I only had to worry about "normal guy stuff."

COMPLICATION #3: COMPLICATED RELATIONSHIPS

I still had to continue relationships with people who had never deeply considered their own stances on sexual violence. Most people do not spend their time pondering rape and its causes, especially men. They talk about these things casually but rarely in a sustained or introspective manner, and many find discussing them to be downright bizarre. I quickly learned that blank stares and strained attempts at humor were to be expected whenever I told somebody that I spent time giving presentations about rape prevention. Others were downright defensive and took my work as a personal attack. This is to say nothing of the times when I was indeed critical of rape-supportive attitudes that I came across, and nobody wants to be that guy who ruins everybody's time by criticizing what others consider to be innocent fun. Because of these things, I sometimes constructed walls between the personal and the political—a reflex born out of a desire to fit in.

This held true for my interactions with girlfriends as well, as some wished me to pick up a more "normal" cause. There are those who find this brand of work to be too much of a break from the standard male playbook and would rather that their male partners behave more conventionally. Telling a woman that you spend your time talking about rape is not the great pickup line that some think it is.

This is a good time to point out some of the labels that the world attempts to affix to men who openly work against sexual violence. From reading accounts from other men who speak on men's violence against women, I know that I am not alone in observing that we are sometimes assumed to have a loved one who is a survivor of violence (or assumed to be survivors ourselves), to be gay, or to be former perpetrators. The first assumption of knowing a survivor is understandable as a personal connection to an issue is quite often the origin of an unconventional position. The others are worth discussing, though.

It is common enough for heterosexual men to divorce themselves from accountability by claiming that anti-violence work is the work of women and feminized or gay men. Many of my anti-violence colleagues are indeed gay, but someone once pointed out to me that to presume all of us to be gay only highlights the depths to which violence against women has crept into heterosexual dating norms. This presumption suggests that men who are not interested in being violent toward women cannot possibly have romantic or sexual interest in them. The logic that those who speak against violence are former perpetrators is lacking as well, as I have never murdered a person or kidnapped a child but I proudly denounce those things as well. Society will do many things to minimize men who challenge sexual violence, and one of its favorite tactics is to push us into narrow boxes that explain us away.

* * *

My life would have certainly been much simpler had I never taken up anti-violence work, but it would not have been better. There is no way that I would trade in the experience, as it has led to tremendous self-growth. When boys and men get together to discuss what can be done to change violent cultures, my experience is that these sessions naturally lead to identifying our own mistakes rather than devolving into self-congratulatory events as you might expect. Few experiences have made me think about my own flaws as profoundly as sitting down to discuss how I can influence other men.

Anti-violence work was the doorway for me to examine manhood as well. It can be disorienting to challenge male training that literally began as soon as you came into the world, but there is a tremendous freedom once you realize that you are free to critique those aspects of manhood that you do not care for. This frees you up to work on those aspects of yourself that you do like or even to find them in the first place.

I even find some of the accusations lobbied at anti-violent men to be helpful because it is healthy for men doing anti-violence work to evaluate their motives. For example, if someone were to accuse me of putting up a front to impress women, it might be a good opportunity to take a step back and examine my intentions and methods. This constant self-evaluation has value and leads to self-growth. However, there is another seldom-discussed label for men of color that does produce a degree of internal conflict for me—a race traitor.

I mentioned earlier that the cultural response to Kobe Bryant's sexual assault trial was a key experience in my development as an anti-violence activist. In the midst of the trial, I had the opportunity to appear on a regional television show that was dedicating an episode to discussing the broader impact of Bryant's trial on attitudes toward sexual violence. Viewers could call in to the show and direct comments toward the participants, so I had considered the questions that I might face. A fraternity brother called me as I pulled into the television studio's parking lot and said something that I was not prepared to face at all. I quickly explained what I was about to do. He wished me luck and closed by saying, "I hope you're defending Kobe. Because you're not Black if you don't." He said this in jest, but there was much truth to it, as he would be far from alone in thinking that the primary relationship between Black men and sexual violence should be in defending Black men who are wrongly accused.

This brings up a barrier to entry that we have to address if we are serious about inviting young Black men to speak up. There is no way to go about anti-violence work without shining a light on problematic behaviors and attitudes. Black boys may fear that racist agendas will hijack this spotlight as evidence that they are particularly prone to violence. This may be especially true in light of the current scrutiny on excessive force used by police officers, where judgments about a person's propensity for violence may literally be a matter of life and death.

Sadly, many boys have interpreted the need to guard against prejudice against Black men to mean that they should always side with Black men accused of violence. Daring to publicly interrogate the violent behaviors and cultures that some Black men feed is readily viewed as collusion with systemic racism. We have a firmly established track record when one of us comes under fire—defend, defend, defend. I saw this mentality on display during Bill Cosby's various legal proceedings pertaining to sexual assault throughout the 2010s. Many observers fully accepted that Cosby faced allegations of misconduct against no less than 60 women and spanning across five decades. They also believed he frequently and illegally dispensed drugs to these women in order to facilitate sexual encounters (I am not arguing what the facts are but pointing out what many of Cosby's defenders believe them to be), yet they still thought it was absurd to consider the possibility that Cosby could be anything other than the target of a racist agenda.

If this fact pattern is not enough for the criminal justice system to entertain a case, then should Black men just ask for an exemption to any harmful consequences of their sexual decisions? If we are so conditioned toward the unmitigated defense of Black men who are accused of rape, how much more lenient are we toward those whose who engage in relatively minor behaviors that create a culture that breeds sexual violence—those who routinely brandish unsavory names for women with whom they disagree, those who are comfortable tugging at body parts and clothing belonging to strangers passing by on the street, and those who feel justified in labeling any woman who dares to come forward with an accusation of sexual violence as an attention-grabbing bitch?

Of course, some Black boys and men very consciously support all Black male defendants, even those who might be guilty. They make a strategic decision to attack what they perceive to be the greater evil and to protect an image of Black men that is often unfairly maligned. They feel compelled to prioritize racial oppression over gendered violence.

Some might say that the pressures demanding Black male innocence hold particularly true when Black men are defending themselves from accusations of violence against White women, but I think that they apply regardless of an alleged victim's demographics. Supreme Court nominee Clarence Thomas famously claimed that he was the victim of a high-tech lynching when publicly accused of sexual harassment by a Black woman. Michael Jackson's camp also echoed this charge when Jackson was publicly accused of molesting White children. We have seen many other prominent Black men who have been accused of sexual violence by parties of various ages, races, and genders routinely compare their detractors to lynch mobs. Black men's regular usage of this defense has likely contributed to the frequency with which we now see even non-Black men invoke it. References to lynch mobs were commonly cited by those who criticized the rush to judgment of Duke University lacrosse players accused of rape in 2006, and former International Monetary Fund chief Dominique Strauss-Kahn also claimed to be the victim of a public "lynching campaign" after he was accused of sexually assaulting a sex worker in 2010.[1]

As the primary purpose of this book is to add to the resources for those raising Black boys who see their racial identifications as key aspects of their identities, I am going to devote the rest of this chapter to addressing the barrier of betraying Black communities. Let me begin by saying that I completely understand the concern of Black boys and men who choose to defend Black men named as defendants. I was once asked to speak to a class of incoming students at a university in the Northeast. I was to present a case study involving a fictional sexual assault for the audience to discuss. My hosts requested that I not bring race into the case study. On the one hand, this was a very understandable request given that discussions of sexual violence can already be quite complex without considering how the race of an alleged perpetrator or victim might change our reactions.

Trying to teach concepts such as consent in a limited amount of time is already a daunting challenge. On the other hand, I interpreted the request to avoid race to mean that the case study should only feature White participants because there is simply no way to feature an alleged victim or alleged perpetrator of color without racial dynamics being a part of the conversation.

The race of the participants is a key concern nearly every time I discuss a real or fictional portrayal of sexual violence with Black boys. Racial politics are inseparable from Black boys' understandings of sexual violence prevention, as many of them rightly recognize that there is a history of not giving accused Black men a fair trial.

I was once again in a barbershop when a discussion arose about the sexual assault allegations against Jameis Winston, eventual winner of the 2013 Heisman Trophy. This was prior to authorities stating that they would not be pursuing action against Winston. Still, the shop was full of definitive claims that Winston was innocent, even though none of us knew anything about what happened beyond the information the media was circulating. Much of the "proof" of Winston's innocence came in the form of stories about other Black men who had been railroaded by vindictive women and racist systems.

To talk to Black men about a given Black man accused of sexual violence is rarely to meet localized arguments informed by context but rather to meet sweeping contentions about the innocence of Black men as a whole. What I would like to challenge is not so much the utilization of an anti-racist argument in the defense of any one man, but more so that these arguments are often laid out so as to squelch the very idea that a Black man could be violent. I have to believe that we can strike a better balance between protecting Black men from racist agendas and protecting women and children from violent men. Both racism and sexual violence exist in abundance in America. We must ensure that our fights against either reality do not consume us to a point where we inadvertently aid the other. *Can we not train boys to work toward a day when neither exists?*

* * *

Some of my most salient memories from growing up revolve around false accusations that I believed were motivated by racial animus. I remember the store where the owner followed my brother and me like a hawk in order to make sure that we were not stealing. I remember the convenience store clerk who accused me of stealing, going so far as to follow me out to my mother's car. I remember the time that I was pulled over by no less than 10 police officers so that they could search my car for drugs. Having false accusations lobbed at you strikes at something deep in the spirit. It makes you want to check out from a society that does not value you. There are stories far worse than mine—stories where life outcomes were affected. Combine these memories with even a rudimentary understanding of America's history of prejudice against Black men and it is only natural that many Black boys routinely side with Black men accused of violence.

Black boys' belief that their place is standing alongside Black, male defendants accused of violence is more than justified historically, but boys will end up unbalanced if they are not also trained to take on power structures such as the systemic misogyny and objectification of women that results in astounding rates of sexual violence in America. Many Black boys are wary of challenging their peers for fear of colluding with the historical demonization of Black men, but they should know that sexual violence prevention is definitively pro-Black. Here are four reasons why I believe this to be true.

BLACK WOMEN AND MEN ARE VICTIMIZED

The most obvious reason why anti-violence work is pro-Black is because Black women and men are among the victims of sexual violence. The regrettable irony of defending an alleged Black, male perpetrator on the grounds that you want to support the Black community is that a Black woman or child is quite often on the other side of the allegation. One of the major themes in the National Crime Victimization Survey that I mentioned in Chapter 1 is that victims of violent crimes tend to identify their assailants as belonging to the same race.[2] This is not surprising, as we know that the majority of perpetrators of sexual violence are known to their victims.

Not to mention the thousands of children, partners, and friends who are witnesses to this violence and its aftermath. I often wonder just how much energy Black communities spend responding to this violence. *What great things could be accomplished if they were allowed to utilize this energy for more productive purposes? How much closer would communities be without the mistrust brought on by knowing that violent men are in their midst?*

FAILING TO ADDRESS SEXUAL VIOLENCE IS ALL BUT ASKING THOSE OUTSIDE OF BLACK COMMUNITIES TO DO SO

Boys with strong community-oriented leanings should recognize that sexual violence is often handled by folks outside of local communities when those communities do not handle it themselves. Knowledge of violence against women does not always make it further than the locale in which the violence occurs. However, when it does find its way out, extra-community forces often deal with it. Responding personnel may or may not have affiliations with the community where the violence occurred; and as you move further away from immediate response toward the policymakers addressing the aggregate violence, the personnel can become decidedly less community-focused. By taking an active role in combating violence, Black men can simultaneously apply localized solutions and dismantle violent stereotypes about themselves.

MANY OF THE TRADITIONAL DEFENSES OF SEXUAL VIOLENCE ARE SUBTLY RACIST

Let us consider some of the traditional statements used to defend men who are accused of rape or sexual assault. One might hear, "She was drunk. What did she think was going to happen?" or "She went up to his room. What did she think was going to happen?" *Are these statements not extremely derogatory of men? Do they not assume men to be mindless automatons whose free will is easily coopted by circumstance and lust?* Furthermore, when used in reference to Black men, they are a shade away from old-school racist arguments that claimed that Black men were animalistic brutes incapable of anything beyond primal motivations.

Let us not forget that such arguments were once key weapons in America's post-Reconstruction era efforts to limit the rights of Black Americans. They basically amounted to saying that the government had to control Black men because we could not be trusted to control ourselves. The energy around such beliefs was captured in the 1915 film *The Birth of a Nation*. For those unfamiliar with the film, it posited the Ku Klux Klan as benevolent warriors defending America from a tide of sexually aggressive Black men. The movie's content alone is not enough to distinguish it from other racist material put out by American media at the time. It is the movie's success that does that. The film is credited for innovating several cinematic techniques and remained the most profitable film in American history for some time. Many consider it to be the first "Hollywood blockbuster." The film is also credited as a primary contributor to the resurgence of the Ku Klux Klan in the 1920s. We recognize it today as the flagship title for a time period where Black Americans were popularly portrayed with little diversity beyond being shown as villains and morons. I would rather not aid any efforts that suggest that *The Birth of a Nation* and its supporters had things right.

Many place the blame for male-perpetrated violence on women who place themselves in vulnerable situations. As a man, I do not see directing women how to behave as my place, but I can speak to the expectation that women take an environmental assessment before deciding to enter certain spaces where men are present. As this expectation pertains to Black men, I find it to be too much in league with the arguments of the American slave state of old. After all, slaveholders were the ones who defended the American slave institution with predictions that the freed and unrestrained Black man would run amok and create a nation where women would need to be on guard at all times. They were the ones who argued that Black men lacked the capacity to control their base urges and required outside forces to prevent them from giving in to animalistic temptation. These are not admissions that I am willing to make.

To place blame on women for male-perpetrated actions is to admit that we need assistance with something that we lack the capacity to control on our own. I would rather challenge Black boys and men to utilize the fullness of the faculties that they possess and on which their forefathers made their claims for freedom—empathy, reason, fidelity, and civility. Appealing to the positive qualities of Black men rather than urging women to avoid our more sinister qualities is certainly pro-Black.

THE BLACK COMMUNITY HAS A STRONG HISTORY OF WORKING AGAINST VIOLENCE

Working to end sexual violence is a continuation of some of the noblest traditions of the African American experience. Resisting violence has been a part of our narrative since the first African was forcibly brought to American shores. Accounts of American chattel slavery are full of sexual assaults against Black women and men alike. We have always cultivated the resiliencies for resisting and surviving psychological abuse stemming from sexual exploitation.

* * *

Many Black boys are raised in an unbalanced manner, as I was. We grow into experts at deciphering race-based violence but are oblivious to gender-based violence. However, we must be careful not to judge Black America too harshly. Peoples and cultures all over the world make a habit of minimizing sexual violence, and each one has its own methods and language for doing so. Additionally, just as racial justice efforts can be clumsily wielded such that they hamper justice for survivors of sexual violence, so too are anti–sexual violence efforts sometimes wielded in ways that rely on racism.

In her classic *Women, Race and Class*, activist and author Dr. Angela Davis contends that even some of the most respected pioneers of the anti–sexual violence movement have bolstered their critiques of rape culture via the demonization of Black men. As someone who was trained by the anti–sexual violence community throughout the early 2000s, there are few authors whose work I consider more foundational than that of Susan Brownmiller. But in reviewing portions of Brownmiller's work, Davis remarks, "It seems as if she wants to intentionally conjure up in her readers' imaginations armies of Black men, their penises erect, charging full speed ahead toward the most conveniently placed white women." She later writes, "Susan Brownmiller's discussion on rape and race evinces an unthinking partisanship which borders on racism. In pretending to defend the cause of all women, she sometimes boxes herself into the position of defending the particular cause of *white* women, regardless of its implications."[3]

Even when shying away from critiques of pioneers like Brownmiller, it is obvious that concern for Black men as allies is not always a front-burner issue for some anti-violence advocates. I once attended a conference that examined pornography's contributions to rape culture, among other things. The organizers decided to show the documentary that I previously mentioned in Chapter 3 that examines manhood and hip-hop culture, given some of the thematic overlap in the content produced by the pornography and hip-hop music industries. The video predominately featured men of color, and one audience member felt comfortable raising her voice in a packed auditorium to ask what a bunch of thugs had to do with her. This was definitely not the only time that I walked away from an anti-violence collaboration convinced that I was in alliance with people who did not care about how Black men might receive our tactics.

Given that the anti–sexual violence movement already wrestles with the proper inclusion of men (as we have not traditionally inspired much confidence as anti-violence advocates), Black boys who choose to pursue alliance with anti-violent causes are doubly forged in the fires of mistrust. The Black men who survive this scrutiny with their desire to help intact are forced to constantly review their motivations for participation. This makes us confident and flexible advocates, as the disingenuous will likely not tolerate waves of mistrust and scrutiny for very long.

At the time of my graduation from college and departure from the peer education program that first recruited me into anti-violence work, I was the only active Black member. This was not for lack of effort. We did succeed in attracting several minority members, but no more Black men. Some outright denied our invitations. Some just had too much on their plates. Some came aboard and then fizzled away for the same reasons that men of all colors have collectively avoided taking action against sexual violence—participation posed too much of a threat to their conceptions of "manhood" or they were unwilling to abandon the privilege and comfort that goes along with denying men's systematic violence against women. Especially painful for me was seeing Black men leave because sticking around proved too much of a surrender of their core identities as Black men—whether that meant yielding to the internal dynamics of our group or to the larger movement we served. One of these men told me in private after separating from the group that he simply did not have the energy to spend educating another group of White men about their contributions to systemic racism. He knew his role in the group would be a contentious one and did not relish the idea of fighting a group of men whose mission he knew to be an important one.

Unlike these men, I was obviously able to reconcile my concerns over racial matters enough to remain around the cause. I have stuck around this work for two decades now and consider it to be an integral part of who I am. I also share a lasting camaraderie with and respect for the multiracial collection of men who served as my initial colleagues in this work. And I have grown tremendously under the mentorship of women of all races who were every bit as concerned about challenging both racism and sexual violence. Still, I deeply sympathize with the Black men who did not stick around. They reflected the tensions for which Black boys who join the effort against sexual violence need to be prepared.

I once heard a comedian joke about how Black men used to be required to step aside when they crossed paths with a White woman on the street, but now it seems that White women are always the ones to cross the street when they pass us in public. He was commenting on the phenomenon of

White women speeding up, altering their paths, clutching their belong-
ings, or casting a wary glance in the presence of Black men. I suspect that
this ritual is familiar to most Black men regardless of upbringing or physical stature. When it occurs in my presence, I usually do my best to dis-
guise my acknowledgment of the situation.

These events generally play out over a few seconds, but they tend to re-
play in my head long after they conclude. I cannot help but wonder if my
stoicism in these encounters is counterproductive to the anti-violent goals
to which I claim to adhere. For all I know, some of the women I pass are
survivors of male violence and have reasonable feelings of vulnerability
when around men of any color. *Would it be so hard to take action that
might mitigate any fear brought on by my presence? Perhaps I could alter my
own path? Or maybe shoot a smile or a kind word to affirm that I have no
intent to harm? Or would that make people feel more uncomfortable?*

An inner voice tells me that I am within my rights to defiantly push
through these encounters regardless of whatever trepidation I might sense
in passersby. I tell myself that I am not violent and this person has no
right to assume otherwise. In a flash, I am able to convince myself that
the woman causing my distress is a racist whose only contact with Black
men has come via mugshots on the evening news. But this reflex might
only serve to reinforce whatever negative beliefs the other person holds
regarding men of color in the first place.

Whether I choose to silently acquiesce to a woman's mistrust of me
or boldly posture against it, I fear that there is no response that would
not trigger some degree of inner turmoil. The former action leaves me
wondering if I have betrayed my sense of racial justice and the latter leaves
me angry for complicity with justified guarding against male aggression.
Neither choice is without regret. Each appeals to a particular aspect of me,
but neither satisfies the totality of who I am.

It is within the margins of this tension that Black boys who speak
against sexual violence will live their lives. They will wonder to whom they
are "selling out" and when it is worth it to do so. When news surfaces that
yet another Black male celebrity has been accused of intimate violence,
they will commit a portion of themselves to hoping that society has not

found its newest poster child for Black male indiscretion and another portion to wishing that America would do more than slap men on the wrist for violent behavior. Even if boys do satisfy their internal conflicts, others around them may remind them of their appropriate place, as I was in that television studio parking lot.

I have at times struggled with striking a balance between being authentic to the communities of Black men with whom I identify and being authentic to the movement against sexual violence that I have come to deeply respect. Loyalty to both can sometimes feel tenuous. I will likely never completely satisfy these tensions, but I have advanced to a comfortable place where I realize that these tensions should not stop me from acting against the rape culture that creates so much violence in America. Men have put this work off long enough.

Of course, I fully recognize that there are entire passages that could be lifted from this book in order to serve as excellent propaganda for those arguing the violent proclivities of Black men. Here is the thing, though. If you know a Black boy who is struggling with similar concerns, I also know that our work could never harm Black men as much as those men who engage in sexual encounters with little to no thought of the consequences. We certainly do less harm than the men who effectively fight for violent Black men to go unpunished. We certainly do less harm than men who teach boys that their manhood is entirely dependent on their ability to access women sexually. And our stance is far more productive than the men who argue that it is normal for men's sexual urges to sometimes supersede their values.

* * *

I have discussed Black boys' awareness of racism as a roadblock to involvement thus far, but the truth is that it can be a tremendous asset as well. That same ability to detect racial prejudice can also be used to detect the social underpinnings for massive amounts of violence against women. Violence does not occur at such horrific rates without cultural norms that support it. Many Black boys understand this rather intuitively when it comes to forms of race-based violence. They might therefore be able to make connections between attitudes held about them and attitudes held about women and survivors.

I was once talking with a prominent African American public speaker on feminism and violence prevention. As we walked along a sidewalk, I remarked that I thought that there was a disproportionate number of men of color in formal anti-violence positions (this is just my belief; I have no real statistic to back this up). He agreed. I then asked him why he thought this was the case. He did not say a word and proceeded to drift into me as we continued walking. He ran me clear off the sidewalk before responding to my question and said, "Black men understand what it means to be invisible to people." He said that we are accustomed to being viewed as less than human and therefore predisposed to react to the inhumanity of sexual violence. His point hit home for me. I could see in retrospect that my racial identification played a huge part in why I responded positively when invited to join the movement against sexual violence. I had already accepted that prejudice and discrimination were alive and well in America, so I did not find it jarring when women started telling me that men held certain behaviors and attitudes that resulted in systemic violence against women.

Playing out this thought experiment, I have identified nine areas that I think allow Black boys to be receptive to anti-violence messaging. In doing this, I obviously cannot address the full spectrum of attitudes held by boys who identify as Black. I can only speak to some common themes that boys express to me that might serve as levers to pull on as you ask Black boys to raise their voices.

THEY UNDERSTAND THAT IT IS NOT ALWAYS ABOUT STATISTICS

Many Black boys and men understand that it is cowardly to tolerate racist beliefs on the grounds that one needs to see undisputable evidence that racism exists before acting. The voices of those who feel devalued ought to be enough for people to ask what they can do to help.

Likewise, there is little value in insisting that somebody provide statistics about sexual violence before you consider it to be a real issue. The voices of women and men who have been victimized are continuous and widespread. That ought to be enough for one to consider helping.

THEY UNDERSTAND THAT ACTIVITIES BEHIND CLOSED DOORS CAN HAVE CONSEQUENCES

Many Black boys and men know that racist jokes, stories, and media matter, even if we consume them behind closed doors. These behaviors condition people to seeing other communities as undeserving of sympathy and can ultimately manifest themselves in mistreatment of those communities. Language choice is one of the primary methods by which the dehumanization of "others" occurs, such as referring to Black men as "thugs."

Conversely, many "harmless" activities such as "locker room talk," pornography, and other objectifying media create a culture that encourages sexual violence. These activities normalize the idea of women as inferior even if intended as entertainment and are often accompanied by dehumanizing language such as "bitch," "hoe," and "thot." Though it would be difficult to place the blame on any single activity, repeating the same messages about women over and over again undoubtedly trains men to see some women as deserving of violence.

THEY UNDERSTAND THAT SOME VIOLENCE IS MINIMIZED AND NORMALIZED

Recent emphasis on police violence has highlighted feelings among Black Americans that violence against certain people is accepted. State violence against people of color is a logical remnant of a system that once overtly sanctioned violence against Black Americans.

It also stands to reason that since those who create and enforce policy have historically been men, society may dismiss violence primarily inflicted on women. Policies may no longer overtly sanction violence against women, but the underlying beliefs that created them did not disappear overnight. Our responses to violence against women often blame women for that violence, minimize the scope of that violence, and trivialize the impact of that violence.

THEY UNDERSTAND THAT METHODS OF OPPRESSION ARE SUBTLE

Most Black boys and men know that you do not have to go around shouting racial epithets and burning crosses in order to exercise racism. Racism is so ingrained into the American experience that those who employ it are often unaware that they are even doing so. This notion is supported by ongoing research on unconscious bias.[4]

By the same token, many men think of sexually violent offenders only as malicious men who intentionally rape using force or threats. However, much violence arises from men going through the motions of how they believe "real" men are supposed to behave and who see their actions as normal even though they may be hurtful to others.

THEY UNDERSTAND THAT BYSTANDERS NEED TO STEP UP

Many Black boys and men understand that the blame for racism rests not only with those who are actively racist but also with those who fail to challenge racist ideologies.

Likewise, most men will never commit a sexual assault or rape. That does not mean that there is nothing for them to do, though. The stories, comments, and actions that men allow to go unchallenged contribute to a culture in which violent men see their actions as normal. We all have roles to play in prevention.

THEY UNDERSTAND THAT THE ACTIONS OF THE CRIMINAL JUSTICE SYSTEM DO NOT ALWAYS ALIGN WITH JUSTICE

The high-profile deaths of George Floyd, Philando Castile, Eric Garner, Breonna Taylor, Tamir Rice, and many others have elevated the concerns of some Black boys and men who believe that the criminal justice system does not always render justice. Those who work in criminal justice are subject to error and prejudice the same as anybody else, and their decisions and actions do not always align with justice being served.

Many men are quick to resist speaking against sexual violence by stating, "What about all of the men who are falsely accused?" or "The courts are going to automatically side with a woman who cries rape." The criminal justice system is far from perfect in responding to sexual violence, but we should understand that weaknesses in the criminal justice system do not discount massive levels of actual violence against women. It is inconsistent for us to turn our backs on this violence just because the courts sometimes mishandle it.

THEY UNDERSTAND THAT LIVING IN FEAR TAKES ENERGY

Living with discrimination can be draining, and calling attention to it can be frustrating. Thus, the voices of Black boys and men may not always be calm and measured when speaking against racism. For example, the sustained cry for police reform championed by efforts such as Black Lives Matter has laid bare a wide range of emotions for public consumption. Sometimes people are incredulous that they have to ask the powers that be for law enforcement that they do not fear as law-abiding citizens. Sometimes they are disappointed in their neighbors and elected officials who do not seem to be listening to them say that they are living in fear. And sometimes they are just plain furious that they have to live in a state of fear when others do not.

All else being equal, women think about sexual violence much more than men. They think about it when they go on dates, when they choose neighborhoods to live in, when they invite people to their homes, and many other times when men typically do not. This is to say nothing of the women who must spend energy recovering from violence already inflicted on them. Therefore, when women do speak up about their right to control access to their own bodies, we should not be surprised if their voices reflect fatigue, pain, or impatience. We should not immediately dismiss them as "feminazis" or something of the sort just because they express anger.

THEY UNDERSTAND THAT THERE SHOULD BE LIMITS TO RETRIBUTION FOR PERCEIVED CHARACTER FLAWS

When a person of color is killed by a police officer, there is a familiar refrain by some to figure out what that person did to justify the attack. There are certainly actions that somebody can take that justifiably require law enforcement officials to escalate their use of force, but the actions that people cite often venture into prior actions altogether such as past criminal offenses. Black boys commonly understand that people can grow beyond past mistakes. They also understand that even if somebody is a "bad" person, that does not mean that he or she deserves to be executed. There are processes for determining the appropriate sanctions for a past misdeed.

By the same token, victims of rape are commonly seen as deserving of assault because of past actions such as prior sexual activity, flirtation, dress, and alcohol consumption. This is not the best analogy in the world, because I do not mean to equate behaviors such as dressing a certain way with criminal offenses and sexual victimization with death. I just mean to point out that both situations involve people justifying applications of violence based on their own subjective examinations of a person's character.

THEY UNDERSTAND THAT THE TRUTH IS NOT
ALWAYS COMFORTABLE

Many Black boys and men know that claims of racism can be jarring for their White peers. Most people consider themselves to be good people, so accepting the presence of racism can be disturbing as it requires people to ask if they themselves are racist in certain contexts. Challenging racism requires people to ask difficult questions about how they may have benefited from privilege.

In a similar manner, men should not expect to feel entirely comfortable when asked to speak against sexual violence. Men have to ask challenging questions about whether their own behaviors are hurtful or support violent men. A certain degree of discomfort is to be expected for men who genuinely take inventory of their contributions to rape culture.

* * *

Most of the parents and guardians I talk to believe their boys to be capable of holding complex perspectives. That means there is no reason for us to surrender them to an oversimplified viewpoint that demands that they always defend alleged Black perpetrators of sexual violence—especially when they may already be primed to ally with the necessary work of standing against sexual violence. Defending Black men certainly has its place in a nation rife with historical and contemporary examples of racism, but it should not prevent us from challenging a nation that is also rife with violence against women. Unfortunately, very few clear examples exist for Black boys wondering how to embody the brand of manhood required for change. Just turn on a news show of your choice to see that sweeping, black-and-white perspectives tend to have more traction than nuanced perspectives that meet the complexities of the world. Boys will understandably stumble on their way to finding where they need to be. Remind them that there is more than one way to challenge stereotypes about Black men's propensity for violence, and one of the most enduring methods is to stand as an example of nonviolence.

How Do We Develop Boys into Allies? A Conversation with Ted Bunch

Ted Bunch is the co-founder and chief development officer of A Call to Men, one of America's premier organizations that provides training on healthy manhood to boys and men. Their website says that they work from the "barbershop to the boardroom" with clients that include the National Football League, the National Basketball Association, and the Department of Justice, along with numerous educational institutions and corporations throughout the country.

Q: You have made a career of having difficult but necessary conversations with men and boys. What advice would you give to the people who want to talk to the boys in their lives about confronting sexual violence but don't where to begin?

A: To begin with themselves. When I talk to high school students, college students, or even professional athletes, I can say to them that whatever they learned about being a man, they learned from my generation. My generation passed down a collective socialization of what a man is to those boys. Therefore, I have to start with myself. This collective socialization—which we call the Man Box—teaches that women and girls are objects, property, and that they have less value than men. We have learned things that are wrong. We have been misinformed. The truth is that we have to work toward valuing women and girls as well as LGBTQ and gender nonconforming individuals in our community. The more I can break out of the Man Box, the more I can become my full authentic self and appreciate the differences in others because I am more aware of who I am.

Q: When I look back over my life, I can clearly see many of the factors that inspired me to speak against sexual violence. Have you had similar revelations? Are there any particular factors that you think translate to activating other boys and men to share their voices to fight sexual violence?

A: There are some wonderful things about being a man that we are passing down to boys. But we have also passed down practices and ways of thinking that devalue women and girls. We often bond as men by talking about conquest, and that conquest is often about women and girls. We want to interrupt those things.

Additionally, when someone who is male-identified in the Black community does not live up to those rigid notions of manhood, they are often ridiculed. The Black community is not a monolith, nor are we a binary where everybody fits into a box for men or women. We never have been. Boys may react to this. When we help them unpack how limiting the teachings of the Man Box are, they can see its faults. Homophobia and heterosexism is the glue that holds the Man Box together. That's why boys feel pressure to ridicule and devalue people who identify as LGBQ, trans, or nonbinary. We need to respect the humanity of all people, and boys understand this when you give them space to unpack what they've been taught about manhood.

Lastly, boys should talk to girls and women about their experiences as well as those who identify as LGBQ, trans, or nonbinary. They should be intentional about this. Be inquisitive and caring. That's how I am learning to be the best man that I can be. As men, if we just have a conversation among ourselves, we are going to have a lot of blind spots.

Q: My personal belief is that Black boys tend to carry some worldviews that make them readymade allies to confront sexual violence. For example, many already understand that there is racialized violence in the world that is minimized and excused. Do you agree with this idea?

A: I do think that they can be readymade allies because oppression has the same principles no matter where you look. There is a construct of those in power oppressing the marginalized group, so I think that those marginalized groups can understand what the others are experiencing. In our work at A Call to Men, we often talk about race in order to make analogies about gender because we have more language around race discrimination. So Black boys and young men can understand the experiences of violence against women because they also have to be very aware of how the world sees them. How they experience policing, whether it's from law enforcement or going into a store and feeling like you have to buy something or else you will be searched before you leave, helps them see that women and girls have experiences that are similar.

When I talk to young men about sexual harassment on the street, they might say they have the right to treat women a certain way because some women are asking for it by dressing a certain way. But then I ask them, "When you have your hood over your head and your jeans hanging low, are you asking for the police to treat you like a criminal and stop you?" They will say, "Of course not. This is the way that we dress." So I point out to them that they are being treated a certain way because of how they are dressed in the same way that they are treating women based on how they dress. It's easy to make connections like this with Black boys. They can be real allies.

CHAPTER 4: PREPARING ANTI-VIOLENT BOYS FOR CHALLENGES

- Boys who decide to speak against violence may face new complications in their relationships, may have to process the stories of survivors, and will be asked to consider personal accountability. Boys can be better prepared for these complexities by practicing how to engage others, connecting with others who are of like mind, and understanding the broader context of their efforts.
- Despite the complexities and challenges that face men who speak against sexual violence, there are positive effects as well:
  - Challenging rape culture requires you to examine your own behaviors and attitudes that contribute to the problem. There is tremendous growth to be had in this constant self-evaluation.

- Deconstructing male norms brings a freedom as you identify and cultivate your own interests rather than just accepting those assigned to you because of your gender.
- In reaction to historical prejudices against Black men, many Black boys have adopted a stance that always presumes Black male innocence in cases of sexual violence. Positions that presume Black male guilt are to be challenged, but positions that presume innocence carry their own harm, as many behaviors of Black men are worthy of rebuke and criticism just as with men of all races.
- Black boys who speak out against sexual violence may experience some degree of tension. This work requires that we challenge violent behaviors and practices, which often means shedding light on our own faults. One might see betrayal in displaying the faults of communities already maligned by prejudice and bias. Additionally, anti-violence perspectives may bring boys into conflict with peers who associate all accusations against Black men with racism. One of the best ways to counter this internal and external conflict is to connect with the growing body of men of color who support anti-violence movements.
- I came to believe that standing against violence is pro-Black for the following reasons. Some may help you connect with boys who you know:
  - Black women and men are the victims of violence.
  - Non-action generally results in intervention from outside of communities.
  - Many arguments made in defense of Black men are subtly racist.
  - Black communities have an honorable tradition of resisting sexual violence.
- Those concerned about negative portrayals of Black manhood should be reminded that few things combat negative images better than supporting anti-violence movements in both words and action.

- A strong desire to challenge negative portrayals of Black men need not be a barrier to entry for Black boys. In fact, recognition of injustice in the world makes them ready allies to challenge sexual violence. Consider leaning on the following insights about rape culture that Black boys may already possess because of their knowledge of race-based violence:
  - They understand that statistics should not be required for action.
  - They understand that activities conducted behind closed doors can have consequences.
  - They understand that violence against some communities is minimized and normalized.
  - They understand that methods of oppression can be subtle.
  - They understand that bystanders need to step up.
  - They understand that the actions of the criminal justice system do not always align with justice.
  - They understand that living in fear takes energy.
  - They understand that there should be limits to retribution for perceived character flaws.
  - They understand that the truth is not always comfortable.

Working Under the Myth
of the Black Rapist

One question that sometimes arises during my conversations with young men is "What does a rapist look like?" I welcome this question, as its resolution demonstrates that society often has an archetypal image of what violent men look like, and it gets audiences questioning if this should be the case. However, every time that this question comes forth, I find myself fearful that somebody might look at me and say, "Well, rapists look a lot like you." It has never been lost on me that I have committed to a cause where my Black male body operates as one of the nation's most enduring representations of the problem. I have spent many hours strategizing and working alongside White women in the name of fighting violence, but it is surreal to do so while wondering if those same women would be preparing for a potential attack were we to meet under different circumstances.

If we are serious about encouraging Black boys to challenge violent conceptualizations of manhood, then we have to also recognize that there is a powerful historical context casting a shadow over them. That is, there is a belief that Black men have a special propensity for forcefully acting out their sexual desires on women. I submit my thoughts on this here; but, truth be told, I am of the mind that Angela Davis has presented the gold standard on this topic in her widely read *Women, Race and Class*.[1] My reverence for this work shows in my adoption of the term "myth of the Black rapist" to capture belief systems about the violent tendencies of Black men. *Women, Race and Class* was published in 1981 but remains poignant today.

Like me, Dr. Davis believes that the extralegal lynching of Black men represents one of the most starkly visible representations of America's fears of Black male sexuality. Black men were far from the only victims of lynching. But it was primarily in the cases of White citizens chasing down Black men accused of sexual violence that we develop a sense that lynch mobs were not chasing individual people accused of independent offenses. Instead, they were chasing an idea, considering all the talk of quelling Black savagery and defending womanhood.

One reporter, writing on a lynching in which the victim had been beaten with "clubs, sticks and whips until his head and body were scarcely recognizable" and then "roasted alive," wrote that "several of the women who witnessed the burning said to *The World* correspondent to-night that they now feel as though they could walk the loneliest country road at mid-night without being molested by a black man."[2] These people were fueled just as much by a belief that they were keeping an animalistic and deviant force in check as they were by the pursuit of justice for an individual.

The remarkable number of lynch mobs who executed the wrong man further demonstrates this point. In their fervor to make a statement against Black aggression, mobs targeted innocent parties all too readily. *The Knoxville East Tennessee News* reports an extraordinary account in which a White woman "regained consciousness just in time to prevent departure of a search party that had been formed to scour the country for 'the big black brute' who had been described in the press as her rapist." Apparently, her attacker had been a White man.[3] The article does not say how this mob formed, but one presumes that the community's hatred of Black, male aggression had led them to conjure up a Black rapist where none existed. I doubt that the mob would have come back empty-handed had it been allowed to carry out its search.

The violence that accompanied the lynching of alleged Black rapists was generally of a brand designed to achieve the utmost degradation for the victim and the utmost fear in Black communities. Consider a story found in a powerful book of lynching photography titled *Without Sanctuary: Lynching Photography in America*. The volume unabashedly presents page after page of the horrors of lynching as recorded through photography. One of the stories it recounts belongs to a Black planter named Sam Hose who met an untimely death in 1899 (as far as I can tell, Hose is referred to as Sam Holt in other sources). As the author tells it here, Hose killed his employer in self-defense after his employer pulled a pistol on him in the midst of a heated argument. Hose was reportedly seeking permission to visit his ill mother and his employer had refused. But the account circulated by local newspapers involved Hose sneaking into his employer's house and burying an ax in his employer's skull while he ate dinner. Hose then purportedly pillaged the house and raped his former employer's wife in the same room where her husband lay dying. Two independent investigators would later recant this account, including a White detective who interviewed the alleged rape victim. In this interview, the wife herself admitted that Hose never even entered their house on the night of the altercation. Mob reaction was nonetheless swift and cruel.

The mob that tracked down Hose stripped him of his clothes and chained him to a tree. They cut off his ears, fingers, and genitals and skinned his face. They doused him, still alive, in kerosene and set him ablaze. Once the flames subsided, the mob removed Hose's heart and liver and proceeded to crush his bones into dust. The mob then fought over Hose's remnants, which would serve as souvenirs. One of the attendees reportedly delivered a portion of Hose's heart to the governor of Georgia. Afterwards, a placard was placed on a tree trunk near Hose's remaining ashes. The placard read, "We Must Protect Our Southern Women."[4]

Commenting on the event, the *Kissimmee Valley Gazette* reported, "For sickening sights, harrowing details and blood-curdling incidents, the burning of Holt is unsurpassed by any occurrence of a like kind ever heard in the history of Georgia."[5] In retrospect, it actually seems like standard fare for an era where genital mutilation, the severing of body parts for purposes of collection, and live incineration were common tactics for making examples of Black men suspected of perpetrating sexual violence.

Keep in mind that Hose was accused of other offenses beyond rape, including murder, but the placard left at his charred remains leaves no confusion as to the offense that most piqued the mob's ire. In defense of the method of Hose's demise, the *Atlanta Constitution* wrote, "Remember the slain husband, and, above all, remember the shocking degradation which was inflicted by the black beast, his victim swimming in her husband's warm blood as the brute held her to the floor. Keep the facts in mind. When the picture is painted of the ravisher in flames, go back and view that darker picture of Mrs. Cranford outraged in the blood of her murdered husband."[6]

At other times, groups publicly deplored extralegal justice *except* in the case of rape. For instance, the *New York Sun* writes of a group for Confederate veterans who were "violently, vehemently, and eternally opposed to the practice of burning a human being for any crime whatsoever" except for the "one unmentionable crime."[7] Even though accusations of murder or attempted murder most prominently led to the lynching of Black Americans, rape had a disproportionate presence in the perpetuation of the institution of lynching. In a time period already noted for its grotesque violence against Black Americans, the charge of rape held amazing power to arouse even greater depravity.

I grant that acts of reprisal against Black men of this sort are mainly the stuff of history books now, but I also believe these tales of horrific mob violence to be the greatest evidence for the contemporary presence of the myth of the Black rapist. Prejudice that can inspire the mass approval of inhumane violence, is arrived at without due process, and is submitted under the appearance of nobility, is not easily extinguished. We are but a few generations removed from the days when a myth could reduce entire communities to frenetic sadists. It would be naïve to think this myth maintains no power in contemporary culture. Black boys who want to work against sexual violence have to learn to work in the face of this myth.

* * *

When comedian and actor Sandra Bernhard made a controversial reference to vice-presidential nominee Sarah Palin and gang rape during a performance, she banked the punchline's success on the perseverance of the myth of the Black rapist. The Associated Press reported her as having said that Palin would be "gang-raped" by her "big black brothers" were she to come to New York, though Bernhard would state that the reported verbiage was inaccurate and that she delivered the lines in the course of a larger piece about "women, racism, freedom and the extreme views of Governor Sarah Palin." If those words were truly spoken, I still struggle to think of a way that Bernhard's routine did not rely on the myth of the Black rapist. I am sure that the comments were meant to be in solidarity with Black men, but bothering to specify the race of men is to appeal to a communal understanding that rape by men of that race is either more common or more egregious than rape by other races. When Bernhard clarified that she was criticizing Palin for opposing abortion rights and challenging whether she would keep a baby "if she became pregnant after being violated by a group of black men in New York," the critique still functions only in an environment where rape by Black men is considered especially deplorable.[8]

A combination of reading and aimless surfing on the Internet brought me across the following jokes:

Why do black men cry during sex?
The mace.[9]

How do you stop five niggers from raping a white woman?
Throw them a basketball.[10]

How does a girl from Harlem practice safe sex?
She locks the car doors.[11]

What do you call sex with a black man?
Rape![12]

The underlying prejudices that allow these jokes to operate are enthusiastically promoted in certain corners of the internet. Anyone with the stomach for it can easily find his or her way to websites where the dangers of Black men are presented as fact and not as jokes. The number of explicit race-related hate sites was estimated at 600 to 800 sites as early as 1998.[13] It is common for these sites to carry their proselytizing into the realm of sexual violence. I came across one that offered endless "statistics," mugshots, and articles highlighting the violent activities of Black men. It even had tips on how to avoid rape such as "Do not 'date' Blacks or Mexicans," "Avoid traveling through Black or Mexican neighborhoods," "There is no law that says you have to give the time of day to a Black or Mexican," and "Remember, the Blacks you see on Television and the Movies are actors and do not represent the typical feral Negro."[14]

I do grant that Internet fuming from self-identified hate groups makes for suspect evidence of the continued presence of the myth of the Black rapist in mainstream culture. It is common enough to stumble across this kind of sentiment in forums that ostensibly have nothing to do with hate, though. I recall an argument that I once observed break out on an espn. com message board after a Black college basketball player was accused of rape and some users referenced the inability of Black men to control their sexual urges. Even if few Americans would openly endorse the basest representations of the myth of the Black rapist, many do adhere to milder representations.

I see these milder representations reflected in media such as *Out of Sight*, a 1998 Academy Award–nominated action/romance film of some success (it had a brief spinoff television series on ABC called *Karen Sisco*) with an impressive cast featuring George Clooney, Ving Rhames, Jennifer Lopez, and Don Cheadle. There is a scene toward the end of the film in which a Black robber, Kenneth, takes a break from a heist in order to attempt to rape a housekeeper. Never mind that he and his crew are in the middle of an attempted burglary potentially worth millions of dollars. Never mind that they have just broken into a house and are clueless as to how much time they have before they are discovered. Never mind that the house is also occupied by two begrudging partners who cannot be trusted (Clooney and Rhames). It is a move so irrational and so contrary to logic that it demands that the writers take some time to explain it. But that exposition never comes. I suppose the movie's architects figured they

had explained it with an earlier scene where the movie's female protagonist (Lopez) is forced to physically defend herself from the character's aggressiveness upon their first meeting. By movie's end, Kenneth's role as an
uncontrollable rapist is apparently so established that the movie's primary
male protagonist correctly predicts the character's intent to attack the
housekeeper. This is not a flattering role for a Black actor, though Kenneth
is actually somewhat faithful to the Elmore Leonard novel from which
Out of Sight was adapted. In the book, the character is intent on having sex
with anything that moves "like a bullfrog."[15]

You generally have to put your civic sensibilities on hold to watch a
mainstream comedy these days, but I found it impossible not to feel similar reservations when I watched *The 40-Year-Old Virgin*. For those who
have not seen the movie, the plot revolves around an eponymous 40-year-
old virgin, Andy, and his coworkers who make it their mission "to get him
laid" once they learn that he is a virgin. The film ultimately comes off as
a critique of Andy's coworkers' dysfunctional relationships, but most of it
follows these coworkers doing their best to push Andy into his first sexual
encounter.

The first tactic they try is taking Andy to a club and advising him to
seek out the most intoxicated woman he can find and take her home. His
primary guide at this point, Jay, helps Andy pick out the drunkest targets
possible, which are said to be the easiest to "run down."

Jay is of course Black. Beyond encouraging Andy to target drunk women,
constantly referring to women as bitches and hoes, and spearheading
an encounter between Andy and a prostitute, one of Jay's more notable
moments comes when his protégé finally lands a potential sexual partner.
In order to prepare Andy for his first sexual encounter, Jay advises him
to "run through a bunch of hood rats" so that he would be ready for the
"upper echelon-type hoe." As Andy's upcoming date is White and Jay's
"hood rats" are presumably Black, this is also a scene that can be viewed as
devaluing Black women.

The list of instances of movie producers and writers presenting Black
men as sexually aggressive or deviant go on and on. I wish I could fully
enjoy movies without social justice critiques kicking in, especially because

many of the movies I find troublesome are comedies or fantasy films that likely are not meant to be taken seriously. Boys are raised in a modern culture that claims that jokes are harmless, but I do not entirely buy this when it comes to sexual violence. Rape and sexual assault are real-life behaviors that are constantly downplayed through humor. It is also a crime that is unfortunately adjudicated according to popular images of what "real" rapists look like. The images and tones the media attaches to it have impact.

It is not so much that on-screen portrayals of Black men as rapists are false. Violent men come in all colors, so to see a Black rapist or a Black man with a less-than-ideal stance on screen is not inauthentic in and of itself. But making a character Black is overutilized shorthand for scriptwriters to quickly convey that a particular character is predisposed to an aggressive sexual mindset. Regardless of intent, they help to keep one of America's oldest prejudices alive.

The inescapable image of Black men as rapists must surely have influenced popular director Quentin Tarantino's decision to situate Ving Rhames as the victim of a forcible rape in his film *Pulp Fiction*. The decision to portray Rhames this way is natural for a director with a reputation for shocking images. Few images possess the power to turn preconceptions on their heads more than that of a brawny Black man on the receiving end of rape.

* * *

There is enough to believe that the race-based prejudices that fueled the lynching institutions of old are still with us. Consider a 1978 study done at the University of Missouri that examined the effects of a victim's race on the conviction rates of rape trials. The study found that given a scenario featuring a Black, male defendant, prospective White jurors were almost twice as likely to vote for conviction when the victim was White than when the victim was Black. A similar phenomenon was found among Black jurors, who were much more likely to convict given a Black victim as opposed to a White victim.[16]

The aforementioned study is admittedly 40 years old at this point; but, if anything, our understanding of how racial biases operate has increased since then. There is now a healthy field of study uncovering the unconscious biases that we hold and their consequences. These unconscious biases hold particular sway when they are fueled by popular images supporting them, and the world is flush with historical and current images of Black men as rapists (this point is apparent to political strategists, who have occasionally leveraged images of Black rapists to generate support for candidates to great effect). Public commentators, jurors, law enforcement officers, prosecutors, and judges are all subject to unconscious bias just the same as everybody else. Biases, unconscious or otherwise, affect all aspects of the criminal justice system, to include charging, sentencing, and jury selection.[17]

Only a few years apart, the state of Georgia provided us with *State of Georgia vs. Dixon* (2003) and *State of Georgia vs. Wilson* (2007). These cases gained some degree of notoriety partially because the defendants happened to be highly recruited high school athletes and sports media took an interest in their stories. As reported by the Associated Press and the *Atlanta Journal-Constitution*, the fact patterns in both cases are nearly identical.[18] Both cases featured Black male teenagers who were accused of raping younger teenage girls. Both defendants argued that the sexual activity in question was consensual and ultimately received lengthy prison sentences after being convicted on statutory rape and child molestation charges. Both defendants served over a year of prison time and were released from prison following rulings from the Georgia Supreme Court. Activists seized on these cases and maintained that the state inappropriately applied laws designed to protect children from adults to situations involving teenage parties of similar age and that the resulting sentences were far more severe than what was reasonably justifiable. One writer for the *Atlanta Journal-Constitution* commented on the *Dixon* case that "Neither our legal team nor the district attorney's office has found a single aggravated child molestation conviction in Georgia in which the two people involved were teenagers close in age—as is the case in this matter."[19]

My intent in highlighting the aforementioned cases is not to challenge the merit of statutory rape laws. States must enforce boundaries between parties where age disparity might result in power imbalances even if doing so might sometimes pose difficulties in deciphering near-age encounters. Rather, I want to point out what the sentencing might suggest here.

Statutory rape laws are widely reviled and mocked. Some district attorneys have spoken out about their beliefs that these laws adjudicate sexual behavior between teenagers unnecessarily. More generally, legal offenses pertaining to sexual violence are notorious for their low conviction rates. If these laws are more consistently used to bring the full force of the law against only Black boys, this would suggest a continued fear of Black male sexuality.

Going back in time a bit, the widely covered case of the Central Park Jogger might be the best case study of whether or not America has overcome its unjust persecution of Black men for sexual violence. In 1989, a White female victim was beaten and raped by what was thought to be a group of youth of color. The attack rightly drew widespread concern, with even the then-mayor of New York City addressing the incident. Though the victim had no memory of the event, five teenagers were convicted using confessions they would later claim the police coerced out of them.

In 2002, a man serving a life sentence for other crimes stepped forward and claimed to have been the sole person responsible for the attack on the woman known as the Central Park Jogger. DNA evidence corroborated his story and the original five defendants had their convictions vacated, although all of them had already served time in prison.

. There are, of course, competing accounts as to what occurred. Nonetheless, I would like us to juxtapose the response to the exoneration of the Central Park Jogger defendants with the fanfare for the White Duke University lacrosse players accused of raping a Black college student in 2006. District attorneys who questioned the procedures of the original handlers of their respective cases vindicated both parties. Forensic evidence was also widely believed to support both parties. However, it was primarily the announcement that charges were dropped for the lacrosse players that was met with widespread support. The players and their families became frequent guests on talk shows, and radio personalities and bloggers commented on their innocence. Media coverage following the announcement revealed a deep disgust for false accusations.

This intense hatred for false accusations seemed conspicuously absent when the accused boys from the Central Park Jogger case were exonerated. This discrepancy was not lost on one of the accused parties in the Central Park Jogger trial. He reportedly stated in 2011 that "TV doesn't even acknowledge us. Where is our justice? . . . We have difficulties when it comes to functioning on a higher level as productive individuals because we never had the opportunity to grow naturally, make mistakes, live life. We didn't have the chances to become lawyers, doctors, police officers, firefighters or Duke lacrosse players."[20] Since 2011, there has been a fair amount of public commentary and media supporting these men, such as Ava Duvernay's 2019 Netflix series "When They See Us," but it was not as immediate or as widespread as might be expected for people who had ostensibly been cleared of wrongdoing in a widely covered incident.

You might argue that the lengthy time period that the Central Park Five spent away from intense media coverage after their convictions explains the inconsistencies in the responses offered. But I think knowledge that some youths had wrongly served sentences over a decade long for one of the most high-profile rape cases in American history would make for quite a story. It is also telling that many officials associated with the case still cast doubt on the defendants' innocence. In response to the defendants having their names cleared, one New York City public official said, "The criminal justice system hit an all-time low here today when we put more credibility in the words of a convicted murderer and rapist than in the hard work of dedicated New York City detectives."[21] Had the case for the Duke students' innocence included a convicted rapist claiming sole responsibility for their charges and presumed DNA evidence supporting this, then any suspicions cast on them by public officials would surely be frowned upon. We saw as much in the extreme disapproval directed toward the district attorney who originally presided over the Duke lacrosse case.

Perhaps the response to the Central Park defendants was tempered because, by many accounts, they came off as troublemakers. Some of them had other offenses to their names, and many observers believed that they were up to no good on the night in question, even if they did not rape someone. This settles nothing, as one of the biggest rallying points in the Duke lacrosse case was the need to distinguish common youthful recklessness from the more serious question of whether or not these young men had raped someone. People who brought up the fact that the lacrosse players were engaged in activity deemed to be improper by some were reminded that other inappropriate behavior does not equate to guilt concerning an accusation of rape (which I would agree with). The argument for distinguishing between guilt of rape and youthful indiscretion should have been extended to the Central Park Jogger defendants as well.

As I stated earlier, my first memory of taking an interest in a Black man publicly accused of sexual violence came when I observed Mike Tyson's 1991 rape trial. I now believe this trial to be among the most enduring pieces of evidence that America still harbors prejudices regarding who is capable of committing sexual violence and who is worthy of being punished for this violence. In order to understand my position, you must first understand that Tyson is a supreme anomaly among prominent professional athletes formally accused of sexual assault. He is an anomaly because he actually went to prison.

Professional athletes accused of sexual violence simply do not suffer criminal convictions as a result of these accusations. In 2003, *USA Today* ran an article in which contributors reviewed 168 sexual assault allegations over the preceding dozen years involving professional athletes and college athletes playing NCAA Division I football or men's basketball. Of these, the article claimed that only 22 ever went to trial and only six resulted in a conviction—this amounts to a conviction rate that the article's authors believed to be far below the already low rate of conviction for the general population.[22]

Now we must consider the man whose conviction defied the odds. Tyson gained what many people consider to be the most impressive individual title in sports and did so in a most dominating fashion. At 21, he was the youngest-ever heavyweight boxing champion and unified the heavyweight titles previously divided among independent boxing associations.

He won 33 of his first 37 professional fights by knockout, including 17 that were decided in the first round. At various points in his career, his management had to come up with creative ways to find opponents for him because much of the available competition was afraid to step into the ring with him. In his biography of Tyson, sportswriter Peter Heller claims that Tyson was, at one point, "the best-known and most financially successful athlete in the world."[23] In another of Tyson's biographies, professor of culture, media, and sport Ellis Cashmore goes so far as to contend that "no account of late twentieth- and early twenty-first century Western culture can exclude the presence of Tyson."[24] This may seem hyperbolic now, but people forget where Tyson once stood in the popular imagination due to the tumultuous later years of his boxing career. At the height of his career, he endorsed brands such as Pepsi-Cola, Kodak, and Toyota. He even endorsed a video game bearing his likeness well before such promotions were common.[25] He was in the prime of his career and as important to his respective sport as any athlete could be.

On top of this, the incident that landed Tyson in jail was rife with stereotypical date rape elements that usually dissuade people from responding objectively to assault allegations. For example, the reporting victim demonstrated some degree of prior interest in her attacker, she voluntarily entered his hotel room, and she chose to tell her story via media outlets after the trial was under way. These are the same elements that often lead spectators to conclude that an alleged victim is leveraging a rape allegation for personal gain. Looking back on the media trail concerning this case, it is easier to find articles maligning Tyson's supposed personality traits than that of his alleged victim. This is not the natural order of things when high-caliber celebrities are accused of sexual violence (or when anyone is accused, for that matter).

It is all too predictable that Tyson is the megastar who went against the grain of professional athletes walking away from sexual assault allegations unscathed. After all, Tyson was no stranger to allegations of misconduct with women long before his rape trial. He once infamously confided to a biographer that the best punch of his career was the one that sent his ex-wife bouncing off the walls of his apartment and even provided the statement, "I like to hurt women when I make love to them. I like to hear them scream with pain, to see them bleed. It gives me pleasure."[26] Tyson can probably hold prevailing attitudes about him as accountable for his improbable conviction as much as his actions on the night in question.

If beliefs about a person's innate faculties can secure an elusive date rape conviction for a transcendent professional athlete, then it stands as strong evidence that America still retains the capacity to apply powerful prejudices in the courtroom. As long as society continues to place extreme value on the perceived personality of alleged attackers, then Black boys and men—who are inescapably subjected to longstanding prejudices—have good reason to be wary of our criminal justice system.

Anecdotal evidence abounds to prove continued prejudice against Black men as perpetrators of sexual violence, but empirical research to support this belief is admittedly mixed. For example, researchers at Michigan State concluded in a thorough 2003 study that, controlling for offense type, "sexual assault cases are unique because they are the only violent crime that shows a pattern of criminal justice adjudication and sanctioning that is more lenient toward minority defendants." It also went on to say that "the leniency afforded minorities charged with sexual assault is so pronounced that it obscures the fact that minority defendants arrested for robbery, assault, and murder are processed more punitively."[27]

There are numerous contributing factors as to why we might see lesser sentencing for Black men (I recommend reading the aforementioned Michigan State study itself for a good summary of them), but one of the most influential surely must be that sexual assault is a crime primarily committed against acquaintances rather than strangers. There is generally less disagreement about a perpetrator's intent when victims are strangers, so it stands to reason that we would see lower conviction rates in cases involving perpetrators known to victims. As most sexual assaults are committed against acquaintances, sexual assaults by Black men are also overwhelmingly committed against Black women. Some studies have found that this particular combination of race and relationship produces the *most* judicial leniency toward sexual assault defendants. Other studies have suggested that more responsibility is assigned to Black female victims as compared to White female victims.[28] Therefore, the historical devaluation of Black women may be a stronger force than the myth of the Black rapist. There are, again, numerous alternative factors to which we can attribute the leniency shown to Black men who sexually assault Black women, but all of them lead back to my original premise that race still matters.

* * *

I need to venture into a realm that some parents would find strange to talk about in order to provide further evidence of lingering racialized myths about rape. I have to talk about pornography. The first time I recall putting any critical thought toward pornography was in the third year of college—the same year I was introduced to the previously unseen network of men working against sexual violence. I was in a dorm suite with several other men when one of them called some guests and me into his room to look at something that had him laughing hysterically. We all filed into the room to get a look at what he was watching. It was a video clip sent to him via email, and he was laughing so hard that he struggled to press play for us. The video featured a woman on her knees performing oral sex on a man as he stood above her with his hand on the back of her head. It then showed her breaking free of the man's grasp and pulling her head away for what looked like a chance to breathe. At this point, the man slapped her and forcefully pushed her mouth back onto his penis. This caused the entire room to burst into laughter. I chuckled, hoping to buy enough time to explain a very confusing moment. I was not sure how I felt about the clip that I had just viewed, but I was pretty sure that I did not find it funny. Yet there I was in a room full of men in tears. I did not possess the courage or the language to question the situation at the time.

Sometime the following year, the all-male peer education organization that ushered me into anti-violence work placed the topic of pornography on its meeting agenda. Some members wondered if a group with our aims should disavow pornography. This proposition proved divisive, with some members calling the idea an unacceptable breach of personal freedom while others found pornography consumption to have no relationship to sexual violence.

I now find it strange that we collectively ignore an institution with the massive reach of the pornography industry. Those who think of pornography as limited to seedy, back-alley shops are woefully behind the times. The pornography industry is big business. It is affiliated with some of the world's most prolific media conglomerates and possesses considerable influence over the direction of policy and media. The technology review site toptenreviews.com claims that U.S. porn revenues exceed that of ABC, CBS, and NBC combined.[29] Precise figures on the industry are somewhat elusive, but most sources agree that we are talking about an industry whose annual revenues are measured in the tens of billions of dollars, if not more.

You might not find it appropriate to talk to boys about pornography, but chances are that pornography is talking to them. The aforementioned toptenreviews.com also contends that the average age of a child's first exposure to pornography is 11, and that 90% of children aged eight to 16 have viewed online pornography.[30] Many other sources echo these numbers. Pornographers likely play a considerable role in developing many young adults' initial perceptions of sex. This alone makes the pornography industry significant.

I know that not everyone shares my concern. Countless discussions have reminded me that many of my peers think of pornography as harmless fantasy. I have never understood this stance from people who are otherwise passionate about media portrayals of Black men and women. *Pornography is full of images and narratives about Black Americans, so what is it about the stories it tells that are so resistant to critique? What leads otherwise media-savvy people to grant the pornography industry a pass and fervently defend its right to produce whatever material it cares to produce?*

In her book *Pornland: How Porn Has Hijacked Our Sexuality*, antipornography activist Gail Dines recounts events that illustrate the double standard that many apply to pornography. She writes of radio talk host Don Imus being ousted in 2007 after referring to members of the Rutgers women's basketball team as "nappy-headed hoes." His removal came amid pressure from prominent African American pundits. Dr. Dines goes on to point out that the pornography company Kick Ass Pictures issued a press release three weeks later "announcing its intention to donate $1 from every sale of its new movie entitled *Nappy Headed Ho's* to the Don Imus retirement fund."[31] This was a brazen slap in the face for everyone who was agitated by Imus's original statements, but this act did not draw even a fraction of the scrutiny that Imus received. Sure, the audience for this movie was much smaller than that of Imus's initial words, but you would think its hostility toward those offended by Imus would have been enough to garner some attention. But even the brashness of *Nappy Headed Ho's* rested behind the baffling shield that protects pornography from rebuke.

It is a shame that the pornography industry has been designated as unworthy of critique, as it has much to say about Black manhood (as it does about men and women of all races). You will find narratives about Black men there that would feel at home among the propaganda of lynch mobs of old. A few quick Google searches bring me to such gems as www.mandingogirl.com, which boasts a "horny natural red-head shared & passed around by big black cock gangbangers,"[32] and www.daddysworstnightmare.com, where young girls "get deflowered by a massive black cock."[33] Most of the websites advertising a specialty involving Black men offer the standard assertions that Black men offer a deviant and more animalistic sexuality not found in any other race of men. They also emphasize a limitless sexual appetite and a preference for violent and domineering sex. We are talking about good old-fashioned racism when we review images and text concerning Black men in pornography—not a brand cloaked in subtlety. Lucrative businesses are intentionally exploiting the basest stereotypes of Black men.

My view of pornography is informed by feminist and feminist-inspired anti-pornography activism. This view sees the pornography industry as having successfully leveraged misogyny, sexism, and racism in order to fuel a multibillion-dollar business. I do not yet know if I believe that the mere depiction of sex for profit is inherently problematic as many of the people who have informed my thinking do. However, I do agree that the particular product that is widely available is harmful and that its creators could stand to be held to more socially responsible standards.

Contemporary pornography is an arena in which acts such as urinating on women, shoving their heads into toilets, choking them, and ejaculating directly into their eyes are presented as normative and pleasurable.

Pornographers are pressured to innovate and to expand their market share just the same as any other business. Within pornography, the drive for differentiation too often results in the development of new ways of marketing the distress of female sexual partners as pleasurable. Take the "ass-to-mouth" genre in which male performers remove their penis from a partner's anus and place it into the mouth of that partner or that of another woman, a practice that anti-pornography advocates rightly point out adds no added physical sensation for men. Whatever additional arousal might exist for the performer or viewer must be entirely due to observing a woman enduring an undesirable activity.[34]

And so it goes with hundreds of other distressing behaviors regularly performed on pornography actresses that the industry conveys as enjoyable to women. Or the actress is indeed distressed and this is the selling point. These behaviors occur enough in mainstream pornography that they should not be viewed as niche or extreme. Even without overt actions to debase women, many depictions of sex within mainstream pornography feature a verbal and physical aggression toward women (and a female acceptance of it) that I doubt is an authentic look into the average sexual experience. Just as I do not believe that most heterosexual encounters end in a man ejaculating on a woman's face—as they regularly do in pornography—I do not accept sex as it is typically rendered by the pornography industry to be authentic to most experiences. It is but one representation of male sexuality catering to male fantasies for docile sexual partners. Even if pornography is fantasy as its defenders contend, we still have to ask why the pornography industry has landed on providing the particular fantasy that it has.

It is no surprise that interracial pornography thrives in this world. Within pornography, the term "interracial" is largely synonymous with content featuring Black men and White women. The popular subgenre stands as one of the strongest contemporary reminders that the myth of the Black rapist is still alive. To understand why, we have to acknowledge the pornography industry's rare feat in popularizing intimacy between Black men and White women.

The humor website Cracked featured an article entitled "5 Old-Timey Prejudices That Still Show Up in Every Movie."[35] The article briefly but pointedly demonstrated Hollywood's continued avoidance of displaying sexual or romantic relationships between Black men and White women. The article set aside movies that have an explicit message about race or where the relationship is only implied or occurs entirely off screen. It then asked readers to "try and think of movies where the relationship is just treated as a normal, everyday thing." I agree with Cracked's conclusion that Hollywood is still afraid to show Black men and White women together. The list of exceptions is certainly growing, but avoiding depictions of relationships between Black men and White women remains the norm, except in cases when an interracial coupling is central to the film's message.

So what, then, do we make of pornography standing in such stark contrast to the rest of the American film industry? How do we interpret the otherwise rare image of Black men and White women together thriving within an industry that takes special pride in displaying the perverse and the taboo—an industry that profits off of images of women being humiliated, harmed, and exploited? I take it as indication that America still associates the Black, male body with sexual aggression and deviance. Seeing these same bodies penetrate White women holds a special appeal within a fantasyland that revolves around the violation and submission of women.

We quietly allow the pornography industry to cash in on some of the most tired stereotypes of Black men as violent and animalistic. Other industries are guilty of the same offenses, but they at least face some resistance to oversimplifications of Black manhood. Suggesting that the NAACP or another civic or service organization place pornography on its agenda sounds absurd to many. We therefore must not attribute any power to pornography's representation of Black men. We say it is entertainment. We say it is fantasy. But nowhere else do we apply this logic. Were a virulently racist movie, song, or television show to be released, its creators would face at least some pressure to apologize or even withdraw the piece from the public sphere—even if the story told was fictional or fantastical. In these instances, many of us intuitively understand that we cannot simply erect a barrier between fantasy and reality. We understand that the images that youth ingest have significance, and we understand that the ways that we entertain ourselves reveal something about our values.

* * *

The peer education group that sparked my interest in confronting sexual violence against women consisted of only three non-White members during much of my time in their ranks—two Asian American students and me. Even within this supportive space, I still faced questions about race. For example, the group had a questionable tendency of selecting me for a particular part in the program we presented to men on campus. At one point in our presentation, we challenged the natural (but generally unproductive) desire of many men to physically assault a perpetrator after learning that a loved one has been sexually assaulted by that person. We would acknowledge this was a natural reaction by saying something along the lines of "I don't know about you, but if I ever found out that a loved one had been raped, the first thing I'd do is make sure the guy who did it got what was coming to him." Then, we would outline why that reaction was ill advised.

Somehow, I became responsible for delivering this part of the program when I presented. When it came time to divvy up the presentation before stepping in front of an audience, it was sometimes suggested that I do this part, presumably because my teammates saw me as convincing at delivering a threat to a would-be rapist. I am of average height at best and was hardly the biggest member of the group. Still, I was deemed the most credible threat by some. Maybe I possess a talent for acting of which I am not aware, but I always read this to mean that assumptions about who is most capable of perpetrating violence had infiltrated even this group of avid myth-busters.

I loved working with these men. I am not sure if I would have remained in this work if they had not initially traveled with me. Some of these men remain among my most trusted colleagues, and I remain a big supporter of the group responsible for introducing me to a field that I have cared about ever since. But I have always known that my experience working against sexual violence would be substantially different than that of my White colleagues. I could recognize their paths but knew that mine required operating under the powerful myth of the Black rapist.

We have come a long way, but the association between Black men and aggression persists. The casual acceptance of this link probably factored into Acura's decision to include a Black male in a commercial for its TL model that ran with the tagline "Aggression in its most elegant form." In the commercial, professional football player Calvin Johnson is stripped of his uniform and refitted in a fashionable suit. Other commercials released around the time followed this motif, but it seems natural that a Black male was chosen to feature prominently in the series about elegant aggression, and this particular version is the only iteration I ever saw air on television.

"You know why everybody is trippin' over this thing at Duke?" a man once said to me while I was waiting for the bus. He was commenting on the high-profile 2006 criminal investigation involving members of the Duke University lacrosse team that I mentioned earlier. "It's because the world is so used to seeing black guys as the faces of rapists. It doesn't know what to do when that face is replaced by a bunch of white boys. This kind of thing crumbles people's worlds." The resilience of the myth of the Black rapist is such that it can serve as a conversation starter for two complete strangers waiting for the bus in the 21st century.

You might be unconvinced by the evidence I have presented for the continued myth of the Black male rapist in America. You might think me paranoid. But many parents and mentors of Black boys also believe that America has particular prejudices against Black male sexuality. They weave its presence into the lessons they teach their boys. They tell their boys that they must guard against women who carry underlying prejudices and who might falsely accuse them of sexual violence. The fact of the matter is that if you happen to be a member of a group that has historically been subject to myths about its propensity for aggression and violence, then you may have some extra work to do in ensuring that your sexual activity is consensual.

It is unfair that Black men are burdened with this extra responsibility, but asking Black boys to embrace this responsibility is perfectly in line with logic already accepted within many Black households. Many already accept that Black boys have to practice extra caution in certain arenas because the consequences of their mistakes are often magnified and the nature of their actions is often misinterpreted. When we coach Black boys on extra steps that they need to take in order to show deference to requests by police officers, these are not arguments against unfairness but instructions about how Black boys should conduct themselves in the face of unfairness. So we could extend the mentality of applying extra vigilance to intimate encounters. Scrutiny of Black male sexuality is imbalanced and rooted in prejudice, but this does not necessarily make the resulting standard an incorrect one. Caution and heightened awareness are perfectly appropriate attributes for boys and men to possess when initiating sexual contact.

Speak to Black boys behind closed doors and they will often agree that the world believes that their sexuality is more violent than that of other men. There are any number of ways to rebel against the unfairness of it all, but one of the many reasons why I love being a Black man is because of our great history of forcing others to acknowledge our humanity despite widespread lies about our savagery. The only reason I currently have the opportunities I do as an American is because generations of Black men routinely demonstrated excellence where failure was expected. I would rather that the sexual arena not be the exception where we do not strive to exhibit the fullness of our humanity.

* * *

A Korean American undergraduate student once shared an interesting experience with me. She said that she went to the library of a local community college to do some research for a project when she was in the 11th grade. In the middle of her studies, a Black man whom she believed to be approximately 30 years old approached her. He introduced himself as a psychologist and flashed some paperwork that he claimed were his certifications. He then asked her if she would assist him in some field-work, for which she would need to accompany him to a different part of the library. The student's instincts troubled her and she began to think of ways to politely tell the man that she was unable to assist him. However, she wondered if she was hesitant solely because the man was Black, and she agreed to help him with his research.

The man then led her to a less-populated floor of the library and then to an out-of-the-way corner. There were other people on this floor, but it was large enough that she was effectively isolated. The man positioned himself between the student and the rest of the library once she had taken a seat.

He explained that the purpose of his research was to evaluate the calming effects of classical music and he would need to monitor her heart rate throughout the experiment. He handed her a set of headphones and she expected some sort of heart-monitoring equipment to follow. When the student asked him about this, he replied by saying that he could get better readings by simply taking her pulse with his hand.

He proceeded to play some music and to measure her pulse by placing his hands on her wrist. He then progressed to taking her pulse from one of her ankles. Throughout it all, he continually referred to a nearby Bible and told her that he was a good guy. The preemptive defenses of his character made the student even more concerned. Internal alarms were blaring. Yet she went on with the experiment and continued to tell herself that she would likely not be so fearful if the man were not Black.

Fortunately, this story does not have a bad ending. The student bolted after the man rolled up her pant leg to take her pulse on the inside of her knee. I took the story as a reminder that our quest to repel the myth of the Black rapist should never become so zealous that we ignore or excuse the very real violence committed by some Black men. Though we are indeed persecuted by a powerful myth, we are nonetheless as capable of wrong-doing as anyone else. Thus, our strategies of resistance must attack false notions of the archetypal Black rapist as well as any truths that support it.

America has not completely expelled the myth of the Black rapist from its system, but only the most cynical of us would deny that we have come a long way from the days when lynch mobs chased Black men through the woods in the name of defending womanhood. We have even come a long way from the days when Mike Tyson's rape conviction seemed a foregone conclusion because he was a Black man with a history of aggression. There is an argument to be made that prejudices against women (particularly Black women) who make allegations of sexual violence are as strong or stronger than longstanding prejudices against Black male defendants.

This brings its own complications. Black men should never lose their vigilance toward racism, but they should seek a brand of vigilance that does not equate to pursuing entitlement to women's bodies. They should seek a brand that is not supportive of predators who lure young women into remote corners in libraries. Acknowledge the very real concerns that Black boys share about the myth of the Black rapist, but also remind them that these concerns cannot paralyze them into inaction. The fight against sexual violence needs their voices. We are just going to have to continue fighting ugly myths along the way.

How Does Pornography Affect Boys? A Conversation with Dr. Gail Dines

Dr. Gail Dines is one of the most passionate people I've ever met. And she's passionate about something that most people don't think about although they should. As one of the world's leading anti-porn activists, she is one of the people who led me to scrutinize the pornography industry. She is the founder of Culture Reframed, a nonprofit organization dedicated to "solving the public health crisis of the digital age."

Q: Many people think of pornography as a harmless rite of passage for boys. If you could give one reason why parents and mentors of boys should care about the messaging in pornography, what would it be?

A: Well, I can't give one. There's tons. We need to worry about pornography in a way that we never had to before since the domestication of the internet. It used to be you had to go out and find pornography. As sexist as it was, it's very different from what the rite of passage into pornography is today, which is via mainstream hardcore pornography on free sites. What is mainstream today would've been considered hardcore pre-internet. It would have been hard to find even in a porn shop.

The first age of using porn is between eight and 11, depending on what study you are looking at. So what happens is a boy who has no experience and who nobody has probably spoken to about this, finds his way onto Pornhub and he's catapulted into a world of sexual violence. This is not what he expected. He did not expect to see women being strangled, being choked with a penis, being called cunts and whores. He's introduced to a world of violence at a very specific age in his development. His brain is not fully developed. At that age, it's wired for novelty and risk-taking. And his sexual template is being formed at that moment. He's got no way to disagree with the images. He doesn't know this isn't what happens in the world because he can't bring any experience to bear on it. And then the text that comes with a lot of scenes are things like, "We know you want it" and "Are you man enough for this?" like he's some vile creep that wants to watch women being tortured. He's not. They're giving him an identity that is not his, but he's got nobody to talk to.

We know that the earlier that boys get to pornography, the more likely they are to become sexual aggressors, to lose capacity for intimacy in relationships, to engage in risky sexual behavior, to experience erectile dysfunction, and on and on. If you want your boy to be the author of his own sexuality—one that is about connection, intimacy, and love—know that pornography is coming in and hijacking that capacity.

Q: To follow up on the link between sexual aggression and pornography, the connection between boys consuming violent media and boys committing actual violence is heavily debated. Do you have reason to believe that such a linkage actually exists?

A: It's not hard to make that link at all. There's a ton of research out there. We have a lot of research around correlation, but now there's longitudinal research about causation. There's no question that the wealth of the research—40 years of empirical research from multiple disciplines—shows that there is both a correlation and a causal link between pornography and perpetrating violence against women and children. Of course, there are debates to be had, and not all kids who look at pornography are going to rape. There are protection and prevention factors to consider as well. But anybody who does serious research will absolutely point to a causation and a correlation.

Q: Pornography has much to say about all men. My personal view is that pornography singles out Black men as being particularly aggressive and emotionless. Would you agree with this?

A: There is a different visual grammar when it comes to Black men. All men in porn are devoid of emotion, conscience, and empathy. But it's amplified for Black men. They are considered to be the most violent. The ideal man in porn is actually the White construction of Black masculinity. When you think of the trope of Black men having animalistic sexuality that started off as a way to legitimize lynching and the wholesale slavery of a people, who better to use in porn than Black men?

Interracial porn usually features a White woman and several Black men. It's for a White audience and it sells very well. This is a country that lynched Emmett Till just a few generations ago for supposedly looking at a White woman. So why are White men now flocking to pornography that shows Black men penetrating White women? I think that pornography only works to the degree that it dehumanizes women. How better to dehumanize a White woman in the eyes of White men than to have her penetrated by that which has been marked as the carrier of sexual deviancy—Black men?

CHAPTER 5: TEACHING BOYS ABOUT THE MYTH OF THE BLACK RAPIST

- Dr. Angela Davis utilized the term "the myth of the Black male rapist" to describe institutionalized fear of Black male sexuality. The myth is present today in the criminal justice system, movies, pornography, and other places. There is an extensive history of extralegal prejudice against Black men accused of sexual violence. We cannot reasonably expect this system to have no lingering presence in contemporary America. Many Black boys agree.
- Black boys who take up anti-violence work may experience frustration that they have to operate within contexts that paint them as violent or aggressive, whereas other allies do not. Be prepared to support them in this.
- Even if they are born out of prejudice, remember that caution and a heightened awareness of responsibility in sexual encounters are perfectly appropriate standards for boys and men to uphold. We must be mindful that rebellion against historical imbalances in standards does not embolden us to unwittingly support rape culture.

Examining Media Representations of Black Manhood

We have established that the teachings of manhood matter in our fight against sexual violence and rape culture. We have also established that Black manhood in particular may be subject to some nasty assumptions. Let us now consider the men who have a disproportionate impact on setting the tone for messages about manhood—those men who have outsized platforms to impact youth cultures because of their talent, their charisma, or just good fortune.

The list of Black celebrities who have faced accusations of sexual violence is indeed extensive. I will not recount them here, but many would be surprised to see just how many Black actors, musicians, entertainers, and professional athletes have formal accusations of intimate violence on their résumés. Furthermore, Black men would appear to harbor the poster boys for every major classification of intimate violence. Kobe Bryant's case led him to become what is probably the most famous contemporary defendant for date rape (perhaps now eclipsed by Bill Cosby for a younger generation). The same goes for O. J. Simpson, who was at the center of arguably the most well-known trial for spousal homicide. Michael Jackson was arguably the most visible figure associated with child sexual abuse before he passed, and the oft-cited Ike Turner's infamy as a wife abuser has transcended generations. Chris Rock once quipped that Black men even compete with one another for prominence as representatives of intimate violence. In his *Bring the Pain* performance, Rock jokingly states:

> You know who I feel for in the O. J. case, who I feel for more than anybody else, man, everybody—O. J., Nicole, Cato, fuck all them, man. You know who I really feel for? Who I feel for more than anybody else? Ike Turner. You know why? 'Cause Ike was king of the women beaters till O. J. took his title.[1]

The multitude of Black celebrities associated with sexual violence in particular hit home for me when I had the opportunity to spend time with a men's anti-violence program consisting of students from a large university in North Carolina. Aside from one student of Asian descent, the group was entirely White as best as I could tell. Some of the guys spoke in heavy Southern accents and argued intermittently about where to find the best barbecue in town. Despite the differences in our upbringing, we recognized one another as brothers in this peculiar fraternity of men who have pledged to fight sexual violence. My time with these men mirrored my own entrance into the movement against sexual violence—a time of discourse between men of various racial and cultural backgrounds united for a common purpose of asking men to do better.

One of the stories these men shared with me involved an idea that they once had to raise awareness of men's violence against women on campus. The plan was to make T-shirts that featured prominent offenders of sexual violence. The group's intent was to show their campus that even people they cherished and applauded were capable of the violence that the group sought to eradicate. It was a well-intentioned project, but the group confessed to hitting a major snag when they sat down to create the list of celebrities who would appear on their T-shirts. It turned out that the prominent offenders who first came to mind were primarily Black men, and the group pulled the plug on the project for fear of looking like "racist bastards," as one member put it.

The group had enough awareness to know that violence is perpetrated by men of all races. The attitudes that support sexual violence are so widespread that they are not constrained to any one subgroup or sub-culture. To paint a picture that suggested anything otherwise might succeed only in demonizing Black men and shielding non-Black men from scrutiny.

We will rarely know which of the celebrities we condemn or support actually committed the acts of which they were accused. Some of them are surely the victims of an overreaching media; but, whether their accusations are deserved or not, their stories contribute to larger narratives. It is not just individual people who are under attack whenever a celebrity is publicly accused of violence. There is no way for me to recall my childhood without memories of devoutly watching *The Cosby Show* with my mother and gradually developing a sense of pride for the accomplishment of a positive, Black family finding its way into homes throughout the country. My very memories and self-identity came under attack when I learned that Bill Cosby was under suspicion for sexual assault. Cosby is now better known to a rising generation for the violence of which he was convicted rather than the positive images of Black family that he previously generated throughout his career. I understand the urge to defend these men, as there is more at stake than their individual livelihoods and rights.

In the midst of his enormously popular run with *The Chappelle Show*, comedian Dave Chappelle featured a sketch in which he is interviewed for jury duty for the trials of O. J. Simpson, Michael Jackson, and R. Kelly (all three of them coincidentally accused of sexual or domestic violence). Chappelle vehemently defends each of the defendants and counters the statements of the prosecutors at each turn. In defense of Michael Jackson, Chappelle looks sympathetically at his inquisitors and pleads that Michael is innocent because he contributed "Thriller" to the world. When asked what he would need to see in order to believe R. Kelly was guilty, Chappelle rattles off an impossible list of demands, including a video in which the alleged victim was holding two forms of identification in the presence of a police officer. Chappelle simply responds, "Sir, my blackness will not permit me to make a statement like that" after being asked if he thought it was likely that Simpson killed his wife.

As is the case with most effective comedians, there is truth in Chappelle's antics. Black Americans can occasionally go to great lengths to protect what is perceived to be a limited and necessary pool of heroes. The need to preserve this pool is understandable, and we do so partially because we know it to be both easy and insincere to point to the faults of Black male celebrities in order to make sweeping generalizations about all Black men.

Black communities are often criticized for holding on to symbols despite their flaws, but this practice is by no means limited to us. We saw this clearly when former Pennsylvania State University head football coach Joe Paterno was widely condemned in 2011 and 2012 for his handling of allegations of child sexual abuse levied against a former member of his coaching staff. The university eventually responded by removing a statue of Paterno from campus, among other actions. The removal of the statue was accompanied by news organizations broadcasting images of deeply disheartened members of the Penn State community. Many of these men and women talked about what Paterno meant to them and their community. They spoke against the tarnishing of Paterno's image. They spoke of the good he had done and the pride he generated for the school. There is nothing uniquely Black about the pressure to defend the heroes and symbols that are integrated into our senses of self and community. This is a human instinct whose value we must consider in reaching out to boys.

* * *

I loved professional wrestlers growing up. Not the ones who perform in collegiate athletics or the Olympics, but the kind who enter the ring to theme music and smash one another with steel chairs. My cousins and I regularly debated who the greatest wrestlers were and simulated their signature moves with couches serving as launching pads and their pillows serving as makeshift weapons. In retrospect, I realize that the superstars of professional wrestling held significant influence during my formative years and today serve as a reminder of the special relationships that boys share with their heroes in the media.

The life of Lionel Tate is a more solemn reminder that boys take cues from their heroes. In March 2001, 14-year-old Tate was sentenced to life in prison after the death of a female playmate two years prior. It was reported that Tate accidentally killed the girl while performing moves he had seen executed by his favorite wrestlers on television. He was the youngest person in modern history to be sentenced to life imprisonment, though he would end up serving only three years before his conviction was overturned.[2] If only the link between Black boys and the violence they inflict on women in the service of imitating their heroes was always as clear.

Most often, this link is beyond the bounds of direct observation and empirical study. It's perceptible only in the hints of fraudulence evident in boys moving about the world in ways that lean a little too much on the media's chosen representatives of cool. And by no means are the linkages to heroes limited to youth. You can certainly see it in the strides of grown men as well, sometimes as obviously as a young boy imitating his favorite wrestler. The displays of male power at social gatherings among men of my age so often appear to be lifted directly from the hip-hop videos of our youth as men unload money, alcohol, jeers, grabs, taunts, and slaps onto the bodies of women. There are countless ways to display male ownership of female bodies, but adherence to scripts set by those with prominent media platforms might explain why we see the same examples time and time again.

Marketers would not spend the amounts of money that they do to acquire celebrity endorsers were it not for the fact that many of us take our behavioral cues from men who we use our wallets, votes, and applause to elect as trendsetters. That is why we cringe when these social influencers do not pass on messages that we approve of, even if we only do so privately. Everything we know about sexual violence prevention confirms our intuitions. It is widely understood that the most effective prevention strategies are comprehensive and provide anti-violent messaging to boys in all phases of their lives.[3] Ideally, they would grow up hearing the same messaging reinforced among their local social circles and the broader communities to which they belong. The heroes of boys undoubtedly matter.

Having already admitted to growing up a fan of professional wrestling, I might as well admit that I count myself among the nostalgic suckers that Hollywood relies on whenever it wants to make money off of some revived property from my childhood. As a boy who grew up in the 80s, my favorite toys were the Transformers—robotic aliens that transformed into vehicles, animals, and weapons. When I heard that they were to be adapted into a live action movie, I knew very well that I would soon find myself paying money to watch them in action once again.

But my viewing experience was ruined one third of the way through the movie. One of the movie's protagonists, Jazz, introduces himself to the audience by spinning like a break dancer and saying, "What's up, lil' bitches?" I spent the rest of the movie pondering the inclusion of this odd bit of dialogue in a movie where children were expected to make up a large portion of the audience, judging by the cross-promotions and toys that accompanied the film.

To understand my reaction, you have to understand that Jazz is widely considered to be the "Black" Transformer. Though he would transform into a white Porsche in the original cartoon series, his demeanor and speech led many of the show's fans to dub him as Black, if there could be such a thing among robotic aliens. This was supported by the fact that he was voiced by African American singer Scatman Crothers. Not to mention that his name was *Jazz*. Apparently, the people behind the 2007 film deemed an impromptu break dance and casually throwing around the word "bitch" to be the easiest way to convey the character's blackness to a new generation of viewers. *Why must the heroes of Black boys be relentlessly linked to disrespect of women?*

Even when we leave the world of robotic aliens and focus on the flesh-and-blood heroes of Black boys, we see that they are not doing much better (though their images are often as fantastical and stylized as those of the giant robots who entertained me as a child). I gave in to staring out of my window one Friday night after seeing a limousine pull up down the street from my apartment on the outskirts of Philadelphia. A Black teenage boy stepped out of a house and excitedly made his way to the limousine. An entourage of older people who I could only assume were family members followed behind. Once he made his way to the car, one of the rear doors swung open and a series of well-dressed boys filed out of the car to vigorously greet their comrade. This led the adults to scramble frantically for their cameras. Given the time of year, I guessed that the young men were on their way to the prom.

The boys had yet to meet up with their dates, but it was clear that the party had already begun. With their audience assembled, they kicked off an extravagant exhibition for the cameras. One young man donned a gaudy fur coat that he gripped while striking exaggerated poses. Another continuously adjusted a top hat in between twirling a cane. And another endlessly held out a limp hand—a gesture that I presumed was meant to request that others kiss his ring. These young men were assuming the stereotypical iconography of pimps.

They probably did not mean any harm by their prom theme. Theirs was a world that included a television show called *Pimp My Ride* and an energy drink named "Pimp Juice." I am hard pressed to think of negative representations of pimps in popular culture. They most often appear like Money Mike, the eccentric rhyming pimp from the movie *Friday After Next* whose antics are exaggerated but rarely portrayed as problematic. They are outright celebrated as heroes in other media like *Pimps Up, Ho's Down*, the best known of several "pimpumentaries" that take audiences into the world of pimps, complete with Cadillacs and player's balls. Pimps have so much crossover appeal in the Black community that a radio station I listened to when I lived in Philadelphia used a recurring character that it dubbed the "Power Pimp" to promote various contests and giveaways.

Another characteristic of pimps in popular culture is that they are undeniably Black. Black skin is as consistent a part of the sensationalized symbolism of pimps as flashy suits and pinky rings. *American Pimp*, another documentary of the pimp lifestyle (this one directed by the Hughes brothers), features a scene where a pimp explains that he has never met a White pimp and that his profession is reserved for Black men. The aforementioned *Pimps Up, Ho's Down* does in fact feature a White pimp, but he comes off as aware that he is meant to play up his unique position.

Prostitution transcends centuries and cultures, but pimping is a Black man's job in mainstream American consciousness.

I might have an easier time swallowing the revelry surrounding pimps if the popular portrayals of them were not so out of touch with the reality of their work. When people use the word "pimp" or any of the mannerisms and styles popularly associated with them, they do not generally mean to reference a profession of selling women's bodies, often through methods that are mentally or physically brutal. They do not mean to recall men who profit off of the sexual exploitation of women and who often achieve this by leveraging the emotional and financial dependence of those women. This is what Black boys tacitly condone when they take on pimps as heroes.

I recognize that I am making condemnations from a relatively comfortable position. I have a college education and have always considered myself to have a realistic opportunity to legally make enough money to pay the bills. Some who ascribe to the mystique that surrounds pimping say that pimps do not choose their profession but are rather "called by the game." If they mean to say that socioeconomic factors play a part in determining the desirability of becoming a pimp, then I cannot disagree. My background might make me an unworthy critic of those who choose such a trade.

While I may be in an unfair position to wholeheartedly denounce pimps for their choices, that does not mean that I have to join in the hero worship that surrounds them, either. I do not have to imitate them at gatherings, name products after them, work the language of pimping into common vernacular, or celebrate them as heroes for boys.

* * *

There is one particular area on which I have clashed most often with my White colleagues in the anti-violence field, that being the suitability of hip-hop artists as heroes. Some of my colleagues believe that no one who is serious about ending violence should have anything to do with hip-hop and its endless depictions of female submission. They would be right in arguing that hip-hop remains a field where one can go on stage and spout lyrics about raping women with absolutely no consequences. Sometimes artists will describe scenarios that can easily be interpreted as nonconsensual. For example, there are an awful lot of lyrics about real or imagined sex acts that artists "make" women perform (rappers David Banner and Lil' Flip rapping "Poke yo' gul up in the throat/And make her swallow the nut/We make 'em swallow the nut/So follow the truck" is one of countless examples).[4] The contemporary wave of rappers have fully embraced this theming, as we now have a generation of music with prominent themes of maintaining emotional distance from and obtaining sexual favors from women.

I can also think of many other times when artists explicitly use the word "rape" in their lyrical storytelling. When artist Rick Ross received massive backlash in 2013 for lyrics wherein he talks about taking a woman home after putting a "molly" in her drink without her knowledge, I was fascinated because I could recall any number of lyrics that were equally or more suggestive of violence against women. The public did not force the artists to apologize or to clarify that the accounts were fictional in those cases.

Even when violence is not spoken to outright, it only takes a cursory review of popular hip-hop songs to find the trappings of rape culture. Listen to the top hip-hop songs on the Billboard charts at any given time and you will likely find usage of violent terminology to characterize sex and sexuality, requests for sexual acts that border on commands, and objectification of women through plentiful references to them as "bitches." The portrayed relationships could very well fit many real-word relationships that are consensual, but we should consider that a lot of this media is consumed by boys with little to no experience with real-world relationships.

I completely understand those who see hip-hop as little more than a vehicle for popularizing rape culture. My reasons for not writing it off are probably selfish in part, as I grew up alongside hip-hop music. However, I do also have two strategic reasons for continuing to follow hip-hop. First, familiarity with hip-hop artists and traditions has assisted me greatly in my work with certain male audiences that idolize it. I have many times used a lyric or artist that an audience is familiar with as a launching pad for discussing anti-violent concepts. Second, I actually see huge potential for hip-hop to be a powerful voice against rape culture. Consider that the late legend Tupac Shakur is best remembered by many for "Keep Ya Head Up," a track whose first verse reads like a feminist treatise, complete with a confrontation of the rape of women, a challenge to raise boys in a manner that is respectful of women and their bodily rights, and a charge for "real men" to get up and do their part in this effort.[5] Whereas some music genres tend to address sexual violence via allusion and metaphors, hip-hop generally pulls no punches.

I am excited to see where hip-hop can go with its particular brand of resistance to sexual violence. Avid listeners are bound to come across extensive commentary on sexual violence as they wade through hip-hop's offerings. As Exhibit A, I submit an artist like Kendrick Lamar. Like many artists, the "New Prince of the West Coast" is rather difficult to fit into a neat category. His catalogue is laced with hip-hop's usual fare but also features plenty of rich social and personal commentary. He is a good artist to focus on because he has both commercial success and broad respect as an artist. In the course of listening to his first studio album, one will encounter "Keisha's Song (Her Pain)," which describes the ordeals of the eponymous Keisha, a 17-year-old prostituted girl.[6] In this song, Lamar does not communicate the popular notion of prostituted women as empowered individuals who love sex but rather describes a profession that is body punishing, that requires the use of coping mechanisms in order to survive, and where prior sexual victimization facilitates one's entrance into the profession. Lamar describes a childhood experience of Keisha's in which she is molested by her mother's boyfriend. The disdain for this man's actions is evident, its consequences are acknowledged, and there is no space given to condone or normalize it as Lamar transitions from its description to Keisha's violent death while on the job.

In other words, what you have in "Keisha's Song (Her Pain)" is commentary that is in near harmony with what is preached by many anti-sexual violence educators, that is set to music by a popular artist, and that is specially crafted for a youth audience to consume. The aid of opinion leaders presenting countercultural messages is quite often what anti-violence educators aim to produce.

However, I can see why many of my anti-violence colleagues do not embrace hip-hop as a potential ally as readily as I do if I look doubly through the very same song by Lamar. My first hesitation is hip-hop's amazing inconsistency. Hip-hop is rife with artists, like the aforementioned Tupac Shakur, who are remembered as champions of both female empowerment and misogyny. There is enough in many of their catalogues and alleged personal histories to make either argument. When considered within the context of an entire album, Lamar's piercing critique of predatory clientele who frequent prostituted girls is admittedly mixed in with language more befitting of unsympathetic johns. It might be the case that all of the awareness that I celebrate in hip-hop is drowned out by contradictory messaging.

My second hesitation is that even when lending its voice to addressing sexual violence, hip-hop does not generally address the types of violence for which its influence would likely have the most profound impact. Like with "Keisha's Song (Her Pain)," I would argue that most references to sexual violence in hip-hop cite child sexual abuse or, when discussing adults, rape that is accompanied by blatant coercion or outright physical violence. While these behaviors occur at inexcusable rates, and I applaud any and all denunciations of them, these are behaviors that are primarily already viewed as harmful.

I do not mean to suggest that rappers should avoid discussion of behaviors such as sexual abuse of children—those lyrics have value in terms of raising awareness, creating empathy for victims, and further marginalizing perpetrators and their facilitators. But I would love for hip-hop to flex its enormous muscles in order to take risks and enter the fray where public opinion is more divided and where boys could stand to see more leadership. *How about some dialogue on appropriate sexual behavior with women who do not physically resist sexual advances but are less-than-active participants, women who are conscious but whose judgment is heavily impaired by alcohol, or young girls who are physically mature enough for sex but legally unable to consent to it?* These are but a few of the situations where the actions of men and boys clearly have impact but contention over acceptable behavior is considerable. I know that the types of violence that I just described are rather complex to put to lyrics, but many hip-hop artists are masters of wordplay who capture social issues just as nuanced as these in limited space.

Lamar closes "Keisha's Song (Her Pain)" by breaking from verse and telling the audience how he shared this song with his younger sister—presumably as words of guidance so that she would not end up traveling a path similar to the titular Keisha's path. Herein lies my third hesitation with hip-hop, in that the majority of its messaging that confronts sexual violence is squarely directed at women. Songs such as Nas's "Daughters" and Ja Rule's "Daddy's Little Baby" that warn young women about predatory men are common enough, but it is much more difficult to find songs that actually discourage violent behavior in boys.

Even when artists do not identify a female audience as clearly as Lamar does here, anti-violence messaging generally feels directed at women. Any individual song about sexual violence primarily intended for consumption by women is not problematic, but taken together they reinforce the common notion that resisting sexual violence is solely work for women. For all their efforts to warn and protect women, I wonder if artists realize that the rest of their lyrics might embolden those same men who are to be guarded against. One of the contributing factors to the lasting appeal and legacy of Shakur's "Keep Ya Head Up" might just be its uncommon insistence on placing a challenge squarely at the feet of men.

With my criticisms stated, the potential for hip-hop to become a prime force in confronting sexual violence remains. The genre is rife with both positives and negatives, as is the case with most cultural expressions. The great irony in hip-hop's continued failure to promote an unmistakable alternative to ideologies that are dismissive of sexual violence is that hip-hop artists should not need to worry about proving their manhood by way of demonstrating their ability to acquire women. By virtue of their talent, charisma, and status, who would really doubt that most of them receive the attention from women required of "real" men? That even they display a continual need to demonstrate control over women's bodies says something about the depth of the culture that we are training boys to confront.

* * *

My work in sexual violence education once took me to Jacksonville, Florida, where I had the opportunity to work with several public schools courtesy of the Jacksonville Jaguars Foundation and other local benefactors. The Duval County School District, in which Jacksonville is located, had brought in a colleague and mentor of mine to speak to its students, and she asked me to join her, given the substantial African American student population in the area (I was more of an opening act to her main event, truth to be told). I readily agreed and we decided on an atypical presentation format that we thought would capture the students' attention. We decided to show popular music videos. We would then facilitate discussion with the students and help them analyze the music videos' content related to respect, gender roles, and healthy relationships.

This actually worked, and the students were hooked and invested. Most of the music videos that we played for the students featured hip-hop artists. A recurring reaction occurred in every single audience as we played the videos for the students. The introduction of each video was always greeted with a loud cheer as the students enthusiastically displayed their disbelief that their favorite entertainers had actually found a sanctioned way into their school. This initial outburst would then give way to the audience quieting down and listening intently. Thirty seconds into each video, the only sounds that could be heard were the shuffling of bodies as students swayed to their favorite songs and a collective murmur as students recited each and every lyric along with the videos.

My co-presenter and I also selected a number of R&B music videos to play for the students because some of them had messages about relationships that we wanted to highlight. I thought that it would be a gamble to feature this material because I believed that hip-hop reigned supreme over the musical interests of our target audience, but I was soundly corrected. Sure enough, a good amount of the middle school and high school students also cheered wildly for the R&B artists and also knew all of their lyrics.

It turned out that the R&B songs were referenced much more frequently than the hip-hop songs when we got into the heart of the discussions. It could be that the students saw a divide between the ultra-staged worlds presented in hip-hop music videos and the realities of their day-to-day experiences with attraction and relationships. Or maybe they just took the hip-hop world at its word since its artists rarely tout themselves as experts on relationships. Many instead create personas that actively distance themselves from having any relationships of meaning with women beyond those that are purely sexual.

Whatever the case, the students' apparent faith in R&B made me wonder why few comment on R&B's contributions to rape culture while hip-hop music cannot seem to find a moment's rest from critique. Because of the high level of collaboration between hip-hop and R&B artists and producers, these genres share a very close association in the contemporary landscape. Yet, accusations of sexism, misogyny, and the promotion of sexual violence generally avoid those artists that categorize themselves as R&B artists.

If we did turn our gaze toward R&B, we might notice heavy circulation of myths and attitudes that fuel rape culture. So many of the genre's most popular motifs would be at home among those who defend violent men. As illustration of this, let us look at a song that was part of my teenage soundtrack—R. Kelly's 1994 single "Your Body's Calling."[7] This song was one of the headline singles off of Kelly's debut album, which catapulted him toward a career as one of R&B's iconic figures. The song is a bit dated at this point, but Kelly and his peers undoubtedly influenced the current crop of R&B artists that dabble in similar themes. "Your Body's Calling" chronicles Kelly's wooing of a sexual partner, like so many other R&B songs, and some of the themes that catch my attention are as follows:

1. *A rejection of verbal communication*: As indicated by the title, the song glorifies the singer's ability to read a partner's intentions entirely through her body language. In the event that a partner's

intentions are not fully known, then there is nothing wrong with verbal communication in order to clarify things. Many women will even say that they find a partner speaking to them in order to clarify their intentions to be attractive. Nonetheless, I know from talking to young men that many do not see verbal communication as a viable option for a sexual encounter. They see it as awkward and would prefer to just push through ambiguity rather than confirm that their actions are consensual.

2. *A need for a partner to make an urgent decision*: At several points, Kelly requests that his partner make her intentions clear to him (somewhat at odds with the general theme that his partner's intentions are already known to him via her body language). There is nothing wrong with this and, as I said earlier, clarification of a partner's intentions is ideal. The problem is that there is an urgency to Kelly's request and an implication that there will be negative outcomes if his partner does not make her intentions known quickly. Taken altogether, this need for urgency can border on coercion. Many men do indeed pursue sexual partners with an unhealthy urgency that can distort their decision-making process.

3. *A premium on convincing a partner to see things "your way"*: There is also the implication that Kelly's partner was initially reluctant to share her affection with him and had to be convinced to do so in some fashion. The art of seduction is timeless and not inherently problematic, but the drive to get someone to "see things your way" has to be tempered by the possibility that a partner might not share your viewpoint about a particular act.

These three themes pop up repeatedly in an R&B genre that has increasingly made sex and seduction its preferred domain. Again, there is nothing inherently wrong with a man reading a partner's body language, requesting that a partner make her intentions known, or wooing a partner such that she changes her mind. Few probably even bat an eye at the themes that I have teased out, and it is a shame that I cannot fully enjoy a song that I like without analyzing it. But over a decade of listening to women share their experiences with sexual violence leads me to believe that many men are not as savvy at reading women as we often claim to be. Many men are not the skillful ladies' men portrayed by Kelly, as evidenced by persistent incidence reports analyzing sexual violence and a massive network of victim support services with steady workloads.

Boys grow into their sexuality in a culture steeped in music that presents men as all-knowing masters of convincing women to see things their way. This makes it difficult for young men to admit that they have discomfort or uncertainty about the courtship processes expected of them. I would love for musical heroes to display more leadership here, though I am sure that many listeners would rather not turn on their radios and hear about fallible men who deeply evaluate their advances toward women because they might be spurned or received negatively. I am sure that many would find lyrics about male insecurity to be silly. However, this again just shows how far we have fallen as a culture when singing about something as deeply human as negotiating the experience of courting romantic partners can be considered silly.

* * *

History records the 2001 film *Training Day* as the one that garnered a Black actor, Denzel Washington, the first Academy Award for Best Actor since Sidney Poitier accomplished the feat in 1964. But contemporaries of the film will recall that Washington's award generated mixed emotions in Black communities. Rather than applauding Washington's accomplishment, many viewed his receipt of the award as destructive and racist. Some viewed the award as the Academy's token gesture to make up for years of discrimination against Black actors. Others were upset at the particular role that garnered Washington's Oscar attention. In the movie, Washington plays a corrupt narcotics officer. Given his illustrious career portraying good guys, many found it curious that the Hollywood elite would finally reward Washington for a portrayal of such a dubious character.

A writer for the *New York Times* asserted that Washington's portrayal failed to transcend age-old stereotypes of Black antagonists as simple agents of moral advancement for White protagonists and that Washington merely played "a demon sent to test the innocence of a young white policeman played by Ethan Hawke."[8] Likewise, the editor of a review site summed up the emotions of a healthy chunk of Black America when she asserted that

> It has not escaped the attention of even the most casual observer of Black film that Washington has finally won the Best Actor award for playing a crooked LAPD narcotics detective, a thug so without heart that he risks the life of his mistress and son to save his own . . . It is just striking, and to many of us more than coincidence, that he is awarded for playing one of our thugs we know well, rather than for playing our "Shining Black Prince."[9]

Criticisms of Washington's *Training Day* character were not hard to find, but it was interesting that hardly anyone specifically disapproved of the character's casual attitudes toward violence against women. Some addressed his predisposition to overt physical violence, others addressed his narcissism or criminality, and some even took issue with his profane language; but hardly a soul wrote of the character's troublesome perspectives on women. The aforementioned review was one of only a few I came across that mentioned the character's relationships with his partner and child in pointing out his flaws. I am sure there were others, but this concern was easily not a front-burner objection. Yet, here was a character who threatens a suspect by saying he is going to have some men rape his girlfriend. In another scene, he callously responds to the attempted rape of a 14-year-old girl (one that he did not attempt to prevent in the slightest) by sending her on her way and refusing to arrest her assailants.

I am actually a fan of *Training Day*, and it got me interested in following the career of director Antoine Fuqua. Yet I also find it, and the response it received, illustrative of how those concerned about portrayals of Black men and boys do not readily look to their contributions to a culture of hostility toward women. There are always bigger fish to fry. To be reminded of this point by a movie called *Training Day* is appropriate because we do so little in the way of training young men to even recognize sexual violence.

I have met many anti-violence colleagues who take issue with the heralded film *Gone with the Wind*. In one of the movie's more memorable scenes, the male protagonist, Rhett Butler, confronts his wife, Scarlett O'Hara. In a fit of jealousy, Rhett repeatedly defeats an angry Scarlett's attempts to walk away from him. He restrains her and carries her upstairs, where he presumably acts on his sexual desires. The following morning, Scarlett is singing with the excitement and joy of the previous night's escapade still fresh in her mind. It is certainly disheartening that a film as iconic as *Gone with the Wind* would imply that nothing could be more romantic than a drunken man threatening a woman, shrugging aside her attempts to physically resist him, and carrying her off. I hope that moviegoers are able to distinguish fiction from the real-world ideals of healthy relationships. If they cannot, then I fear the impact on generations of Black youth raised on movies where violence in relationships is common and often not even identified as violence.

I still vividly remember the hype surrounding the 1991 release of *Boyz n the Hood*. I was 11 years old and the television was abuzz with the approach of the John Singleton–directed film. I watched as reporters interviewed moviegoers waiting in lengthy lines for their chance to check out then-24-year-old Singleton's movie. From what I could gather, people were excited about the film for two major reasons: First, *Boyz n the Hood* was one of a handful of major releases to feature inner-city Black youth as primary protagonists and second, the film was believed to be the vanguard of an era in which African Americans would tell their own stories in major releases.

Many expected Singleton and his class of Black directors to bring a more diversified Black experience to the big screen. But what we received when I look over the films that featured during my journey to manhood is debatable. If we fast-forward 10 years from Singleton's *Boyz n the Hood*, we find Singleton's 2001 film *Baby Boy*. At one point in the film, the primary character, Jody, faces an accusation of infidelity from his off-and-on girl-friend and mother of his child. Their quarrel becomes physical and ends when Jody slaps his partner to the floor. Jody is immediately remorseful and rushes to console his partner. When Jody realizes that his attempts to comfort his partner through touch and speech are not working, he carries her into the bedroom and conceives the brilliant idea to pull down her pants and perform oral sex on her. This produces magnificent results and the situation is forever resolved, never to be mentioned again.

A nearly identical scene unfolds in the Hype Williams–directed *Belly* (1998). Williams is best known for his work directing the music videos of hip-hop superstars such as LL Cool J, Kanye West, and Notorious B.I.G. His first foray into feature-length work includes a scene in which a main character named Tommy (played by rapper DMX) is confronted by his partner after she learns that Tommy has a sexual relationship with an-other woman. Like *Baby Boy*'s title character, Tommy strongly rebuffs the charge of infidelity and ultimately ends the confrontation through aggres-sive initiation of sexual activity. The aggressiveness plays out a little more explicitly in this scene as Tommy initially confronts his partner by force-fully grabbing her and screaming, "Shut the fuck up!" The tactic of using sex to sedate angry partners once again works perfectly. The director goes to noticeable lengths to convey Tommy's partner as sufficiently calmed and satisfied by the event, portraying her in true Scarlett O'Hara fashion. These movies model aggressive initiation of sex as an effective means of resolving relationship conflicts.

The two sexual encounters that follow violence in these films are argu-ably rapes themselves. Both encounters occur in close proximity to phys-ical violence, without the benefit of explicit communication, at moments that many would not recognize as socially expected opportunities for sex, and within the context of relationships lacking in equity. There are some troubling elements here. Both scenes are presented as unhealthy and highlight flaws in their characters, but one does not walk away from these scenes with a sense that the characters' sexual decision-making is what is meant to be analyzed. The sexual activity they initiate is more of a plot de-vice for temporarily resolving the "real" problems that the characters are to overcome. I doubt that these were key moments that challenged the young men who made up much of the audiences of these films. Most viewers are unlikely to identify the sexual activity as problematic. As proof, the Wikipedia entry for *Belly* tellingly describes its aforementioned scene as a "passionate night" between Tommy and his partner.[10]

Interestingly enough, *Baby Boy* has another encounter that is, in fact, internally labeled as an attempted rape. It differs from the scenes that I described earlier in that its perpetrator is both undesired by the victim and acknowledges the maliciousness of his act. This scene's victim even uses the word "rape" during the scene. The stark contrast in tones between this scene of a "real" rape and the two sexual encounters described earlier only further cements the normalcy of "good" men aggressively pushing for sex on their own terms.

This is the kind of messaging about Black male sexuality that was common during my adolescence, and you may find similar messaging when you take inventory of what the young men in your life are consuming. To be sure, Tommy, Jody, and other depictions of Black men are more nuanced than many of the Black protagonists who graced the big screen before them. They are rightly complex because humanity is complex. I just wish that they had ushered in a more sophisticated discussion of men's relationships with their partners. Movies could be a site for some advanced discussion on healthy relationships, but the "bad guys" are still generally identified as such by tone and the actions of the "good guys" are rarely interrogated—at least in the sexual arena.

To this end, many have criticized what they view as a lack of leadership by celebrated director Spike Lee due to a scene in his debut feature-length film *She's Gotta Have It*. The movie follows the exploits of Nola Darling as she attempts to entertain three intimate interests in her life. One of her suitors, Jamie, eventually grows impatient with Nola's insistence on keeping multiple men in her life and rapes her in a moment of frustration and anger (the film itself internally defines this scene as a rape as it is later referred to as such in a conversation between Jamie and Nola). Jamie asks Nola, "Whose pussy is it?" in the middle of the encounter and ignores her cry that he is hurting her. He concludes the incident by pushing Nola onto the bed and stating that he enjoyed it. Some might say that this scene represents the nuance in Black, male protagonists that I have been looking for, but I do not see much nuance in such a conscious and domineering rape. I just do not think that many young men would see themselves in Jamie's shoes. We also do not get any insight into the reaction of Jamie's peer network, so the audience also is not invited to discuss the community's responsibilities.

Many find this scene to be out of place in a film ostensibly intending to champion the sexual empowerment of Black women. I found that I could read it as representative of men's negative reactions to the growing sexual independence of women. However, if this is indeed the point of the scene, it feels strangely done, with the victim seeking advice from a friend soon after to discuss her remorse over making her rapist so angry with her. Then, she even meets up with Jamie and it is Nola who does most of the apologizing.

She's Gotta Have It is not widely known and was an early feature directed by Lee, who was then relatively unknown. I do not find it to be as dangerous as so many releases by lesser-known directors adorned with rappers, hypersexuality, street violence, and all of the trappings that many Black boys have been seduced into believing confirm their authenticity. Most of the criticism that came Lee's way for *She's Gotta Have It* was probably due to his regard as one of Black America's most successful film directors. There is a worry that if Lee cannot get it right, then things are not looking good for the masses of directors who have less acclaim and less interest in telling a productive narrative about Black men.

We could also look to Tyler Perry, another of Black America's most successful directors. I cannot call myself a huge fan of Perry's work, nor am I sure that I sit in his intended audience. But I am a fan of Perry himself. I believe he is very skilled at writing for his target audience, I believe that he is a great model of entrepreneurial success, and I respect his efforts to carve out his success on a foundation of positive messaging. Perry is often criticized for providing heavily clichéd characters, but I respect him for at least wielding these characters to advance messages about hope, community, and empowerment.

This is what I must remind myself when Perry touches on sexual violence, which he does with some frequency, often in service of explaining
a character's personality via past victimization. I would like to see him try
something other than coverage where the rapists are clearly demarcated as
villains, something where the shining knights who romance the heroines
have issues of their own. The rapist could be a guy going through the
motions of normalized male behavior, perhaps someone who is aware that
his partner is not entirely involved but who never stops to ensure that his
partner consents to his activities—someone who does not begin to think
that his actions are violent because he has not employed physical force or
overt manipulation. Imagine the dialogue that would be generated if a director with the reach and ability to stir up conversation like Perry decided
to feature a character such as this.

This may have been the intent behind the character of Bill in *For Colored
Girls*, the Perry-affiliated film adaptation of Ntozake Shange's 1975 stage
play *For Colored Girls Who Have Considered Suicide / When the Rainbow
is Enuf*. Bill rapes Yasmine, one of the film's many protagonists, but his
inclusion nonetheless feels odd in a film that seemingly wants to demonstrate that rapes by acquaintances are no less valid and damaging than
those committed by strangers. He is not an everyman but a calculating
predator with malicious intent. When he is ready to make his move, all
prior charm and subtlety quickly evaporates as he transforms into an irrational being who starts removing his clothes almost as soon as he enters
the victim's apartment and who resorts to overt physical force at the first
sign of physical resistance from his victim (though not her first signs of
resistance, to be sure).

I am not suggesting that rapes of this nature do not occur, nor am
I suggesting that more conventional acquaintance rapists are not every
bit as hurtful and calculating. I just think that few boys and men would
relate to Bill either as someone in their cohort or as the man who they
might be. There is a lost opportunity to generate introspection into the
male experience, which is ultimately responsible for the violence that the
film wishes to decry. Empathizing with Yasmine's experience might spark
this introspection, but Bill himself likely will not. After the rape scene in

question, Bill is not seen again, with the exception of a single scene that informs the audience of his death. He simply fades back into wherever it is that these kinds of men go. There is no insight into the culture that created him or how that culture received him after the assault. The type of precision and depth that I am asking for may be unreasonable within a film seeking to tell the stories of nine major characters. Not to mention that all of the things on my wish list probably have little place in a film so clearly interested in releasing the voices and perspectives of women, and that has obligation to Shange's award-winning source material. The title of the film practically dissuades men from engaging with it and any statements it makes about male culture.

While I am on the subject, I do wonder why so many of Perry's rebukes of sexual violence are delivered by his recurring female protagonist Madea (played by Perry). It is obvious that Perry sees the sexual abuse of women and children as serious issues to be addressed, but is the confronting of this violence so firmly entrenched as women's work that Perry feels obligated to assume a female persona in order to say anything meaningful on the topic? Perry is easily one of the most prominent contemporary represent-atives of Black America. If he or the male protagonists whom he crafts were to lend their voices to the cause to end sexual violence, that would go a long way toward rightly establishing this work as community work.

In fairness to Perry, I am not familiar with his entire body of work, particularly with his stage and television productions. I remain a fan of Perry's insistence on bringing messages of personal and community up-lift along with him during his rise to a member of the Hollywood elite. I ought to just be happy that he consistently denounces sexual violence in his work. Someone with less willingness to vilify sexual violence could certainly be in his shoes instead, and so I count him among the allies for developing Black boys. There are also plenty of survivors of rape and child sexual abuse who might caution me that my push for portrayals of sexual violence that challenge young men is premature since so much violence perpetrated every year is every bit as conscious as typically portrayed in movies. When I remember that the stories that people have shared with me include men discussing plans to incapacitate and rape women at parties and stories of men threatening to have their associates gang rape a teenager if she reported a previous rape to authorities, then I am reminded that any director who would use screen time to say that rape is wrong deserves applause, no matter how simplistic the statement might be. The people who commit these acts should know that they will find no sanctuary that approves of their behavior, even when escaping to a movie theater.

Boys quite often express an overly simplistic world where men can be either calculating sadists who rape women with weapons in hand or "good guys." This oversimplification is often reflected in the visual media that boys consume. Few boys see themselves in the shoes of blatantly violent men, and they need to know that all rapes are violent no matter the methods employed—that "good guys" can also be violent if they go through the expected motions of sexual interaction and fail to ensure that they have obtained consent.

This may be where we are headed, as the last few years have seen several well-received movies, such as *Moonlight* and *Dope*, that focus on Black, male teenagers wrestling with societal expectations of manhood. Today's boys are also growing up watching the unparalleled success of the Marvel Cinematic Universe (MCU). For those unfamiliar with the MCU, it is a movie franchise owned by the Walt Disney Company and based on superheroes created by Marvel Comics. It is easily the highest-grossing movie franchise of all time, an accomplishment that could not have been achieved without a massive following among boys. I bring these movies up to point out that they are a far cry from the action movies that dominated my childhood. Those movies starred actors such as Sylvester Stallone, Arnold Schwarzenegger, and Bruce Willis and often featured heroes who personified the extremes of the "man box." The MCU has its share of characters who use force and aggression to solve problems (these are action movies, after all) but dedicates an awful lot of space to examining the appropriate applications of that force. Boys and their caretakers have demonstrated overwhelmingly with their wallets that there is space for Hollywood to move on from the status quo.

* * *

I intentionally chose a song by R. Kelly to represent some of R&B's un-healthy messaging earlier because he himself represents our collective in-ability to insist on media figures who can lead the way on challenging rape culture. As of this writing, he is imprisoned on account of charges of child pornography and kidnapping, but negative consequences for trou-bling allegations are a relatively new development in his career. He had previously been battling accusations for over a decade. His success was not due to criminal exoneration but in spite of it. He garnered an NAACP image award and continued to produce top-selling records not because the public gave him the benefit of the doubt but, from my perspective, be-cause the public did not really care if he was guilty of the charges against him. A man I know once summed this up when he said, "I don't care if he raped and pissed on a little girl or not because he makes some bangin' tracks." Many people firmly believed that he had committed violent acts but did not take that into consideration when deciding where to place their dollars and support. Whereas the classic defense of our heroes is "He didn't do it," Kelly was protected by a common refrain of "So what if he did?"

That's not the full story, though, because there are so many examples of consumers demanding accountability from entertainers. We could point to the many blogs and podcasts that denounced A$AP Bari of the hip-hop collective A$AP Mob after a video surfaced of him demanding a sexual act from a woman who was verbally resisting. Or we could point to the wave of industry and grassroots figures who reacted to Rick Ross's aforemen-tioned lyrics about drugging a woman without her knowledge and pulled a public apology from Ross, compelled at least one sponsor to drop him, and even pushed the primary artist on the song to release a version that did not feature Ross. Or we could point to the many outlets and universities that questioned the lyrics in the Robin Thicke and Pharrell collaboration "Blurred Lines," which referred to women as animals and told them that they knew they "wanted it." Both men ended up issuing statements to ex-plain the context of the lyrics and their potential impact on rape culture.

The prevailing thinking of the prevention community agrees that we are correct to interrogate the heroes of boys, because their words and actions matter. Many public health advocates, to include the Centers for Disease Control and Prevention, apply approaches to preventing sexual violence that are informed by the social-ecological model.[11] The social-ecological model was initially formulated by Urie Bronfenbrenner and, in its simplest form, holds that behaviors are only fully understood by considering the individual histories, interpersonal relationships, community values, and societal influences affecting them. So to understand why we have outrageous levels of sexual violence, one has to account for the policies we write, the messages we receive in our households, and the messages we receive from societal opinion leaders.

As evidence of the power of opinion leaders, consider the Harvard Alcohol Project, which was based at the Harvard School of Public Health and is credited by many with severely decreasing alcohol-related traffic fatalities, thought to be one of the leading causes of death of young adults in the late 1980s. The Project achieved this milestone by enlisting the aid of public figures and infusing the concept of the "designated driver" into American pop culture. In partnership with writers at CBS, NBC, ABC, preventive messaging about drunk driving (including usage of designated drivers) was written into the scripts of a variety of popular television shows, including *Cheers*, *L.A. Law*, and *The Cosby Show*. The Project also facilitated the primetime airing of public service announcements supporting designated driver usage and earned the support of public figures and organizations throughout the nation, such as President Bill Clinton, Mothers Against Drunk Driving, and the National Basketball Association. The Project's efforts were so successful that the term "designated driver" found its way into dictionaries only a few years after the Project began.[12] Today, "designated driver" is a household term and the practice of utilizing designated drivers is well established. Most of the high school and college audiences that I work with see intervening if they observe the potential for drunk driving as perfectly normal, whereas this idea was controversial in prior generations. Healthy behavioral changes can be rapid and far-reaching when backed by public figures.

If the heroes of boys were to get involved in the fight against sexual violence, we might see attitudinal and behavioral shifts that are every bit as effective as what we witnessed with drunk driving. If boys coming of age were to constantly witness their heroes refrain from intimate contact with women unless they were absolutely sure that the contact was welcomed, then boys would grow up believing that these behaviors were as acceptable as using designated drivers. You might argue that the idea of designated drivers is far less polarizing than the racial and gendered politics that surround sexual violence, but this argument is partially a testament to the utter transformation of attitudes toward drunk driving. The now fairly conventional idea of empowering third parties to restrict the rights of others to drive was polarizing in the early 1980s. It was seen as a matter of personal freedom. Only after intense community work did America come to embrace it. Today, it is provocative to say that men who initiate sexual contact have a responsibility to ensure that consent is present in any and all situations, but it might be significantly less charged over time if it was also publicly supported by media figures.

For the sake of teaching young men that one's popularity and authenticity are not diminished by standing against sexual violence, we have to encourage public figures to take a stand and not label them as childish when they do. There are no perfect men to deliver this message, but remember that the pictures that boys see of their heroes are generally incomplete anyway. They know them only through the imperfect glimpses provided by the media, where makeup, editing, and lighting mask the blemishes. We need to highlight efforts like that of Dru Hill, an R&B group popular in the 1990s, who create music that inspires their fans to speak out against sexual abuse (Dru Hill's 1997 video for the song "Never Make a Promise" was included in the Rape, Abuse & Incest National Network's school-based education program and reportedly encouraged at least one girl to report abuse by her father).[13] We could point to John Legend providing a cover of the classic song "Baby, It's Cold Outside" and revising lyrics that evoked a man pressuring an uncomfortable woman who is attempting to leave. Then there are many public figures, such as Will Smith and Steph Curry, who use their platforms to challenge traditional definitions of manhood in search of finding our best selves.

Dru Hill's career has now come and gone. Boys today likely have no idea who they are, and I doubt that very many of their fans were aware of the group's association with violence prevention even when they were thriving. Had one of its members been rumored to beat his wife or been publicly accused of sexual assault, that might have been common knowledge. As much as we might push public figures to assume positive stances, their negative and salacious incidents often end up defining them.

I once attended a seminar for anti-violence educators where someone mentioned a scene from comedian Martin Lawrence's sitcom *Martin*. The series had long been off the air, but its mention evoked a strong reaction from several attendees who looked upon the comedian unfavorably due to Lawrence's alleged sexual harassment of a co-star. Some attendees felt that anyone claiming to have anti-violent goals had no business supporting Lawrence and his show, but this pronouncement also brought sharp criticism. One attendee said that we would have to go home and stare at the wall if we stopped following everybody accused of wrongdoing. Some felt uncomfortable criticizing someone who had never been proven guilty of anything in a court of law, and some saw private indiscretions as wholly independent from one's public contributions. Still others claimed that no men are above reproach and that we have set unfair goals for public figures to uphold.

What is the correct standard to which we should hold the heroes of boys? At what point should we cast them out as unworthy role models? At what point do their transgressions outweigh their talents—and does it even matter if they do?

There is no standard that I might submit to answer these questions that would satisfy everyone. To throw our hands up in defeat does not feel good, either, because boys will be subject to media messaging regardless of our action. Many parents have confided to me that they feel overwhelmed in tracking all of the media sources talking to their children. This is a task that was challenging enough before young adults were walking around with personal devices that allowed around-the-clock access to media. So what should we do while we are waiting on media cultures to change?

For one thing, we can use media figures as discussion enhancers. The activities of boys' heroes can open the door to powerful conversations about consent and healthy relationships (both the activities that they simulate in performance and those that they are alleged to perform in real life). I often contextualize comments that I hear from boys against a well-known song, movie, or quote from a professional athlete and then watch as the energy picks up. Sometimes it helps to connect what we are trying to teach to existing points of reference.

In the end, it will likely come down to local heroes to get it done—the formal and informal teachers of young men who interact with them daily. Remember that the social-ecological model of prevention holds that individual, community, and societal factors all influence behaviors. This means that you yourself play a part. Protective factors that you instill in boys can counteract risk factors that they pick up elsewhere. If enough of us take it upon ourselves to challenge violence-supportive behaviors, then we would not worry as much about the antics of any given celebrity.

I am suggesting that we become the heroes who we keep waiting on the public arena to produce. But we must be mindful that we may run headlong into the same frustrations we have with entertainers, professional athletes, and the like. We might be exempt from the cameras of the paparazzi, but we are still beholden to expectations once we raise our voices. There will be those expecting us to be perfect spouses, boyfriends, fathers, and citizens.

Fear of scrutiny is actually the primary reason it took me over a decade to write this book. I have spent the better part of a chapter nitpicking entertainers while knowing full well that my own life and works might not withstand the same spotlight. I have a fiercely introverted personality and a constantly wandering mind that can manifest as social awkwardness. For someone whose subject matter involves women, I have admittedly failed every girlfriend I have ever had in one way or another. And that is just scratching the surface of regretful moments in my life that were driven by lack of attention, ignorance, or apathy.

But I must remind myself that the violence we challenge thrives off of silence. You should remember the same if you care about the welfare of a rising generation of boys. Requiring perfection of those who wish to speak against sexual violence adds yet another barrier to participation when this violence already persists largely because boys and men are afraid to openly challenge it. It is critical that those who wish to challenge sexual violence constantly examine their attitudes, intentions, and effectiveness; but we should also recognize that our opponents do not the share the burden of getting things exactly right. Our insistence on becoming perfect role models effectively allows those with no intent to make the world better to have their fill of unchallenged airspace.

WHAT ROLE DOES—AND CAN—MEDIA PLAY? A CONVERSATION WITH AISHAH SHAHIDAH SIMMONS

Aishah Shahidah Simmons is the producer and director of "NO! The Rape Documentary," a 2006 feature length film centering Black female survivors of sexual violence. With an accompanying study guide and supplemental video, "NO!" is used in schools, rape crisis centers, and governmental programs around the world. Aishah is also the organizer and editor of the 2020 Lambda Literary Award-winning anthology, love WITH accountability: Digging Up the Roots of Child Sexual Abuse (AK Press, 2019), a collection of writings by diasporic Black survivors and advocates that focuses on healing from and disrupting childhood sexual violence.

Q: You use media to address sexual violence. What do you say to those who argue that media—such as books, movies, video games, etc.—do not impact people's actual behavior?

A: I completely disagree. Media does matter. Media informs, educates, and teaches for better and for worse. My mediums have been film and written word, as well as spoken word. I learned from my teacher, the late Toni Cade Bambara, that the role of the artist is to make revolution irresistible. There are multiple revolutions but mine is around healing from and disrupting sexual violence. People who haven't really thought about the long-term impact of sexual violence on survivors have told me that my film has played a role in changing their thinking.

Contemporarily, I think of the incredible series produced by Dream Hampton, Surviving R. Kelly, and we see how it changed a national dialogue around sexual violence in Black communities. We have been talking about sexual violence for a while, but that series really centralized the voices of Black survivors. I think that media is very powerful. I think that it helps us to see images of and hear the voices of survivors in particular. We don't get to see that often—the vulnerability, the trauma, as well as the healing and resiliency. Media plays a role in shaping and transforming society, and my hope is that we can use it to make society more whole.

Q: It has been several years since I have watched "NO! The Rape Documentary" but the scene that most stuck with me over the years was the sequence highlighting some of the community response to Mike Tyson's release from prison following his conviction for rape. Some people celebrated his release not because they believed he was innocent, but because he's one of us. That was 30 years ago though. Where do you think we are now in defending media icons for problematic behavior?

A: I feel like my own understanding keeps growing, transforming, and hopefully deepening. I strive every day to be an abolitionist. I don't see the criminal justice system, especially prisons, as a holistic solution to society's problems. RAINN talks about how only 8 people are convicted out of 100 sexual assaults so what are we going to do with the other 92? There are other forms of holding people accountable. And I say that as a survivor of child sexual abuse and adult rape. I also say that as somebody that believes that every survivor has to figure out how they want to move in the world. This is my personal, political, and even spiritual ethic that I strive to embody.

I wanted to lay that out to look at somebody like Bill Cosby. What we are grappling with is not being able to hold the complexities. It's very clear that Bill Cosby and his wife have done incredible things in terms of philanthropy. And he's been convicted of raping at least one woman while a whole slew of other women came forward about the harm that they have experienced. We move in a space of binaries. Good and bad. Cosby's alleged acts are definitely heinous and he's done this other good work. I think that if we could learn how to hold both of those ideas, then we can get closer to disrupting and ending sexual violence. In our minds, we say that "he's done all of this good work so therefore he couldn't have done that." No, he can do both. Most who commit sexual harm are both. If we could only hold those tensions and think about what accountability might look like outside of the prison industrial complex. What would it look like if Bill Cosby's wealth could be shared with organizations that are doing work to end violence against women? What would it be like for him to hear the testimonies of those whom he has harmed? With our icons and heroes, there has to be space for the reality that many have caused harm.

Q: In this book, I focus on Black boys not because I do not care about boys of other races but because many Black boys see their racial identification as central to their identities and how they engage the world. I find that it's impossible to meaningfully discuss the context of sexual violence without considering race. Much of your work focuses on intersectionality. Why do you believe that race is inseparable from the conversation?

A: This country was founded on the genocide of indigenous nations and enslavement of African people. It's foundational. We cannot talk about sexual violence in the United States without talking about race. I would offer that this is true for most places in the world, particularly in the West. To act as if race isn't a part of how criminal justice and society view who is the harm doer and who is the victim is a tremendous disservice to anyone that is trying to disrupt sexual violence.

How do we have very important, and yet delicate and complex, conversations in the instances when Black men and boys have committed harm against Black women and girls? How do we talk about the harm committed in the context of white supremacy? So much of the silence in Black communities is about protecting Black boys and men from a racist criminal justice system. If we don't talk about the horrors of the criminal justice system, while we also talk about the horrors of the sexual violence, then we are not going to unearth what allows these harms to proliferate. I think it's also important to remember that Black boys are sexually abused and think about how we must see them as needing protection, healing, nurturing and care since they, like Black girls, have been so continuously dehumanized since enslavement.

CHAPTER 6: TEACHING BOYS TO EXAMINE MEDIA REPRESENTATIONS OF MANHOOD

- We should not consider the celebrities who boys follow to be inconsequential. They matter. There is a long track record of public figures directing culture for good or for bad.
- Media can serve as an excellent entry point to discussing violence with boys because many relevant themes are prevalent within music, video games, movies, and television. If boys are already consuming this media, consider using it as a launching pad to discussing how they can fight violence and rape culture.
- Those unhappy with the selections from which boys choose their role models should always remember that they have the option

of becoming one themselves. Serving as a role model can be challenging, but there are consequences for simply refusing to try. Sexual violence already thrives because people are afraid to speak against it. Waiting for perfection before we step up as role models only contributes to the silence. In the meantime, we surrender airspace to interests primarily seeking financial profit and not moral profit.

Understanding Our Power to Harm

In Chapter 3, I provided a brief listing of the self-protective behaviors that many women employ. Let us flesh that list out more for a woman preparing to go on a date or spend time with a man in whom she has some interest. Consider that the following list does not even include behaviors designed to protect against violence from strangers. These are behaviors aimed at men who are presumably known, liked, and trusted on some level.

Before a woman even heads out of the door, she may inform others of her intended whereabouts or send them a picture of her date in case something happens. She may do a background check on the man. She may scrutinize her intended attire so that she does not send the wrong messages. She may employ the "buddy system" and enlist a friend to accompany her.

During the date, she may keep an eye on her alcohol consumption lest somebody take advantage of her in a vulnerable state. She may also closely monitor those drinks out of fear that somebody might tamper with them. She may make special effort not to lead her date on such that he misreads her intentions. She may covertly check in with friends in order to notify them that she is safe. And then even once she has returned home, she might check in with somebody and let them know that she made it back safely.

Many would consider these activities to be prevention strategies, but many anti-violence educators would identify these behaviors as risk reduction strategies. We have to ask different questions to get at primary prevention such as "Do we have to accept that there will always be violent men for whom women must prepare?" After all, the violent men that we train girls to defend against were presumably once impressionable boys with adults in their lives who could influence their views on respectful behavior. But many of us find it impossible to imagine our own boys as violent. We see rapists as masked men who lurk in the shadows and consciously plan to assault women with weapons and force. They are not the boys whom we know and love.

It is not surprising, then, that some boys grow into men who also cannot fathom how they can be violent when they do not behave like stereotypical rapists. The past decade has seen several prominent trials involving teenage boys accused of rape who provided much of the evidence used against them through text messages and social media. They simply did not see their actions as problematic even though they were involved with nonconsenting peers. Or they were indeed aware that something was wrong and were unable to resist the inertia of their peer cultures. They are simply products of coming of age in a rape culture.

* * *

Boys who want to help change the appalling rates of sexual violence have access to unprecedented levels of resources. There is an ever-expanding array of organizations, research, and media to aid them. This is thanks to brave pioneers who got the ball rolling in the 1970s, 1960s, and even earlier.

Despite the considerable strides taken by the movements to end sexual violence, it is arguable as to how far prevailing attitudes about sexual violence have shifted. Our instincts still place the primary burden for prevention on women. I was once eating lunch with a group of coworkers when I mentioned that I was working on this book. Two men at the table then stated that they agreed with preventing sexual violence and went into a list of habits that they encouraged their daughters and wives to take up, such as dressing modestly in public and maintaining skepticism about the intentions of men who befriend them. They felt strongly that women should always remain vigilant concerning their surroundings. This led the lone woman at the table to ask if they were perhaps placing the blame for sexual violence on the wrong parties. She was met with the response that "Life isn't fair."

There was nothing abnormal about the responses of those fathers. One day I came across an episode of rapper T.I.'s reality show, *T.I. & Tiny: The Family Hustle*, in which he sat with his teenage daughter and had a discussion with her about her clothing. T.I. (whose given name is Clifford Harris) advised his daughter to avoid wearing provocative clothing that would lead men to make assumptions about what kind of woman she was and presumably pursue her sexually. *What if Harris additionally held an on-camera discussion with his sons about how they did not have the right to unilaterally determine a woman's sexual availability no matter what she might be wearing?* I do not claim to have watched very much of the series, so Harris may very well have had this conversation. If he did, that would have pushed the point that we would not have to train young women to avoid predatory men if these men did not exist in the first place. They exist because we do very little in the way of breaking boys out of perspectives on sex and women that are patently misogynistic, selfish, and violent.

Our instincts often place prevention responsibilities on women and victims even when we are talking about attacks by strangers in public. ABC News responded to a series of women who were murdered while jogging by providing a list of "what women should know to stay safe." Tips included switching up your routines and not wearing headphones.[1] ABC News ran this spot in 2020, not 1970.

It is certainly understandable why fathers would show concern for their daughters by preparing them for an uncertain world. They after all have little control over the world that their daughters must face but do have some measure of control over their daughters. It is also perfectly understandable why a television news show would aim its messaging at concerned female viewers rather than at men with ideas of attacking strangers in public. They probably do not have much faith in their ability to reach the latter audience in a limited news segment. I do not think that placing prevention responsibilities on women would be nearly as problematic if it was situated against parallel messaging to men about their roles in the matter. It is true that we cannot control the broader world where assault is so common that we teach women to protect themselves from it, but men have agency as well.

I am sure that plenty of people in positions to influence young men do regularly have conversations with them about their perspectives on sex and sexuality, but I am also confident that they do not occur with the same regularity that we pull aside young women and talk to them about violent men. The sexuality of young women and girls that we care about often figures prominently in our understanding of how to best prepare them for the world, but sexuality is less of a factor when we consider how to prepare boys. This is a disservice to boys, as they have as much opportunity as girls to make sexual decisions that have lasting impact on themselves and others. T.I.'s fellow artist Nas reflected the unequal attention that we heap on girls when he closed out a 2012 song dedicated to his daughter (the aptly titled "Daughters") with the line, "When he date, he straight, chip off his own papa/When she date, we wait behind the door with the sawed off."[2]

Even when we do actually pull young men aside to discuss sexual responsibility, we do so most often to discuss self-protective measures such as how they can avoid unwanted pregnancies, sexually transmitted infections, false accusations, etc. These topics are important but represent an incomplete view of responsibility. Young men coming into adulthood are often greeted with nothing but praise when their sexual exploits become known. How consent for that activity is ensured is rarely discussed.

Let us consider one natural window through which we can generate conversation about the importance of obtaining consent with boys: helping them to think about how they can minimize their risk of being wrongly accused of sexual misconduct. Whereas adolescents often have difficulty imagining negative outcomes for their behavior, this is definitely not the case here. If you sit down to talk to young men about sexual violence, they will likely bring up this risk on their own. Personal risk is front and center for boys, so we might as well use it as a launching point for conversation. While boys may instinctively point to unethical women, imperfect laws, or gender biases as the reasons for accusations, we can help boys to consider the risk that is within their power to control. They could, for example, demonstrate the self-control to clarify the intentions of sexual partners when they have doubt, actually get to know partners before engaging in intimate acts with them, pay attention to the cues that a potential sexual partner is providing, and respond appropriately when those cues suggest anything other than mutual enjoyment. Self-protective factors such as these also happen to go a long way toward protecting others. The broader culture teaches boys that sex is carefree and casual, but we know from the statistics in Chapter 1 that there are plenty of potential negative outcomes. A healthy fear when choosing to enter another person's intimate space is not a bad thing.

* * *

Many men accused of sexual violence as expected maintain their innocence. I am of the mind that this defense is often genuine concerning violence against acquaintances. I believe that many perpetrators sincerely do not believe that they have done anything wrong (not that this lessens their culpability or impact). This would not be surprising, considering that most boys move well into adulthood without ever having a serious conversation about sexual responsibility that is not about abstinence or condom usage. They may have never heard someone tell them that rape does not have to involve women who resist violently and/or verbally. They may have never heard someone tell them that hesitation on the part of a sexual partner might be cause for clarification of intent rather than a signal to step one's game up or push through the uncertainty. They may have never heard someone tell them that women are not monolithic beings whose desire for sexual contact can primarily be determined by their dress, reputation, and context of meeting. They therefore spend little to no time thinking about sex as the mutual activity that it is and never develop skills around recognizing or obtaining consent from a partner.

We saw the potential relationship between boys and their training when a 19-year-old student athlete at Stanford University was convicted of sexually assaulting an unconscious woman behind a dumpster in 2015. The incident that led to conviction was so off-putting that two passing graduate students intervened. Following the conviction, the perpetrator's father wrote a widely criticized letter in defense of his son in which he stated that the conviction was "a steep price to pay for 20 minutes of action."[3] That the father believed that sexual activity with an unconscious person could be classified as "action" gives some indication of the lessons that informed his son.

Some anti-violence advocates have noted that even the language that men use to refer to sex connotes an activity that does not require mutually consenting partners. That is, words commonly used to refer to sex include "screw," "bang," "nail," "fuck," and a host of others that reference an act that has an active doer and someone to whom the act is done. Casual interaction with Black boys or the entertainment outlets they frequent reveals even more violent references to sex such as "cutting," "slaying," "smashing," and "beating up the pussy," to name a few. This is not language born out of a culture that fully expects all sexual encounters to be mutually consensual and mutually satisfying. It is language born out of a culture that expects some degree of predation and subjugation in sexual encounters. Sure, it would be difficult to prove a direct connection between using this kind of language and actually perpetrating violence, but history is rife with examples of language being leveraged to acclimate people to violence against particular communities (for example, Nazis referring to Jews as rats, which one exterminates, during the Holocaust). It is fantastical to believe that this language reflects nothing about men and their understandings of sex.

Exploring these concepts with adolescent boys can be difficult, but we cannot abandon their education at precisely the ages when they are beginning to act on their worldviews about sex and women. Many parents and guardians have trouble accepting their boys as sexual beings. Many others fully accept this but simply find boys' sexuality to be confusing or intimidating. Either way, the outcome is a reluctance to have tough conversations with boys. But if you avoid these conversations, you run the risk of a dangerous definition of sexual violence, often influenced by the entertainment industry (including pornography), going unchecked.

Let me explain exactly what I mean by boys carrying dangerous definitions. I have had enough conversations with boys to observe some commonalities in their understandings of sexual violence that are mis-aligned with most criminal statutes and school policies, not to mention misaligned with the way that many parents and mentors view their boys. Again, I cannot speak to every school policy and state law, and federal guidance is forever evolving, but sexual assault is broadly defined as any sexual activity committed without a person's consent. Seven of the most glaring misconceptions carried by boys are that their definitions:

1. Require resistance
2. Require intent
3. Contend that alcohol absolves one of wrongdoing
4. Minimize the importance of consent
5. Identify consent in irrelevant activities
6. Ignore that consent can be withdrawn
7. Ignore male capacity.

THEIR DEFINITIONS REQUIRE RESISTANCE

Boys are quick to inquire about a victim's level of resistance in order to determine if a sexual act was violent or not. They will want to know if he or she physically resisted, and they presume the victim has some obliga-tion to do so. At the very least, they will want to know if he or she made some effort to communicate with the alleged attacker and make it clearly known that contact was unwanted. However, many statutes and policies do not require that a victim resist in any fashion. It is the initiator's re-sponsibility to obtain consent. Even if resistance might help tell a story for an adjudicating body, boys ought to have some tools for determining if their actions are unwanted short of somebody physically resisting them. Additionally, boys' ideas of resistance often ignore passive forms of resistance, such as a partner who is simply inactive.

THEIR DEFINITIONS REQUIRE INTENT

Many boys consider an alleged perpetrator's intent to be a critical factor in identifying sexual violence. Simply put, they do not see an act as violent if the perpetrator did not intend it to be violent. But like physical resistance, intent from a perpetrator is also not required for many school policies and criminal statutes to identify a sexual assault. This is for the best, since I have yet to meet anybody who self-identified as a rapist.

Boys often have difficulty identifying behaviors that are coercive and violent because a certain measure of persuasion is expected in contemporary culture. Boys are encouraged to employ methods of convincing a partner to have sex. However, persuasion that becomes coercive or dismissive of a partner's wishes remains coercive even if the person employing it does not intend for this.

THEIR DEFINITIONS CLAIM THAT ALCOHOL
CONSUMPTION ABSOLVES THEM OF WRONGDOING

Boys consistently view alcohol consumption as an exonerating factor for perpetrators. They have difficulty assigning fault to someone who is intoxicated, but this position does not align with many school policies and criminal statutes. If a man were to get intoxicated and initiate sexual contact against a party who does not or cannot consent, then he would be responsible for the offense just the same as if he had committed any other policy violation while intoxicated. Boys (and quite often their parents too) find a great deal of unfairness in knowing that men can be held responsible for actions committed while intoxicated; however, consider that somebody would have to answer for their actions if they were to get drunk and physically assault or even kill another person. Sexual assault is no different.

THEIR DEFINITIONS MINIMIZE CONSENT

Boys quite often recognize a person's consent as an important factor in determining sexual violence, but consent is not just *a* factor: It is *the* factor. Just as many school policies and criminal statutes view consent as of central importance, boys need to reorganize their understandings such that they view partners' consent as essential. They need to develop tools for ensuring that consent is present rather than assuming it is present because of context.

THEIR DEFINITIONS IDENTIFY CONSENT IN IRRELEVANT ACTIVITIES

On the subject of consent, consent is not something that is given to any and every activity for an unlimited amount of time. When determining the presence of consent, it matters not if somebody consented to another sexual activity or even to the activity in question at a prior time. Yet many boys infer consent from irrelevant behaviors such as a person's dress, a person's reputation, and past consent to other sexual or intimate acts.

THEIR DEFINITIONS IGNORE THAT CONSENT CAN BE WITHDRAWN

One particular aspect of perceiving consent in irrelevant activities deserves its own spotlight. Boys do not always account for the fact that partners can rightfully withdraw consent. There are countless reasons why somebody might be comfortable engaging in a particular act only to later change their mind. Somebody changing their mind before an act occurs, or even while it is occurring, should be immediately respected by others. Boys sometimes throw out the scenario of somebody changing their mind after a sexual act has already begun as if it presents an unreasonable expectation for them to stop. Consider identifying this situation for them for what it is: They are describing a willful disregard of awareness that consent is not present.

THEIR DEFINITIONS IGNORE MALE CAPACITY

Following up on boys' minimization of consent, they also employ definitions of sexual violence that greatly minimize their ability to ascertain if a partner is consenting. Boys frequently express confusion (or anger) in pondering how exactly they are supposed to know another person's wishes. Whatever confidence they might have in pursuing sexual activity quickly disperses when it comes to discussion of sexual assault. Then, we are told that men are not mind readers and women need to communicate verbally and explicitly if they are uncomfortable. Men presumably need their partners to do nothing less than fight them off if they are to have any indication that something is wrong. Never mind men's ability to infer intentions from body language, situational context, facial expressions, level of involvement, or anything else that a compassionate being could utilize in order to evaluate if a partner might not be comfortable with a particular activity or might not be able to consent.

The minimization of male capacity is sometimes a selfish excuse from boys who cannot be bothered to challenge normalized but dangerous practices, but it is often a genuine confession of confusion. Boys will only possess what they are taught, and they are rarely taught about methods to ensure that consent is present. One of the most obvious ways to ensure that consent is present is to verbally speak to a partner, but many boys regrettably find this option to be unrealistic.

* * *

Boys who possess the aforementioned flaws in their definitions of sexual violence are simply dangerous. If boys view sexual assault as only the stuff

of men who intentionally ignore physical resistance, then they may understandably have trouble recognizing violence in other contexts. They
are capable of violence toward others without even having recognition of
their harm.

In saying all of this, I have still met men who I believe were intentionally violent—men who just did not care if they harmed others. I quite
honestly do not know what to say to men like this. But I assume the boys
who you have in mind as you read this book are not people who wish to
be involved in experiences that others remember as painful. If this is the
case, then you cannot assume that boys will organically develop the skills
that they need. They have to be developed.

Too many of the stories of sexual violence I have heard boil down to
a man pursuing literally a few minutes of sexual activity with a partner
who was not mutually engaged. Even if there is no intent to harm, it is
still troubling that many men carry out the accessing of another person's
body without undeniable assurance that the access is wanted. Stories upon
stories from survivors of violence tell us that access to another person's
body should not be taken lightly. These transgressions occur within a context in which one's proximity to and interaction with a partner are elevated
so far beyond usual social behavior that one ought to have heightened
awareness of a partner's comfort level. There is ample opportunity for men
to clarify any ambiguities if they choose to do so.

A final flaw in the definitions of sexual violence held by boys is that
many boys define sexual violence as an act that cannot involve a male
victim. Many boys honestly do not understand how a male can be raped
or sexually assaulted when informed that laws and policies allow for this
possibility.

There may not be a clearer example about how boys are trained to
welcome all sexual encounters than this. They are so trained to pursue
any opportunity for sex placed in front of them that they cannot picture
scenarios in which a man might feel aggrieved by an unwanted sexual
advance. Much of this inability to picture male victimization also comes
from their lack of experience with expressing their own pain and discomfort. It is true that the majority of sexual assault victims are women, but

the number of male victims is considerable in its own right. For example, the National Intimate Partner and Sexual Violence Survey administered by the Centers for Disease Control and Prevention estimates that one in 10 men experience sexual coercion (defined as "unwanted sexual penetration that occurs after a person is pressured in a nonphysical way") in their lifetimes.[4] Some sources estimate even higher rates.

If you yourself are having difficulty understanding how male victimization can be as common as estimated, then first consider that most sources claim that a good deal of male victimization occurs when boys are young. Young boys are every bit as vulnerable to predatory adults (most often men) as are young girls. Secondly, growing attention on gay and bisexual communities has confirmed that they suffer from many of the same problems with intimate violence that occur among heterosexual relationships.[5] Men are not exempt from messaging that intertwines sex with control and power simply because they do not identify as heterosexual. Also, no discussion of sexual violence against men would be complete without consideration of incarcerated populations. Though it is typically played for laughs in popular culture, there is truth to some incarcerated populations witnessing and experiencing sexual violence at troubling rates.[6] Lastly, realize that a woman can assault a man. If the initiator of unwanted activity is female and the target is male, this is still violent behavior even if men have not traditionally been trained to consider their own comfort levels in these situations.

* * *

I want to return to the factor of alcohol consumption and give it a little more attention. It is impossible to genuinely review boys' understanding of sexual violence without considering the complications that alcohol presents. Studies have repeatedly confirmed the heavy linkage between sexual violence and drug or alcohol usage, either by a victim, perpetrator, or both.[7] For example, if we look at the National Institute of Justice's Campus Sexual Assault Study that I referenced in Chapter 1, we find that the majority of completed sexual assaults were identified as "incapacitated sexual assaults," which the researchers defined as

> any unwanted sexual contact occurring when a victim is unable to provide consent or stop what is happening because she is passed out, drugged, drunk, incapacitated, or asleep, regardless of whether the perpetrator was responsible for her substance use or whether substances were administered without her knowledge.

This was true both for incidents experienced before college and since entering college.[8]

Schools have increasingly reacted to the realization that many victims consume alcohol prior to assaults by implementing what are affectionately referred to as "good Samaritan" policies. These policies aim to encourage victims to come forward even if they are worried about being punished for prior alcohol or drug consumption. Administrators are given freedom to lessen or avoid sanctions altogether for alcohol and drug offenses in these situations.

Combine these good Samaritan policies with the fact that alcohol consumption by a perpetrator is not generally a valid defense for assaulting another person and many young men see a biased system that is set up to "get them." Here are a few arguments that I have found helpful in talking to young men about their responsibilities when mixing sexual activity and alcohol:

1. *Consider what the alternatives would be*: Those who find it harsh to hold men accountable for their actions while intoxicated should consider the implications of what they are requesting. If there were no expectations of intoxicated individuals, we would be creating a world in which all one had to do to avoid fault would be to make sure that one was sufficiently intoxicated before an assault. That would obviously represent a massive hole in our policies, laws, and morals.

2. *Consider if stereotypical drunken encounters reflect your actual life*: When young men describe the situations that they find to be unfair, they often describe a situation in which two people are "completely wasted" or something of the sort. They wonder how it is fair to assign blame to either party in this case. From my time in student affairs, I must say that I have rarely encountered this situation when listening to actual stories that students shared with me. After all, somebody has to possess the capacity to coordinate an encounter. I more often heard stories involving a person at one level of capacity interacting with somebody at a different level of capacity. I am not saying that it is impossible for two highly incapacitated parties to engage in sexual activity; I am just saying that it does not map to the experiences that many young men find themselves in, if they are honest. Boys quite often describe themselves as "buzzed" rather than incapacitated when they really think about it, and that difference is significant because they then presumably still have some capacity.

3. *Do not forget that the policies protect you as well*: Young men sometimes lose sight of the fact that most policies are gender-neutral. If a woman were to be intoxicated and initiate sexual activity against them that is nonconsensual, then that woman would theoretically be accountable as well. I say "theoretically" because there are admittedly societal assumptions about men as the initiators of sexual activity. Furthermore, many young men are not trained to recognize sexual acts committed against them as problematic. Men typically do not have social permission to acknowledge and voice their own trauma, but it remains the case that policies exist to protect them as well.

4. *Reserve some of your anger for the youth and media cultures that lie to you*: Many young people are immersed in "hookup cultures" that tell them that sexual activity while under the influence is normal and even preferred. You might recall from the definitions in Chapter 1 that parties who are temporarily incapacitated due to the effects of drugs or alcohol cannot even

effectively consent to sexual assault, so there is a great irony
in the world convincing young people to mix sex and alcohol/
drugs. At the very least, they are being trained to increase their
risk. They may respond positively to identifying the ways in
which marketers, media, and others who do not have their best
interests in mind have put them at risk.

5. *Uncertainty about incapacitation should produce caution*: Recall
   that most school policies use the word "incapacitated" to indicate
   when a party cannot effectively consent, not "intoxicated" or
   "under the influence" as is often understood. Incapacitation
   is generally understood to be a state beyond simply being
   under the influence of drugs or alcohol. Possible signs that
   somebody is incapacitated would include difficulty walking
   steadily, vomiting, memory loss, lack of comprehension, and
   incomprehensible speech. Somebody who is unconscious
   would obviously be incapacitated. Incapacitation could present
   differently in different people and even in the same person
   over time, so this requires young men to have awareness. It
   also requires them to show restraint when they are uncertain if
   somebody is incapacitated. If they cannot determine if somebody
   is incapacitated themselves, they should not run the risk of later
   having an adjudicating body decide for them.

*   *   *

This may be the point where you are wondering how to tell if you know a
boy who is at particular risk of perpetrating sexual assault. Truth be told,
there are quite a few risk factors for perpetration suggested by research.
Here are a few of them, in no particular order:

- Pornography consumption
- Belief in traditional gender roles or "hypermasculine" values
- Early age of first intercourse
- Hostile attitudes toward women

- Frequent engagement in casual sex
- Adolescent delinquency
- Prior history of sexual victimization
- Greater alcohol consumption
- Belief that alcohol increases sexuality
- Belief in rape myths (rape myths are false beliefs about sexual violence that typically shift blame to survivors. Think back to the victim-blaming beliefs discussed earlier for examples.)
- Possessing anti-social personality traits (impulsivity, lack of empathy, etc.).[9]

Looking through the list probably triggered some areas that you can focus on in your talks with boys. However, I do want to provide two massive points of caution in doing so.

The first is that research surrounding perpetration is often contested. Many of the aforementioned factors are identified in competing studies that find no correlation to violence. Measuring perpetration is difficult for a variety of methodological and ethical reasons. Limiting research to convicted offenders is problematic because this population may differ substantially from offenders who go unpunished. Researchers often utilize anonymous surveys to identify self-reports of perpetration or association with rape-supportive attitudes and beliefs in order to identify perpetrators. One can see where this approach opens itself up to critics who question if these methods accurately measure perpetration. There is also the standard question of whether the aforementioned risk factors actually cause perpetration or are simply correlated with it. For example, it stands to reason that those who drink alcohol and engage in casual sex more frequently would be more frequently involved in sexual assaults because they have more opportunity for sexual violence to occur.

As for the second caution, focusing on risk factors in order to determine if you need to talk to your boys would be to miss the forest for the trees in my opinion. While there are a number of credible risk factors, the larger message gleaned from decades of studying perpetration is that offenders tend to look quite normal. These are people who function in society just fine and do not always come with glaring warning signs. I think that the aforementioned risk factors have value in helping us refine our messaging to boys but should not be used to identify boys who need to receive our interventions. We should be talking to *all* boys, as all are immersed in rape culture to varying degrees.

Taken as guidance to focus how we talk to boys, we do see some tangible goals emerge. We can spend our time helping boys to deconstruct rape myths, challenge traditional gender roles, appreciate sex as a consequential activity, and develop empathy for women and victims.

You may recognize from the discussion of social-ecological models in Chapter 6 that the risk factors that I listed are primarily individual-level risk factors. There are also several suggested risk factors that extend into community, such as affiliation with athletic teams and fraternities. I hope that my membership in a fraternity allows me to single out this particular factor. There are examinations that do suggest a credible link between fraternities and perpetration.[10] Fraternity members are also linked to stronger adherence to rape myths such as believing that "good guys don't rape."[11] Researchers then have to tackle the question of whether or not these organizations actually encourage perpetration or if they simply attract those who are more predisposed to perpetration. Either answer returns the same path forward for us as we engage boys. They both confirm that culture matters, and we have to instill boys with the courage to act on their own values even if the cultures around them say otherwise. If enough boys do so, then the violent cultures around them are the ones that will ultimately adapt.

* * *

No matter how many questions or insecurities they might possess, boys must unfortunately spend much of their time interacting with boys and men who claim to have it all together. This affords few opportunities for growth because boys are not free to even admit that they need help.

We have to teach boys that if a sexual partner resists contact, then they have an obligation to both recognize this and to respond accordingly no matter what form the resistance might take. Boys may genuinely need some help navigating their responsibilities. Here are some points that generally resonate with boys when I get the chance to work with them:

1. Think about when seduction turns into coercion.
2. Verbal communication is one of your best tools.
3. Walking away from a high-risk encounter is an acceptable option.
4. You are free to set your own higher standards.

As always, I think the best ways to reach boys are those that are authentic and personal, but feel free to borrow from the following messages if it helps.

THINK ABOUT WHEN SEDUCTION TURNS INTO COERCION

Recall that most sexual assault and rape policies speak to coercion. One cannot obtain consent through threat of force, unreasonable pressure, blackmail, or anything of the sort. This demands thought, as the conventions of courting a partner expect and perhaps even require some degree of initiation and pressure. We might broadly refer to this pressure as seduction. Consider outright asking boys how they can tell when seduction becomes coercion. In helping boys to think through this question, they will see that initiation of sexual contact is not a passive act but one that requires active communication and attention. They will get practice on recognizing when they may be crossing the line with a partner and begin thinking about available tools to help them determine when they have. I can even suggest one of their best tools to do so.

VERBAL COMMUNICATION IS ONE OF YOUR
BEST TOOLS

Taking them at their own words, many boys and men have concerns about getting punished for well-intentioned behaviors where they simply misperceive another person's desires. It is a shame, then, that they disregard and mock one of their most potent tools for figuring things out. That is, they could try actually speaking to their partners and clarifying any uncertainty that might exist. Many boys consider the suggestion of speaking to a sexual partner to be absurd. They think that it would be awkward to do so; however, most do not speak from experience in saying this and might be pleased to know that many women state that someone verbally checking in with them would actually enhance the experience. Besides, even if it is awkward, the potential consequences of engaging in sexual activity based on incorrect assumptions are devastating.

It is not surprising that many boys do not see speaking as a viable tool when there are so few venues modeling this behavior. For example, think about the last movie or television show that you watched where sexual partners verbally confirmed that their intentions were acceptable before an intimate encounter. Characters generally just have an unspoken understanding of what their partner wants.

Toward this end, I watched the Jordan Peele–produced series *Lovecraft Country*. The tension between the primary male protagonist, Atticus, and the primary female protagonist, Letitia, builds through the first two episodes and explodes in the third. Letitia is freshening up in the bathroom when Atticus suddenly appears behind her. *Lovecraft Country* is a show that has horror elements, and this sudden appearance is even framed as a jump scare. He then quickly and aggressively initiates what turns out to be Letitia's first experience with sexual intercourse. And all of this goes down after another man challenges Atticus to claim Letitia and he proceeds to grumpily stare at Letitia while she dances with another man.

Without some communication between the two characters, I was honestly uncertain as to how I was supposed to interpret this encounter while

I was watching. I was not sure if it was a negative or positive scene. I am not suggesting that two people cannot achieve a mutual understanding without speaking. That can and does happen. I am just saying that it is a good idea to speak when somebody is not absolutely certain of his or her partner's intentions.

Why rob yourself of one of your most effective tools? Boys seem to understand this just fine when playing sports, completing school work, or even playing video games. I often point out to boys that they seem more comfortable initiating sex acts with people than they do actually speaking to those same people. This often produces a laugh and they recognize that they might not be as ready for certain activities as they presumed if they cannot even muster the courage to talk about them.

WALKING AWAY IS AN OPTION

I was once speaking with a college football team and I suggested to them that they should look to pull aside teammates who might make a questionable sexual decision, such as a teammate preparing to leave a party with a woman who is too intoxicated to consent to sexual activity. I further suggested that this practice would not be altogether different from some behaviors in which they already engaged, such as pulling aside a teammate who was preparing to drive a car when too intoxicated to do so safely. These suggestions went over well enough with the majority of the audience, but one mountainous lineman raised his hand in order to object. He said, "Preventing a teammate from driving drunk and preventing him from raping a girl are not the same because I can drive my man home if I need to but I cannot get him off."

The implication of the student's statement was that his friend going home without a sexual encounter was not a valid option. However, this option simply has to be on the table if men are to be responsible. I just believe that men are beholden to more than their sexual desires, and boys tend to understand this just fine when you point out how they might restrict their own range of choices.

Young men often ask for my thoughts on how to navigate some scenario where they have a potential partner whom they just met and who is at some indeterminate level of intoxication. A drunken encounter with somebody you do not know may be normal according to popular culture, but it is nonetheless high risk, as young men may not have much certainty about their partner's intentions, habits, or capacity. There is no getting around some level of risk here. Sometimes the best way to mitigate risk is to remove oneself from the situation, and sometimes the responsible course of action is just to make sure that a partner makes it home safely.

YOU CAN SET YOUR OWN HIGHER STANDARDS

Young men often ask me questions such as, "Would it be rape if . . . ?" before laying out scenarios with very precise details. While these questions may come from an honest place of trying to understand the extent of policies and laws, they can sometimes feel as though young men are trying to ascertain the limits of what they can get away with. They should not be hanging around the boundaries of what is acceptable. They should be steering well clear of them.

I can sometimes see lightbulbs come on when I tell young men that they are more than free to determine their own standards of responsibility. If navigating school policies and state laws is too muddy for them, there is nothing stopping them from choosing a higher standard to govern their behaviors. When you think about it, avoiding actions that carry potential criminal or school sanctions should be the minimum standard anyway. Harming another person in some fashion ought to be what we are trying to avoid.

Many of my colleagues who counsel survivors of sexual violence have told me that they frequently encounter people who want to talk about situations that they cannot even properly identify. These people do not know if what they experienced was a crime or a policy violation, nor are they interested in pursuing a judicial response. They just know that it made them feel bad. If boys carried themselves in such a way that they steered clear of becoming a terrible memory for another person, then they would probably be well clear of any standards set by states or schools anyway.

* * *

Most of us will be confronted with another person's vulnerability at some point in our lives. In those moments, boys must decide if they will help that person or if they will exploit the person's vulnerability. As it involves sexual encounters, they must make this decision in spite of years of social training that tells them to barrel through and figure out the consequences later. They are going to have to learn to override that training if they want to abolish the possibility of becoming a painful memory for another person.

In closing this chapter, I want to visit the life of Daisy Coleman, a well-known activist who advocated for victims and worked to prevent sexual assault in schools. She is perhaps best known for a Netflix documentary that featured her story of victimization by a classmate and the ensuing cyberbullying she endured at the age of 14. Her name sadly made it back into the news because she took her life at the age of 23. Her mother's statements following her death indicated that she never fully recovered from her childhood assault.[12]

Daisy's passing is a stark reminder of what is at stake when boys choose to initiate sexual contact. The consequences of treating others as disposable can be life-altering for those involved. Not only is there the risk of criminal and civil sanctions against the initiator, but there is also the potential trauma that can be inflicted on another person. There is also the potential to forever ruin one's reputation and that of one's school, team, family, fraternity, etc.

All of this risk of changing the trajectory of a life is brought on by what is quite often just a few moments of gratification. Considering what is at stake, you would think that boys would be eager to get their hands on as many tools as they can in order to ensure that their actions are consensual. They should be having active conversations about the merits and flaws in potential approaches to ensuring consent. In short, they should be practicing a skill set that many grown men do not possess.

CHAPTER 7: TEACHING BOYS THAT THEY HAVE THE POWER TO HARM

- Parents and mentors tend to contribute more energy to protecting girls from violent men than they do to ensuring that boys do not become violent men. A more balanced approach would result in more men who possessed an accurate understanding of sexual violence.
- Discussions about sexual responsibility with boys often focus on definitions of responsibility limited to behaviors such as avoiding unwanted pregnancy, sexually transmitted infections, and false accusations. "Not harming others" needs to be added to conventional understandings of responsibility.
- Sexual assault is broadly defined as any sexual activity performed without a person's consent. Yet definitions of sexual violence held by boys are often flawed in at least seven areas:
  - Boys believe that a victim's resistance is required for a sexual assault to occur.
  - Boys believe that intent to harm is required for a sexual assault to occur.
  - Boys minimize the importance of consent.
  - Boys believe that alcohol consumption absolves them of wrongdoing.
  - Boys infer consent from irrelevant activities.
  - Boys fail to realize that consent can be withdrawn.
  - Boys minimize their capacity to determine unwanted sexual activity.

  Boys with appropriate definitions of sexual assault understand that consent is not necessarily present just because a partner is not resisting, just because he has no intent to harm, and just because a partner previously consented to some level of contact.
- Boys often lack the confidence to obtain confirmation that consent is present. One of the clearest ways to do this is to

verbally communicate, but many boys unfortunately do not see this as a viable option.

- Research-identified risk factors for perpetration provide some areas to hone in on as we talk to boys, such as deconstructing rape myths, questioning traditional gender roles, and increasing empathy for women and victims. We can also help them recognize sex as an activity of value with potential consequences rather than as a disposable act.
- Many boys express a fear of being falsely accused of sexual violence. If this fear is genuine, then it presents an opportunity to talk to boys about consent. While they likely do not have the ability to change the criminal justice system, they can change personal decision-making that might make them susceptible to an accusation. Digging into that decision-making naturally leads one to consider how one can prevent harming others as well.
- Some key lessons for boys to incorporate into their understandings of obtaining consent include:
  - One has to recognize when seduction crosses the line and becomes coercion.
  - Verbal communication is a potentially effective tool for ensuring that consent is present.
  - Walking away from a potential sexual encounter might be the most responsible option when the presence of consent is uncertain.
  - You are free to set your own behavioral standards that are higher than what policies and laws expect of you.

Becoming an Active Bystander

As a senior in high school, a few of my friends and I went to see the comedy-drama *The Players Club*. In retrospect, the film was an early vehicle for several Hollywood stars such as Jamie Foxx, Bernie Mac, and Ice Cube. The story revolves around a strip club aptly called "The Players Club." There is a scene that stuck with me afterwards in which a woman is raped at a bachelor party. She screams and cries for help such that every attendee is fully aware of what is occurring. The men who are present look to one another, express their disapproval, and collectively walk out of the party. I wrestled with the scene afterwards. *Why did the men in the scene not intervene and interrupt what was clearly a rape? At least they did not condone the violence, but could they not come up with a more productive response than simply walking away?*

Now I think that the scriptwriters for *The Players Club* might deserve more credit than I originally gave them. The idea of men walking away from violence is very much grounded in reality. Many sexual assaults arise out of social situations in which outside parties could have interrupted the proceedings if they had chosen to do so. The Steubenville High School rape case is perhaps the best known of many stories involving youth where a group had some awareness of what occurred before and/or during an assault. That case featured assailants and witnesses documenting repeated assaults of an unconscious victim on social media and text messages.[1] Stories involving groups who share some awareness of an incident are common enough even if they do not all get the same level of media attention. There was a 2020 incident where charges were brought against eight men after a mother found a video on Facebook of her unconscious 16-year-old daughter being assaulted.[2]

As an example of another commonly cited experience, observers might notice a man walk off with a woman who is potentially too intoxicated to consent. Or they may witness a man applying steady pressure toward a woman who appears to be uncomfortable with his advances. None of these situations guarantee that an assault will occur, but they do beg for someone to check in and confirm that all parties are safe. Still, boys and men too often respond by looking in another direction.

* * *

I have a personal story that demonstrates men's hesitancy to act against potential violence. I was in a club in Washington, D.C., celebrating a friend's birthday one evening. I rode to the club with another friend and his cousin (let's call her Tiffany). At the end of the night, security went about directing us out of the building and it quickly became apparent that Tiffany would not be leaving entirely under her own power. She had drunk more than any of us had realized and was too intoxicated to do much of anything other than sleep (as I confirmed when she was later unable to recall any of this story). Her cousin left to pick up the car, leaving the task of seeing her to the car to me.

The process was a slow one. We had to go from the third floor of the club to the first and then around the block. I began to feel self-conscious about escorting a barely conscious woman. I must have looked as questionable as I felt because I received a number of comments during my exit such as "She's too far gone, bro." All of the people who spoke up noted the fact that I had a semiconscious woman draped across my shoulder. Interestingly, all of them were men. The tone of all of their comments suggested they were meant to be jokes, but they all contained an innuendo that I was carrying off this woman in order to have sex with her.

These comments stuck with me long after Tiffany was safely delivered to her cousin's house for the night. *Did my actions set off alarm in others around me, or did the whole event just blend into how people are used to behaving at social outings? Out of those who noticed and presumed some form of sexual activity was to follow, how many of them interpreted the scene as an emergency and how many of them did not care what was about to happen? Out of those who did experience discomfort, how many of them held their tongues because they were unsure if it was their place to interrupt the private affairs of strangers? How many of them wanted to check in and ensure that I had Tiffany's best interests in mind but were afraid of being "that guy"?*

I do not know the answer to any of these questions, but I do know that most of us are entirely unpracticed in the art of interrupting potential sexual violence. You might say that the lack of a response occurred because bystanders had no real way of knowing whether or not something bad would happen if they allowed me to walk away. But how often do we have assurance that a negative outcome is about to occur? We more often have to make decisions based on the mere possibility of a negative outcome.

Some of the jokes directed my way while Tiffany and I left the club may not have been delivered by men who wanted to callously make light of a presumed rape. It is possible that some came from men who were executing the only socially acceptable intervention they could come up with in the moment. After all, their comments did alert both me and others to the fact that I was escorting a party who was unfit to consent to sex. Nonetheless, the fact remains that I would have faced little resistance had I harbored ill intentions for Tiffany, despite literally being surrounded by people with opportunity to intervene. We would not expect boys who are still growing into themselves to fare much better.

I want to acknowledge two points before criticizing boys too harshly. One is that I have certainly heard powerful stories where young men did indeed display the courage to say "not on my watch." The second is that we should not be surprised if boys fail to intervene in emergencies if they are never taught the skills to do so.

I mentioned earlier that you are likely to find a peer education program if you walked into a high school or onto a college campus and looked for the public face of the school's antiviolence efforts. There is also a good chance that you would find a program employing at least some facets of what might be broadly labeled as a bystander intervention program. Quite often, these programs will be one and the same, with peer educators providing bystander intervention programming. There is a vast spectrum of bystander intervention programs, but most of them take on the goal of activating third parties who observe potential or actual violence. These programs attempt to give attendees the motivation and skills to interrupt violence. They acknowledge that the required skill set is not innate and give attendees the space to develop and practice.

If you are at a loss as to what this practice might look like, keep in mind that there are now quite a few bystander intervention programs and educational models in existence. They are designed to teach people how to respond to a range of social ills, and quite a few of them focus on sexual violence. If you have a boy in your life who you want to develop as an active bystander, consider putting him in touch with a local bystander intervention program (many were designed with adolescents in mind) or teaching elements of their curricula that are publicly available and that you find appealing.

In full transparency, there are several prominent criticisms of bystander intervention programs. Some take issue with the word "bystander" in the first place as they feel that the term connotes somebody who is passive or outside of the community. As is usually the case, some question the effectiveness of these programs (though many of them have demonstrated results in affecting the attitudes of audiences). Others ask if intervening escalates the potential for violence and if intervention should be left to trained professionals.

Be mindful that intervention need not always mean bystanders directly intervening, as I discuss shortly. One of the key elements in the development of bystander intervention skills is giving thought to what is within our control to interrupt and recognizing the full range of options available to us. It is also about recognizing resources to assist us when we encounter situations that are beyond our capability, such as law enforcement, faculty and staff, or even just friends for additional support.

* * *

When I ask boys why they find it difficult to intervene in situations where they observe some potential for a sexual assault, three common themes emerge. Interestingly enough, I almost never hear them talk about how they are afraid for their own physical safety (they could just be afraid to admit this in front of me or their peers, though). This is what I hear instead.

BOYS ARE AFRAID OF DAMAGING RELATIONSHIPS WITH THEIR FRIENDS

There is no getting around the fact that questioning the behaviors of peers could result in strained and severed relationships. Boys have to decide if maintaining relationships with potentially violent peers is more important than their right to influence the kind of world that they want to live in. Fortunately, boys often reveal that this fear of alienating peers is grounded more in theory than reality. Many young men have told me stories in which questioning a problematic behavior ended up earning the respect of their peers. Others have even told me that they were later thanked by those they cautioned before engaging in high-risk behavior.

BOYS HAVE NO WAY OF CONFIRMING THAT THEIR INTERVENTION IS NEEDED

Boys retreat from inserting themselves into potentially violent situations for fear of making a big a deal out of nothing. They do not want to wrongly accuse another of wrongdoing. But the expectation that they must always exercise perfect judgment is unrealistic when it comes to confronting a brand of violence in which many perpetrators do not always properly identify their own behaviors as violent themselves. Courageous boys will have to act on situations that merely have the potential for violence. Acting in the face of uncertainty is what is required.

BOYS ARE AFRAID OF BREACHING THE CODES
OF MANHOOD

If you spend time with young men, you are likely familiar with the concept of "cock blocking"—a pejorative term applied to situations in which
one person hinders another from participating in a sex act. Young men do
not want to be labeled as a "cock blocker" or any associated term as this
is considered a violation of the codes of manhood. Since fear of breaking
up a possible hookup features so prominently in male cultures, men must
learn to distinguish between disrupting a consensual sexual encounter and
disrupting a potentially violent encounter. Remind them of the definitions
of sexual assault and rape.

* * *

There is a healthy amount of social science research examining the factors
that dissuade or encourage people to intervene when they observe threats to
themselves and others. This research is dedicated to exploring exactly why
people fail to stop harmful events when others are present. Two of the most
influential researchers in this field are John Darley and Bibb Latané, and one
of their lasting contributions is a model that outlines everything that one
must do in order to react to an emergency. The model contains five steps:

1. Notice the event.
2. Interpret the event as potentially dangerous.
3. Decide that you have a personal responsibility to help.
4. Decide what you should do to help.
5. Decide how to do it.[3]

This model was not developed specifically for sexual violence, but
I have always liked it as a reminder of just how much needs to be accomplished when somebody notices an emergency. When you see something
bad happening, you have a lot to think through and generally a limited
amount of time to execute.

A program called Green Dot, which is present at many educational
institutions throughout the country, has helped to demonstrate the

range of actions available when "deciding what you should do to help" by popularizing what they call the three D's. One could intervene in a potentially harmful situation by directly approaching one of the involved parties (direct), activating a third party who is better equipped to intervene (delegate), or creating a distraction to diffuse the situation (distract).[4]

Talking through the "decide how to do it" step with boys can yield some really engaging conversations. Even if a boy is inclined to speak to somebody when he observes a potential problem, he is still left to think about exactly what he is going to say. *What might one say to somebody who is a friend as compared to somebody who is a complete stranger? What can one say that will not sound completely awkward? Does it even matter if an approach comes out awkwardly?* It may be a good idea to connect boys with other young men as they think on questions such as these so that they can hear what worked and what did not work from the lived experiences of others in their peer culture. They might also observe that the negative consequences of speaking up are not always as dire as imagined. Nearly every time that I lead a discussion with young men about what they can say when they observe a troubling situation, I have the good fortune of hearing somebody describe how they intervened and how things went much more smoothly than expected.

My job brings me into contact with a fair amount of active and retired members of the U.S. Armed Forces. Some of these women and men have shared their stories of training for elite units with me. They talk of how they spent hours upon hours drilling at the same activities so that they could be counted on to perform once bullets started flying or their aircraft started falling from the sky. People can generally act more quickly during a crisis if they have already practiced their response.

Likewise, boys may be more likely to react to potential violence if they have thought about their responses in advance. The barriers that make choosing silence the easier choice are varied and understandable. There can simply be a lot to process and a lot of options to consider when you are called upon to act, so remember that boys can do some of the processing in advance.

* * *

The full potential of bystander intervention to prevent sexual violence is debated. After all, much of this violence occurs in settings where victims are isolated and there is no opportunity for a bystander to intervene. Even still, all boys will have opportunities to flex their intervention skills when faced with everyday behaviors that encourage violence. Even if we have no opportunity to prevent a violent act, we all have opportunity to tell violent men our opinions of their behavior. A typical day could include overhearing someone casually toss around the word "rape" (e.g., "My football team got raped last night") or having a discussion with someone who defends violence against women or children in certain instances.

If boys and men are ill equipped at interrupting actual violence, then we probably also have difficulty interrupting more casual acts that contribute to a culture of minimizing violence against women. I was once in a locker room when a man said, "I hope that bitch burns in hell," in reference to the reported victim in a sexual assault trial of a professional athlete. I had seen the man around but never spoken to him, which made his statement part of his way of introducing himself to me. He did not know my personal politics and probably figured the statement would build rapport between us as men. But I did not agree with the tone and the rush to judgment as I believed that this kind of language was exactly why many survivors are afraid to come forward. The statement demanded a response on my part, and I thought about the best way to proceed. What could I say that would effectively state my position without taking an hour to explain? Whatever I said, I needed to come off as relatable. I did not want to incite the other men in the room to jump in and take this man's side.

I ran through an entire dialogue in my head. By the time I was ready to respond, the man who issued the comment had already gone on his way. I took it as a stern reminder that bystander intervention is not easy, even if one is only interrupting words and thoughts. There are still some steps that you have to work through, including whether or not your intervention is even needed.

Recall that the second point of Darley and Latané's five-step model is to "interpret the event as potentially dangerous." Boys typically demonstrate massive amounts of disagreement as to whether nonphysical elements of rape culture are potentially dangerous and worthy of intervention.

Consider the conflict that my undergraduate peer education program experienced when some members wanted to challenge pornography consumption. This was vital to confronting rape culture for some members but a bridge too far for others. Truth be told, jokes are the area where I most often see boys expressing disagreement. Some see somebody telling a joke that belittles sexual violence as worthy of interruption, while others see them as entirely harmless or dependent on context.

When video surfaced of then-presidential nominee Donald Trump talking about grabbing women "by their pussy," he responded by claiming that the comment was just "locker room talk," the implication being that this talk was harmless. On this, I can identify at least two reasons why I think that the ways that we joke and talk with one another have impact.

First, we know for a fact that many survivors do not report their experiences precisely because they do not feel as if they will be taken seriously. Therefore, the ways that we interact have a confirmed impact on whether or not victims seek out help in their recovery and hold violent men accountable. Second, accounts from perpetrators of sexual violence reveal that many do not know that they have done anything wrong. I have to think that spending time in environments where people joke about sexual violence contributes to them failing to correctly understand their actions.

I currently live outside of Washington, D.C., where I observed the grooming of perpetrators that boys must learn to confront one evening. In Adams Morgan, a neighborhood in northwest D.C. that serves as a popular hangout, it only took 15 minutes of hanging out on the street to observe a group of three men address nearly every woman who passed them in remotely revealing clothing as "Hoe." One man slid his hand up the dress of an unsuspecting woman. Yet another man grabbed a female passerby so forcefully that she was swung around and almost fell over. When she reacted by wrenching herself free, the man responded by yelling, "What the fuck is wrong with you, bitch?"

Some will see these kinds of behaviors as entirely distinct from rape. *But what are these behaviors if not rigorous training to disregard female resistance to breaches of personal boundaries? What are they if not validation*

for a method of sexual interaction whereby men are to impulsively barrel in
and sort out the consequences later? These kinds of behaviors have everything to do with sexual violence.

Dr. David Lisak, formerly of the University of Massachusetts-Boston,
and his colleagues have presented influential studies toward our understanding of nonincarcerated perpetrators. One of them explains how
the antiviolence community can hold seemingly inconsistent beliefs
that sexual violence is rampant and that most men are not perpetrators.
They explain that this is possible because nonincarcerated rapists tend to
commit multiple offenses over time.[5]

Understandings of this sort present an interesting view of the world
in which a relative handful of violent men interact daily with and are
surrounded by nonviolent boys and men. These nonviolent men might do
very little to check the behavior of the perpetrators in their midst. They
may consider the sexual exploits of other men to be none of their business and keep their mouths shut. At worst, they may excuse the violent
behaviors that come to their attention. The violent men then live their
entire lives without anybody forcing them to reconsider their behaviors.

Surrounding violent men with peers who will challenge and even rebuke them is one of the most direct means we have of challenging sexual
violence. However, boys do not come into the world with the skill set to do
this. It is up to us to speak to them about the art of intervention.

When we do take a stand against something that we overhear or see,
we will undoubtedly make some mistakes. The transcripts of our dialogue
and actions will not always stand up to the scrutiny of hindsight. We will
probably walk away from some of these encounters thinking there was
something that we could have done or said better. This reality should not
paralyze us, though, as even the clumsiest of interventions is generally
better than inaction.

I believe that many boys possess some discomfort with the cultural climate around sexual violence. Long before I consciously acknowledged
it in myself, possessed the language to articulate it to others, or had the
courage to express it, I was at least aware that I spent a good deal of time
feeling uncomfortable. I was uncomfortable hanging out with my friends

as they discussed their pursuit of women in a similar fashion to hunters pursuing prey. And I was uncomfortable when they shared the fruits of the hunt through sensationalized expositions devoid of any real acknowledgment that we were discussing other human beings. The world told me that "boys will be boys" and that this type of fraternization was wholly distinct from the actions of the rapists of the world. But my spirit disagreed and hinted that we were paving the way for those men, if not outright preparing ourselves to join their ranks. We have to give boys the space to explore similar feelings of their own. Boys would be more confident in voicing these feelings if they knew that others around them had similar feelings. I do not think that it is a coincidence that I became an outspoken advocate after I was introduced to a cohort of men who were also willing to speak up. So do not forget to remind boys that they are not alone.

* * *

Perhaps the boys you know will live a life that is completely different from mine. They might find interaction with rape-supportive language, behaviors, and peers to be less common. This does not excuse them from developing response skills, because there is still a very good chance that a survivor of sexual violence will ask them for support.

Recall the appalling lifetime victimization rates for women that I called out in Chapter 1. Boys will come to know survivors, and some of these survivors may choose to make themselves known. I once met a man in his 40s who told me that every single woman he had ever dated had survived violence, including his wife. Boys may even hear disclosures from their male peers as victim advocates continue to empower victims of all genders and sexes to tell their stories.

Effective victim advocacy requires extensive training and experience, but boys should at least have a basic preparation in the event that a survivor discloses to them. Rather than reinvent the wheel, I will point out some basic skills for responding to disclosures of victimization that were taught to me by the peer education program that first trained me.[6] Several of them assume a survivor who is disclosing a recent experience, but most of them are relevant even for experiences that occurred long ago:

1. *Medical and safety needs*: It is important to direct survivors to medical attention soon after an assault. Not only can they be treated for acute medical injuries, but medical personnel can collect evidence should they later wish to pursue judicial action against an attacker. Many hospitals have personnel specifically trained to respond to survivors of sexual violence. With this said, survivors should never be forced to go to the hospital. The decision to seek medical attention is ultimately theirs.

2. *No more violence*: Many boys and men respond with anger upon learning that a loved one has been assaulted. They may want to assault the attacker, but this reaction generally does not aid a survivor's recovery and can even hinder it by giving the survivor more to worry about.

3. *Listen*: It is generally better to talk less and to listen more. Furthermore, your questions about what happened and why can easily come off as judgmental.

4. *Believe her*: Many victim advocates contend that the single most important factor in a survivor's recovery from assault is whether or not she feels believed. Most criminal justice organizations believe that the number of unfounded reports is extremely low, including the FBI, which believes that only 8% of reported rapes are false reports. Also, do not blame the survivor or agree with her if she blames herself. Even if you believe that she made poor decisions, remember that nobody deserves to be raped.

5. *Help her regain control*: Encouraging a survivor to make decisions, no matter how small, can go a long way toward helping her to regain control. As with seeking medical attention, you should avoid forcing a survivor to make particular decisions even if you do not agree with her choices. This includes sharing a survivor's experience without her permission. This

person reached out to someone she trusted, and disclosing her experience without permission violates that trust.

6. *Realize limitations*: Be patient. Recovering from sexual violence does not happen overnight. Recovery is a process. Those helping survivors should refer them to counseling services for long-term support if needed. On this note, hearing about violence suffered by a loved one and helping that loved one through recovery can leave boys with their own feelings to process. They should consider seeking counseling themselves rather than discussing negative feelings with a survivor.

Believing victims may not come naturally to boys raised in cultures where stories of assault are commonly dissected. They may even want to get to the bottom of what happened. However, boys are not typically trained to adjudicate cases, nor do they occupy roles where they are asked to do so anyway. They are approached because someone is in need of their support. If they are approached as a friend, then they should respond as a friend and not as an investigator.

Many boys possess only a stereotypical understanding of how a survivor of sexual violence will behave. Reactions to trauma are far more varied than many boys assume. Should they ever have the opportunity to help a friend or family member who discloses to them, they will learn about the real decisions that real people make when recovering. Prepared boys who are ready to help will likely emerge as more effective antiviolence advocates.

CHAPTER 8: TEACHING BOYS TO INTERRUPT VIOLENCE

- Interrupting violence is difficult and requires practice. Commonly cited reasons as to why boys do not consistently act to prevent violence include:
  1. They are afraid of damaging relationships with friends.

2. They have no way of confirming that their intervention is needed.

3. They are afraid of breaching the codes of manhood.

4. They are afraid of creating awkwardness with peers.

- Social science researchers Latané and Darley developed a five-step model for intervening in emergencies. It gives insight into what boys must process when deciding how to respond to everything from actual violence to jokes about violence. The steps are as follows:

1. Notice the event.

2. Interpret the event as potentially dangerous.

3. Decide that you have a personal responsibility to help.

4. Decide what you should do to help.

5. Decide how to do it.

- Many boys see jokes as harmless, but they contribute to a climate where it is more difficult for survivors to be taken seriously and where perpetrators are emboldened. Equipping boys with a sense of the harm caused by minimizing violence as well as a personal responsibility to help will make them more adept at bystander intervention.

- Consider utilizing resources from existing bystander intervention programs as you empower boys to interrupt violence and rape culture. There are many such programs, and they often have resources available to the public or offer avenues for young men to connect with them. Some of the more popular programs that employ bystander intervention strategies include Green Dot (https://alteristic.org/services/green-dot/), It's On Us (https://www.itsonus.org), Hollaback! (https://www.ihollaback.org), and Mentors in Violence Prevention (https://www.mvpstrat.com).

- The program under which I was initially trained (The Men's Program) also incorporates bystander intervention components. In addition to the program content, a training curriculum, advice for peer educators, and other resources are available at https://www.johnfoubert.com/the-men-s-and-women-s-programs.

- One of the most underappreciated ways in which boys can challenge rape culture is to aid the recovery of survivors. Some immediate tips that people can use to help survivors are as follows:
  - Attend to immediate medical and safety needs.
  - Do not pursue any further violence.
  - Listen to survivors.
  - Believe survivors.
  - Help survivors regain control.
  - Realize personal limitations.

Finding a Home in a
Global Movement

Even if men were to chalk up a significant percentage of the reports of sexual violence to false reports and research methodology problems, sexual violence remains an all-too-common experience for women. It would remain the case that we can fully expect a large percentage of the daughters, sisters, female partners, and female friends in our lives to have a memory of a hurtful sexual experience (or several memories).

We have historically asked women to deal with this violence. Star tennis player Serena Williams reminded us of the expectation of female responsibility for violence directed toward them by sending a tweet in 2012. She did this when she used an avatar featuring her wearing high heels and matching undergarments soon after a man was arrested for stalking her. Many saw the picture and accused her of being hypocritical and of not doing enough to ensure her own safety. As one blogger put it, "if she wants to put her body on display for the public that's her decision, but she shouldn't complain about stalking or tongue-wagging comments that accompany it."[1] Some in the public saw no distinction between Williams sharing an image of herself with the public and having someone use her Twitter updates to locate her and show up in her dressing room, which is what the man arrested for stalking was accused of doing.[2] Williams was within her rights to choose what types of access to her body were permissible. The reaction she faced is reminiscent of what many victims of sexual violence must face, wherein they are held solely responsible for dissuading unwanted contact and wherein consent to *some* intimate contact is seen as consent to *all* contact.

I am reminded all of the time of just how much more women are forced to think about the prospect of violence than do men. When a friend looking for an apartment asked me about my neighborhood and I told her that I had no issues with it, she responded by saying she would still like to see the neighborhood a few times at night because things would be different for her as a woman. A single drive through had been enough for me to decide it was safe for me, but she needed more information in order to feel secure. Another time, a friend who was looking to hire someone to paint her house asked if I could come over to her home while the work was being performed. I told her that I was not much of a painting expert, only to have her tell me that she just wanted me there so that she would not be alone with men whom she did not know. I have never made that kind of consideration for myself. I can think of environments where men worry about violence more than women do; but in general, the threat of violence does not cross our minds as much as it does theirs. This is especially true in potentially intimate encounters: Most men probably do not devote a single thought toward establishing their personal boundaries, whereas many women give it a lot of thought before, during, and after encounters.

There is nothing wrong with women and girls working to reduce their susceptibility to violence. But the expectation that women are solely responsible for ensuring that men do not harm them is problematic when it is the sum total of our violence prevention efforts. Doing so excuses perpetrators who are ultimately responsible for their own actions. Say what you will about Serena Williams's Twitter habits, but she is certainly not more deserving of criticism than a man who stalks her.

Placing the burden entirely on women also leaves everyone who does not identify as a woman or as a potential victim—namely boys and men—to believe that they can do nothing but urge the women they know to be more careful. The rates of sexual violence make it clear that simply advising women to avoid victimization is ineffective. We have tried that approach and have seen the results.

Men's violence against women has always said more about men than it has about women anyway, so boys might want to have a say in the prevailing stories told about them, especially since many boys resent being stereotyped as potential perpetrators in waiting. Boys might resent this, but the stereotypes exist whether or not we call attention to them. For example, when a woman goes out on a date and engages in protective behaviors like monitoring her drinks, informing others of her whereabouts, or being definitive about her intentions for the evening, her actions are often based more on her expectations about men as a group rather than her date as an individual. If boys and men expect women to be responsible for their safety, then we cannot also be offended by their attempts to defend against our potential transgressions.

Antiviolent boys have options for responding to our collective faults that go beyond clashing with those who bring them up. We have to get more boys to the table so that they can lend their voices toward solutions. The good news is that once you get past surface conversations with boys, they can think of all kinds of ways to help. I believe that a silent majority of boys and men are fiercely opposed to sexual violence and willing to help if properly engaged. This is where guardians and mentors are needed to invite them to the table.

With this said, boys who raise their voices follow traditions that have primarily been pioneered by women. Men should not enter as saviors set on overturning the existing foundation and patting ourselves on the back for good deeds will likely lead to conflict. We should not expect universal acclaim from women for stepping up. Some women justifiably harbor mistrust toward men after generations of men condoning and excusing their collective violence. Black men are not exempt from this mistrust just because we often identify with the underdogs aligned against the ruling class. When it comes to sexual violence, we are members of a privileged class. This change of perspective can be dizzying, but one of the best methods for boys and men to navigate the complexities that I mention is to seek out guidance from women and experienced educators.

Fresh ideas and perspectives are needed, but incoming contributors should do their best to avoid the pitfalls of past efforts that were well intentioned but counterproductive. People who have not spent a substantial amount of time thinking about sexual violence prevention are just going to have very different ideas about how to solve this violence and run the risk of alienating those already invested in the work.

An example of a counterproductive effort would be a 2011 ad campaign titled "Control Tonight" by the Pennsylvania Liquor Control Board. One of the messages in the series featured an image of a woman's legs with her underwear around her ankles accompanied by the text "She didn't want to do it, but she couldn't say no." Additional text referenced how bad decisions about alcohol consumption can make one vulnerable to "dangers like date rape."[3]

Many antiviolence advocates reviled the ad because it placed blame on victims rather than perpetrators. Many called for the ad to be pulled. I am sure that the ad's creators were well intentioned, but they were unable to find universal support from those who ostensibly shared the same goal of ending sexual violence because they were disconnected from prevailing ideologies within the movement to end sexual violence.

Fortunately, America now boasts an expansive network of rape crisis centers, policy advocacy organizations, and volunteer groups that are equipped to incorporate new ideas and volunteers. This network has largely been established by women but also features a growing supply of male-oriented and male-facilitated organizations and resources. If you know of a boy who wishes to help, chances are there is a resource nearby to provide structure.

If you are wondering if the boys in your life have the time to contribute amid their already busy schedules, know that boys do not need to go anywhere to help. This issue has a way of coming to them as they go about their lives. Everyday conversations and interactions are the battlegrounds. They should spend some time in formal training; but, outside of that, they just need to stand in place and share their voices.

* * *

Like all institutions of higher learning, my alma mater, the University of Virginia, has its hallowed traditions. I opted out of some of them, such as the timeless ritual of streaking across the campus. I enthusiastically participated in others, like living on what is known as "the Lawn" during my fourth year on campus. The Lawn consists of a terraced stretch of land and the surrounding facilities that served the original residential and academic purposes of the University. It is one of the more well-known components of founder and former President Thomas Jefferson's vision of the University. Today, the Lawn and its surrounding grounds are listed on the esteemed World Heritage list alongside the Taj Mahal and the Great Wall of China.[4]

The University is wary of meddling with Mr. Jefferson's original "academical village," and its physical infrastructure remains much the same as it was in the 1800s. For example, the housing units on the Lawn contain no restrooms, and residents must brave the elements in order to take a shower or relieve themselves. Oddly enough, residence on the Lawn is considered an honor and not a punishment. What the Lawn lacks in amenities, it makes up for in community. You cannot help but feel a bond with those who choose to live under the same peculiar circumstances.

During the only winter I spent there, one of my residential companions approached me with something that was bothering her. She was White and told me that her sister was dating a Black man who was physically abusive. He would frequently come home angry and take it out on her sister. As my friend told me this, it was apparent that she felt that she was describing a gross anomaly. My friend was telling a story, but her tone and eyes suggested that she was also asking a question that she was uncomfortable asking directly. Eventually, I believed I understood. She was pondering how Black men—so familiar with being on the receiving end of unearned contempt and so aware of the realities of societal injustice—could turn around and subjugate a woman through violence.

Linking systemic violence against women to systemic racism could be a powerful point to push Black boys to action, but we must exercise caution here. Most Black boys are nowhere near as skilled in identifying gender-based oppression as they are in identifying race-based oppression. They are not afforded as much social permission to speak against the byproducts of sexism and objectification of women and therefore simply have less practice in this area.

I remember 2008 discussions around the *National Post*'s reports that the Chicago White Sox had erected a shrine in their locker room featuring blow-up dolls surrounded by "strategically placed" bats doing "naughty things."[5] I also recall the 2007 discussions around a Dolce & Gabbana print advertisement that featured a man forcibly holding a woman down by her wrists while other men looked on. I can recall countless discussions about women in hip-hop music videos routinely shown draped across our favorite rappers as possessions. In all of these cases, my peers told me that the images were largely irrelevant. They were harmless entertainment with no bearing on actual behavior. They were only being discussed because of overzealous political correctness.

I received an entirely different response from the Black men I knew in reviewing an infamous print advertisement that Intel ran in 2007. It featured a White man standing with his arms crossed and six Black sprinters in a start position at his feet. As stated by Intel in its apology for the ad, the intent was to "convey the performance capabilities" of its processors "through the visual image of a sprinter."[6] I see what the company was trying to communicate, but they were clumsy in their execution by relying on the image of multiple Black men kneeling before a confident White man. Many of my Black male friends agreed. This advertisement provoked a visceral response in them—one that admitted that images reflect and contribute to our attitudes, that our attitudes cannot be wholly separated from our behaviors, and that a creator's intent matters little when it comes to the effects of an image.

As I have stated, my self-identification as a Black man helped usher me into the international movement to end sexual violence. In addition to wanting to take an active role in eliminating archaic stereotypes of Black men as rapists, I found the transition to be fairly smooth because I had already accepted the modern-day existence of prejudice against particular populations that is institutionalized, systematic, and so deeply ingrained in culture that it is invisible to many. I also understood what can happen when people who hold negative beliefs about another group of people are placed in situations of power over them. Thus, when I heard women commenting on the widespread disrespect of women and the resultant violence against them, I was always able to quell the guttural reflex to label them as man-hating fanatics who cherish victimhood. I found common threads between our lived experiences.

The same determination that I found to shake up the status quo is present in thousands of men all over the country. I would like to thank an undergraduate student at Harvard for confirming this. While I was a staff member at the university, I was going through items left by my predecessor and came across a research paper written by a student with whom I had a pretty good relationship. She was heavily involved in sexual violence awareness work on campus and had conducted qualitative research on men who did similar work on campus. She wanted to know what drove some men to go about the strange business of speaking up on a "women's issue."[7]

Some men got involved through personal connections to survivors of violence. Some stepped up because they themselves were survivors. Some followed in the footsteps of friends who had preceded them in the work. Black-identified men chimed in, too, to provide reasons that were specific to them. One got involved because he had a strong urge to confront the myth of the "violent and oversexed 'big Black male' rapist," another because the voices he identified with were absent from the cause, and another thought that dealing with sexual violence forced him to look at the health of Black communities more holistically.

I have never much cared what attracts boys and men to the movement against sexual violence, because you generally have to train us before we can do any good anyway. Well-intentioned but untrained men are prone to pedagogical errors that alienate and misinform. Fortunately, nearly all of the men I have come across in the field have naturally found paths of self-development after taking the first few steps. The foremost challenge is getting men to take the first steps.

Those first steps can be difficult in a world that often claims that we need to choose sides. I watched commentators on Twitter accuse the NFL and NBA for supporting rape culture because it allowed players to make statements of solidarity with Jacob Blake. Jacob Blake was shot multiple times by a police officer in 2020 as he leaned into a vehicle with his young sons in the back seat. He also reportedly has a past sexual assault charge. In the same Twitter session, I observed somebody respond to a survivor of sexual assault celebrating the conviction of her attacker with a statement about how meanwhile there are plenty of people walking around who should be locked up for killing Black Americans. A fight naturally broke out about whether sexual assault survivors or slain Black Americans were more deserving of justice.

Dr. Martin Luther King, Jr., famously wrote from a Birmingham jail cell that "Injustice anywhere is a threat to justice everywhere. We are caught in an inescapable network of mutuality, tied in a single garment of destiny. Whatever affects one directly affects all indirectly."[8] The urge to fight one form of injustice and forsake all others is a false one. As I found with my journey, observing injustice against others can unite as well as divide.

* * *

Though some Black women also met their demise at the hands of lynching (and many non-Blacks as well), many of us remember Black men when we conjure up the faces of the victims. With that said, the person perhaps best remembered for speaking out against lynching is Ida B. Wells—a Black woman. She and many other women and women's organizations were front and center in the effort to end the lynching of Black men. The tradition of Black women confronting violence that applies disproportionately to Black men was established early in America and continues to thrive today. I can attend a meeting or rally to address street violence or racial profiling in Black communities—phenomena that more frequently involve men rather than women—and fully expect women to be well represented. Women will likely even be the vast majority of attendees. We are also accustomed to women bringing most of the noise when the discussion of violence against Black men moves to social media and other venues. The presence of women is understood as that of people marching for loved ones and of people aware that violence affects entire communities. We identify their works as acts of solidarity with family and community, and we would probably label them as selfish or short-sighted if they were absent.

There is no parallel tradition of Black men standing up for violence primarily directed toward women. Attend a conference or rally on sexual violence, domestic violence, or any other public health concern that dis-proportionately affects women and you can fully expect women to dom-inate the audience. The gender politics that have created this situation are complex, but it may be partially due to the simple fact that Black communities cannot easily recall men akin to Ida B. Wells who left behind strong legacies of combating violence against genders besides their own.

Should you need to provide an example for Black boys, know that Black men have resisted sexual violence in some form or another for the entirety of our tenure on American soil. Examples of this resistance are widespread even if you may have to dig to find them. A fairly public mobilization occurred in 2007 when the New Black Panther Party seized on the afore-mentioned accusations of sexual assault against Duke lacrosse players and held a demonstration in support of the alleged victim near campus. A poster for the event reportedly featured the words "Had enough of dis-respect and racism from Duke University? Demonstrate your discontent! Stand up!"[9] Naturally, the media spotlight followed. Many took issue with the New Black Panther Party's politics and with anyone who sided against the lacrosse players, who were ultimately successful in having the charges against them dropped. Regardless, an organization inextricably linked to Black manhood welcomed the national spotlight in order to make a state-ment against sexual violence.

In 1987, 15-year-old Tawana Brawley was reportedly found in a trash bag in Poughkeepsie, New York. She was smeared with dog feces and the words "KKK" and "nigger" were scrawled on her body. The deputy who first responded to the calls that led to Brawley's discovery said that the stench from inside the bag had "nearly overwhelmed him." She was in-itially silent and unresponsive to questions. When she finally spoke, she claimed that six White men had abducted, raped, and beaten her over a period of four days.

Brawley's account of her whereabouts during the four days during which she was missing eventually came into question and a grand jury decided that she had fabricated the story, though there are parties who claim the truth of her story to this day. The initial response of Black men to Brawley's account was vocal and uncompromising. Mike Tyson, then heavyweight boxing champion, reportedly gave Brawley his Rolex watch and offered to pay for her future college expenses. Bill Cosby and magazine publisher Ed Lewis posted a $25,000 reward for anyone who could provide information about the case. The Rev. Al Sharpton, then relatively unknown on the national scene, became perhaps the best remembered of a team of strident advocates who ensured that the incident remained in public consciousness. Black men and women in the New York area participated in numerous protests, many of which linked the incident to other cases of perceived racial injustice, including a recent incident in Queens, New York, in which three Black men were assaulted by a mob of White men.[10]

In her book *I Will Survive: The African-American Guide to Healing from Sexual Assault and Abuse*, Lori Robinson recounts a response to young Black women being systematically raped and robbed near bus stops in Chicago's South Side throughout 2000 and 2001 (in total, 16 Black girls and women aged 14 to 23 were raped). "Operation Defense," spearheaded by the Rev. Al Sampson of civil rights fame, held weekly community awareness forums attended by the Nation of Islam and area pastors. Others recruited African American motorcycle clubs to patrol neighborhoods, created an escort service of men to accompany women using public transportation, and offered free self-defense classes to women. "Operation Defense" helped direct media attention to crimes that had previously received very little, and three suspects were eventually apprehended.[11]

Those searching for a more contemporary inspiration from a Black male need look no further than the 44th President of the United States, Barack Obama, who chose then-Senator Joseph Biden as his running mate. Biden also happened to be the senator best associated with the Violence Against Women Act (VAWA) and a man who continues to publicly raise awareness for dating and sexual violence. VAWA funds a number of initiatives promoting community and criminal justice responses to sexual violence, among other things. The Act has, for the most part, received bipartisan support throughout its lifespan and is widely credited with positively altering the national landscape for sexual assault victims. President Obama became chiefly associated with the Act when its 2012 renewal was contested. Obama's defense of the Act and his association with one of its most recognizable architects make him an ally in my mind. Former Vice President Biden cleared up any doubt that he stood against rape culture by issuing an open letter to a survivor of sexual violence at Stanford University in 2016 following a high-profile ruling that many condemned as too lenient.

Under President Obama, the White House Council on Woman and Girls also rolled out the "It's On Us" campaign. The campaign was aimed at ending sexual assault on college campuses, and it is exciting to see the first Black-led presidential administration house such a program and for President Obama to lend his voice and face to associated public service announcements. I was also pleased to see that President Obama did not idly sit on the fence when Representative Todd Akin made controversial comments about "legitimate rape" in 2012. As a public response, he submitted that "the idea that we should be parsing, qualifying, slicing what types of rape we're talking about doesn't make sense to the American people. It certainly doesn't make sense to me."[12] I am not so naïve as to believe that political jockeying had nothing to do with this response to a Republican representative, but affirmation for antiviolent causes from a man who is arguably the most visible Black man in the world is always welcome. Former President Obama even pledged at one point that he would not speak at any schools that did not take sexual violence seriously. In my mind, President Obama, who entered office with two young daughters in tow, is the most outspoken president on the issue of sexual violence prevention that America has ever witnessed.

The aforementioned examples of Black male activism are promising as they demonstrate that Black men have it in them to organize to great effect. When inclined to speak out, the voices of Black men can garner great attention and have power to alter the national discussion. At the same time, it is telling that Black men seemingly rally in most force against

sexual violence when it takes on particular forms—namely when the alleged aggressors are White or are faceless strangers, the victims are Black,
the violence is overt, and/or the violence is suggestive of its perpetrators
having racist motivations. There appears to be more hesitation to mobi-
lize when the target is not a faceless stranger or looming White patriarchy.
This is problematic because, by most accounts, the vast majority of sexual
assaults are both intraracial and committed by someone known to the
victim.[13]

A contributor to *The Black Scholar* touched on a possible explanation
for the imbalanced responses from Black men in writing, "You are not a
man in this patriarchal world if you do not control women, if you cannot
protect your women from white men, if you do not have control over
and access to your women's sexuality as we do."[14] There is a possibility
that Black men are most motivated to act when our sense of manhood is
threatened by other people attempting to control "our" women. Never do
we muster the strength to stand and say that rape is wrong as strongly as
when our pride and perceived manhood are on the line. It is a shame to
read such a negative thread into seemingly positive efforts, but Black men
leave themselves open to such interpretations by not lending a more consistent voice to the fight against all forms of sexual violence. We can do
better. We will do better.

* * *

In the summer of 2007, I was honored to receive an invitation to a
roundtable discussion in the Boston area. All of the invitees were men who
worked against sexual violence in some fashion or another. Some were
men like me who held formal positions tasked with preventing sexual violence. Others provided their voices outside of a formal position. Many of
these men were my heroes. They wrote the books that helped me understand how men can help to end sexual violence. They gave the speeches
that inspired me to grow as a man doing this work. They marched alongside the women who had established the centers and organizations that
I counted as critical resources. All were men who overcame socialization

that taught them that "real" men did not do things like speak out against rape (either by incorporating this cause into their definition of real manhood or by rejecting the notion of real manhood altogether). All were men who understood that now was the time to correct an ugly reality that friends and loved ones experienced violence at the hands of a man far too commonly.

The roundtable attendees were of various races and sexual orientations. They hailed from nearly every region of the country, some from outside the country. Their experience ran from fresh-out-of-college to decades-old veterans of the work. The organizers understood that it takes a vast and diverse coalition of men to transform prevailing notions of manhood.

Throughout this book, I have written toward a finite mission of encouraging the parents and guardians of a particular demographic. I have spoken almost entirely to the guardians of heterosexual boys of African descent. I did this to focus my material so that it might better resonate with a particular audience and to speak to specific forces targeting Black boys. This decision made sense to me from a literary standpoint but makes less sense to me from a social justice perspective. We need men of all walks of life to speak up, as was demonstrated during that summer in Boston.

I soaked up as much as I could in those two days, but the most lasting expression those men left with me was regret. Several of the White men who had been around the movement to end violence against women for decades spoke of how multiracial collaboration should have occurred much earlier. They felt as though they had made a critical mistake in not inviting men of color into the fold sooner and admitted this with deep sadness.

That overdue invitation is now extended. My invitation came via an unexpected letter that found me in my third year of college and asked me to join a peer education group. The invitation for so many other boys is coming soon. It might take the form of a peer or loved one who says they are in need of help. It might occur when they find themselves involved in public conversation about a notable sexual assault case. It might occur when they overhear someone making a joke about rape. For a growing number of boys, it will come from a respected guardian or mentor who tells them that their voices are needed.

I grew up in a time when men were far too comfortable risking their livelihoods and values in pursuit of "hooking up." A rising generation may have a different experience. Many will choose the response expected of men and conclude that men should think about sexual violence only when it happens to one of their loved ones. But I am confident that more and more boys will decide to act in a manner that is truer to who they are. More and more boys will decide to extend their social justice perspectives to include gender-based violence. More and more boys will decide to repel age-old myths about their inherent violence by becoming visible allies. More and more boys will donate their time and financial resources to organizations throughout the country that carry the mission of providing an alternative to a socialization that trains them to be predators or apathetic bystanders. The number of Black men stepping up for change grows every day. These men are aligned with other men of all races and are collectively bolstered by the leadership and foundation set down by visionary women.

One of my favorite movies is *Glory*, the Academy Award–winning 1989 release portraying the story of the 54th Massachusetts Volunteer Regiment, one of the first African American units to fight in the American Civil War. For years, I have played it when I need a reminder of society's ability to transcend an ugly past. When I first moved to Massachusetts, my first stops were to the Boston Common and Harvard University's Houghton Library—the former because it features a monument to the 54th Massachusetts and the latter because it houses Captain Robert Gould Shaw's letters on which *Glory* is partially based.

The movie ends on the following triumphant words:

As word of their bravery spread, Congress at last authorized the raising of black troops throughout the Union. Over 180,000 volunteered.

President Lincoln credited these men of color with helping turn the tide of the war.[15]

This is not purely the work of Hollywood's imagination, as many historical scholars would support this statement. Harvard professor of African and African-American studies John Stauffer contends that President Lincoln knew that "without the support of blacks it would be impossible to win the war."[16]

History repeats itself, and the age-old war to end sexual violence in America needs an influx of Black men in order to tip the scales. The Black men who I know are absolutely relentless in interrogating social injustice. They are comfortable with maneuvering in the face of pressure as they accept stacked odds but rise to face them every day. They operate out of a legacy of pride and defiance that oozes out in an unmistakable swagger imitated around the world. Many of them already maintain a preference to resist the dominant culture rather than to acquiesce if it means sacrificing their self-identity. I know that someday soon, Black men will once again make a tide-changing addition to the ranks and that we will help bring about change that humankind has struggled for since its inception. This time, we do not stand against Confederate rifles but against the unfortunate truths that many men are violent toward women and that many more men are apathetic to this violence. The formerly disenfranchised and forgotten will once again play a role in turning the tide.

Can Sexual Violence Be Prevented? A Conversation with Dr. Susan Marine

I count Susan Marine among the long line of women who have mentored me. She has the distinction of being the initial director of both the Office of Sexual Assault Prevention and Response and the Women's Center at Harvard University. Today, she is an associate professor at Merrimack College, where she teaches higher education. She is the editor of several publications addressing sexual violence in higher education and has decades of experience studying strategies to address sexual violence.

Q: We now have several decades' worth of research on programs designed to prevent sexual violence. It seems like every program that catches on also has its share of detractors, though. Have any clear best practices emerged in your mind?

A: I do not think there is consensus on this topic. We still have very little evidence that any prevention program actually lowers the rate of perpetration, which is what you and I would call prevention. There's lots of programs that have fairly convincing evidence that they change attitudes or belief or knowledge. So, for example, there is quite a bit of evidence around bystander intervention. When students go through those programs, they come out thinking differently and they say they will act differently. Programs appear to have an effect on changing norms and attitudes, but they do not have a definitive effect on intervening in situations and, of course, bystander intervention doesn't even scratch the surface of trying to get perpetrators to change the ways they behave in the world.

Q: Then what is the value of prevention programs?

A: Prevention programming is still important to do because it does help change norms and culture. And by changing norms and culture, one of the things that we're doing is making it less likely that people will allow sexual violence to happen.

Q: Much of the research that we have obviously comes from observing college students. Do you think that the lessons learned in college settings can be translated to other environments?

A: My theory, which I think is probably accurate based on years of looking at this stuff, is that most research is in colleges because that's where the researchers are. Most of this research is done by psychologists, a little bit maybe by criminologists, and probably a little bit by sociologists. Since they work and teach on a college campus, they develop interventions and they look around and go, "I can go to my Psych 203 class and run this intervention and do outcomes testing." And that's what they do. I think you and I would both agree we need to be doing interventions with sixth graders on up.

We've learned that doing prevention education work with youth is way more complicated than we thought it was in the 1980s and 90s. We used to do these one-size-fits-all interventions where we focused on consent, on not hurting other people, and on how alcohol impairs our ability to make good decisions. I think we know now that it doesn't work to talk to everybody the same way about sexual violence.

Q: Having spent years observing and cultivating youth activism against sexual violence, what would you say is the current climate toward accepting contributions from young men of color?

A: Very little prevention programming that's targeted at young Black men is culturally relevant and addresses their very real concerns and needs as people who are constantly racialized in this society. Young Black men are already hypervigilant about being targeted by police. That all has to be taken into account, and I'm guessing that most prevention programming is done by nice, middle-aged White ladies like me. I think it's a really exciting time for activism and especially student activism on this issue. I am so energized by talking to these young people. They are so committed to what they're doing. They are so thoughtful about what they're doing. They are so strategic. It truly is a movement that is not just White women.

CHAPTER 9: TEACHING BOYS THAT THEY HAVE A PLACE IN A GLOBAL MOVEMENT

- Instilling boys with the drive to stand against violence is only half of the battle. They will be best suited to make a difference if they give some consideration to their roles as men in a movement traditionally populated by women and if they take the time to study the efficacy of past efforts. Fortunately, there are many resources throughout the country with training programs specifically geared toward young adults and men.

- Intuitive educational efforts to fight sexual violence might have unintentional consequences. After all, we were all raised in a culture where sexual violence is normalized. It is best that boys who want to help seek out training and guidance from more experienced educators.

- There is an international movement to end sexual violence against women. Joining it does not require boys to join any organizations or attend any conferences (though they should consider doing so in order to acquire much-needed training). They can contribute just by sharing their voices in their existing environments.

- Examples of Black men organizing against sexual violence are out there for those who care to find them. In organizing, Black men must be mindful that they are not motivated by a need to control Black women. Motivations matter.

- Many Black boys possess a heightened ability and willingness to detect race-based prejudice. They can utilize these faculties in order to recognize the cultural forces that create sexual violence.

I wrote this book because I saw a hole in the literary resources available to caretakers of boys. With this said, there are many books that go deeper into subject matter covered in this book or touch on different aspects of it. The available library is truly filling out. Consider the titles listed here if you have a reader in your life or are looking for additional reading yourself. Many of these books helped to develop me along my personal journey.

I have limited this list to titles that I have read personally. There are many other great books that I simply have not read, so please research further if you need more. I have included the publication dates as some of these books may use reference points that are dated depending on the age of the reader. I should also warn that most of the referenced authors talk openly and candidly about their experiences with sex, sexuality, and violence. You might want to preview them if you are uncertain if they are age-appropriate.

If you are looking for a deeper dive into the scope of men's violence against women, consider the following:

Arrested Justice: Black Women, Violence, and America's Prison Nation by Beth E. Richie (2012)
Violence in the Lives of Black Women: Battered Black and Blue by Carolyn M. West, Ph.D. (2002)

I largely glossed over sexual violence from the perspective of survivors. Here are some good titles if you are looking for their perspectives as well as insight into the process of recovery:

I Will Survive: The African-American Guide to Healing from Sexual Assault and Abuse by Lori S. Robinson (2002)
Surviving the Silence: Black Women's Stories of Rape by Charlotte Pierce-Baker (1998)

There are many other men who examine manhood and its connections to violence. Here are a few of my favorites. Several of them are also by African American authors if that is something that you are looking for:

Breaking Out of the "Man Box": The Next Generation of Manhood by Tony Porter (2015)
Cool Pose: The Dilemmas of Black Manhood in America by Richard Majors and Janet Mancini Billson (1992)
Who's Gonna Take The Weight?: Manhood, Race, and Power in America by Kevin Powell (2003)
The Macho Paradox: Why Some Men Hurt Women and How All Men Can Help by Jackson Katz (2006)
You Throw Like a Girl: The Blind Spot of Masculinity by Don McPherson (2019)
The Tough Standard: The Hard Truths About Masculinity and Violence by Ronald F. Levant and Shana Pryor (2020)

If you are looking for a Black woman's perspective on Black manhood and its contributions to violence, bell hooks is one of the best in my mind:

We Real Cool: Black Men and Masculinity by bell hooks (2004)
The Will to Change: Men, Masculinity, and Love by bell hooks (2004)

You are welcome to disagree, but I believe that pornography's contributions to boys' development are vastly ignored. Here are a few titles that explore the pornography industry and its potential effects in greater detail:

Getting Off: Pornography and the End of Masculinity by Robert Jensen (2007)
Pornland: How Porn Has Hijacked Our Sexuality by Gail Dines (2010)

Lastly, if you are looking for an overview of men's historical involvement in the American movement to end sexual violence, then I recommend *Some Men: Feminist Allies and the Movement to End Violence Against Women* by Michael A. Messner, Max A. Greenberg, and Tal Peretz (2015).

Helpful Tips for Productive Conversations

I have learned a lot in talking to male audiences about sexual violence. Most of these talks have gone well but others have not, so I want you to learn from my experiences.

BOYS WANT TO TALK

First and foremost, do not ever forget that boys want to talk about sexual violence. They may not necessarily want to talk to *you* about it, but they do want to talk to someone. I have many times led discussions with boys in school settings only for faculty and staff to remark on how boys who do not normally speak up had things to say. Boys have fears. Boys have hopes. Boys have questions. Boys have opinions on the laws, policies, and norms that govern sexual behavior as well as the cultures that surround it. They just need a venue to release those thoughts and feelings.

THERE ARE RESOURCES

I was fortunate to get into antiviolence work at a time when there were a host of books, videos, and organizations that I could turn to as reminders that I was not alone on my journey. Things get better every year, and there are now even plenty of resources on social media and video-sharing platforms that you can turn to if you need backup. Many of these resources are free and available to the public. If you are having trouble finding the right words, try visiting YouTube, Google, or Twitter and you might be surprised at what you find.

BOYS DO NOT NEED TO GO ANYWHERE IN ORDER TO MAKE A DIFFERENCE

You may be thinking that the young men to whom you want to speak are not really the types to be standing on stage and sharing their voices. Or perhaps they already have a lot going on and cannot possibly cram another activity into their schedules. Note that they do not need to join any groups or even change their activities in order to help. While it would be ideal if boys linked up with personnel who could train them, the issue of sexual violence has a way of finding them regardless. It will find them when discussion of the latest high-profile case makes it into their classrooms and locker rooms. It will find them when one of their friends makes a joke about a survivor getting what she deserved. It will find them as they grow into adulthood and have intimate experiences where their consciences do not align with their instructions as men. And it will find them when loved ones reveal hurtful experiences. I went through most of these experiences without anybody previously talking to me about what to do. Fortunately, your boys have you.

TIME IS ON YOUR SIDE

When I work with audiences, I generally only get one shot at it. I have to tell them everything that I want to say in a condensed period with no chance for follow-up. That is usually just enough time to scratch the surface of the conversation that needs to occur. The good news is that you have the opportunity to follow up if things do not initially go well.

You can also break up the conversation into smaller portions in order to allow for time to process and reflect. In my personal life, I have had several conversations with men who were defensive at first, only for the same men to return at later times with different perspectives. Time can be a valuable ally.

Here are a few websites that are helpful resources for informal antiviolence educators:

www.rainn.org
The Rape, Abuse & Incest National Network is perhaps best known for maintaining a 24/7 hotline for survivors. Their site also features an extensive library of statistics, policy briefs, and summaries of criminal statutes.

www.nsvrc.org
The National Sexual Violence Resource Center is a nonprofit that provides resources for preventing and responding to sexual violence. Their site offers podcasts, blogs, and publications that are searchable by topic.

www.bjs.gov
The Bureau of Justice Statistics, an agency under the U.S. Department of Justice, regularly publishes consolidated reports on violent crimes throughout the country. I particularly like using their work because it is a little more difficult for people to discredit the Department of Justice as having an agenda to overinflate violence statistics as people may do with other sources.

www.itsonus.org
Launched out of President Obama's White House, It's On Us is a wide-reaching educational initiative targeting young men that features a truly impressive list of supporters. The boys who you know will surely have an organization or celebrity who they admire among them. It's On Us focuses its prevention education on bystander intervention, education on consent,

and survivor support, so it operationalizes many of the concepts in this book on a national scale.

www.cdc.gov

Given the scope of sexual violence, the Centers for Disease Control and Prevention rightly views it as a public health concern. They have created a fantastic collection of publications with content on preventing sexual violence.

www.culturereframed.org

If you want to further explore the impact of pornography on boys, Culture Reframed is a nonprofit organization that has compiled resources to assist with this. Their website features books, videos, websites, and research articles. They even provide free parent programs to assist parents in facilitating conversations about pornography with children and adolescents.

Here are some myths that you are likely to encounter when you have open conversations with boys:

1. *Most reports of sexual violence are false reports*: The belief that most women and men who formally disclose victimization are lying is not at all supported by research. Research consistently finds that false reports are extremely rare.

2. *Most assaults are committed by hyper-violent masked strangers*: Research points to sexual violence as somewhat normalized behavior. Many of those who perpetrate it are not overtly violent outcasts but "normal" guys who function in society just fine.

3. *"Real" victims physically resist encounters and report them to authorities immediately after they occur*: Any professional who works with survivors of sexual violence will likely tell you that they have encountered all kinds of responses to violence. They probably have met people who froze during assaults while they processed what was happening, people who made conscious decisions not to resist for fear of escalating violence, people who got angry and fought back, and on and on. They probably have met victims who decided to immediately report to authorities after assaults, victims who wanted to make their story public after years of deliberation, and victims who wanted to keep things as private as possible. There

is no universal response to violence, and we cannot use a victim's response as a definitive revelation of what occurred.

4. *Sexual assault does not have anything to do with you*: Perhaps the clearest message from statistics is that a boy is an extreme anomaly if sexual violence does not touch him in his lifetime. Almost assuredly he will have a friend or family member who has survived this violence, will survive it himself, or will even perpetrate it himself, knowingly or otherwise.

Leading Case Studies Involving Celebrities

INTRODUCTION

There is seemingly always a celebrity facing a publicized allegation of sexual violence. Because the national conversation about these allegations is intense and widespread, these cases offer a window into public attitudes about sexual violence and its aftermath. Chances are that the boys in your life already have opinions about these cases, so they offer an opportunity for intergenerational conversation about sexual violence in which all parties have at least a basic understanding of "the facts." Here are a few ground rules and key lessons that you may want to consider during your conversation.

KEEP THINGS NEUTRAL

Rapes and sexual assault are vastly underreported crimes. Many victims never disclose what happens to them to the criminal justice system or to formal counseling personnel. From listening to survivors, we know some of the most common reasons why victims do not report. Top among them are fears of being ridiculed or not being believed. Therefore, the ways we choose to discuss allegations against public figures or anyone else have an impact on how survivors view the cultural climate and whether or not they choose to report. Furthermore, while celebrities are in the public domain, many of their reported victims are not. You do not have to get into the weeds of an alleged incident in order to have a productive conversation about acceptable behavior.

FOCUS ON BOYS

Many boys will naturally gravitate to discussing the behaviors of reported victims. For example, they might want to know why somebody would wait years to report or delve into the intentions of a woman who voluntarily consented to some form of a relationship with the alleged perpetrator. You should assess the value of such questions in talking to boys and ensure that they are not distracting boys from considering their own behaviors— which is ultimately why we are talking to boys.

CONTEXTUALIZE THE DECISIONS OF SURVIVORS

Many people place some or all of the blame for what occurred on victims by pointing out their decisions that led to the assault. Many of these decisions make perfect sense once you consider that these people were interacting with somebody who they trusted. To the extent that you find it useful to discuss the actions of an alleged victim, help boys understand the factors that contribute to the decision-making of victims before, during, and after assaults. Most importantly, remind them that they cannot speak for the intent and feelings of another person.

KEY LESSONS TO LEARN

The general public will never know exactly what occurred between an alleged perpetrator and an alleged victim in many cases. Most of us only have the allegations and rumors circulated by the media and our peers to go on. Nonetheless, there are generally some conclusions that we can draw with certainty. Each of them makes for a vital lesson to be learned by boys:

Many People Do Not Understand Consent

There are many conceivable reasons why a woman would voluntarily seek out contact with a celebrity. Some may be seeking the approval of a respected member of their career field. Some may desire a deeper relationship with a trusted friend or mentor. Some may indeed want some form of sexual contact. None of these scenarios precludes somebody from betraying their trust and committing a sexual assault.

A large portion of the public believes that consenting to being alone with a person or consenting to intimate contact of any form counts as consent to any and all sexual activity. However, this belief is not reflected in the majority of criminal laws and school policies. Boys who believe this run the risk of wrongly assuming that they have obtained consent from a partner.

Sexual Behavior Has Impact

There are profound consequences to the choices that celebrities make behind closed doors beyond the potential loss of their freedom and livelihood. Communities are divided and involved parties have their lives affected in irrevocable ways. Disruption to community and family is by no means specific to allegations against big-time celebrities. It is rather common for incidents to be tried in the court of public opinion regardless of whether or not participants are household names.

Many young men articulate a fear of being wrongly accused of impropriety, and we often see these fears projected in the defense of men publicly accused of violence. If they are so worried about such things, remind them that they have agency in choosing how much risk they are inviting. For example, if they choose to engage in sexual encounters with partners whom they do not know well and/or they believe to be capable of maliciously accusing them, then they must accept the risks introduced by these choices.

Young men who are fearful of false accusations should also be reminded that they can create personal behavioral standards that are well above those required by laws and policies. It should be enough for them to avoid sexual encounters that run the risk of partners feeling disrespected even if these encounters do not rise to the level of a criminal or school violation. Fear of harming another person or a community ought to be enough to drive the decision-making of boys and young men.

If You Are Approached as a Friend, Then Respond as a Friend

Responding to a public accusation involving a celebrity is one thing, but boys should strongly reconsider talk of false accusations if a friend discloses an experience to them. Feeling believed is a vital contributor to a survivor's recovery process. There are personnel and systems in place tasked with determining what occurred, so boys do not have to take on that role. They should focus on their role as a friend when supporting a survivor.

Talking to Boys About False Accusations

If you are going to work with boys, you absolutely must expect discussion of false accusations. "What's to stop somebody from lying and destroying an innocent person's reputation?" boys might say. Boys are not alone in thinking this. Somebody brings up false accusations every time that I am required to take a training on sexual assault at my workplace.

The issue of false rape accusations is complicated. On the one hand, we cannot ignore the fact that they happen, and I do not want to discount anybody who has been falsely accused. If you or someone you know finds themselves in this situation, it is only right to defend yourself. But many boys automatically respond to any and all claims of sexual violence by saying that the allegations are false. This promotes rape culture and damages growing societal awareness of sexual violence and its impact.

It is important to know that every credible measure of false accusations shows that they are rare. Many boys do not find this very reassuring, though. They would likely have concern if even one case out of a hundred was false. Here are some additional arguments that I have found helpful in discussing false accusations.

FALSE REPORTS AND SEXUAL VIOLENCE ARE NOT MUTUALLY EXCLUSIVE

1. There are epidemic levels of violence in America.
2. Some people make false claims for perceived personal gain.

Both of these statements are true, and neither can be ignored. Often when I talk to somebody about the latest allegation in the headlines, they respond with a story about some man whose life was ruined by a false accusation, as if one person's reality invalidates that of another.

Rape culture and the nature of sexual violence are far too complex to be summed up by believing that every person who comes forth with an allegation is either telling the truth or is maliciously lying. The much messier truth lies in between these extremes. We live in a country in which some routinely violent men are admired by their peers, while some nonviolent men unjustly spend years behind bars or in infamy. We have to elevate our awareness and our conversation to match the complexity of these issues.

WE HOLD REPORTS OF SEXUAL VIOLENCE TO A DIFFERENT STANDARD THAN REPORTS OF OTHER CRIMES

Those who complain about the potential for abuse of sexual assault allegations are not wrong. Some complainants exaggerate or outright falsify their claims. Juries and judges cannot be wholly separated from the prejudices that they hold. And the court of public opinion often makes up its mind irrespective of what a judicial body says. But the same can be said for most crimes.

While our judicial processes are imperfect across the board, sexual violence is the most likely baby to get tossed out when we examine the dirty bath water of the criminal justice system.

There are few human institutions, if any, that people cannot abuse for personal gain. But we cannot allow the very real potential for abuse to prevent us from taking a stand against very real violence that affects hundreds of thousands of Americans. One could argue that sexual violence is especially prone to false accusations and their effects because conclusive physical evidence proving or disproving consent can sometimes be difficult to identify. But demanding a flawless criminal justice system before we take allegations seriously is to ignore very real violence that takes place every day. People have the right to seek justice for acts committed against them even if we have not figured out how to perfectly process accusations—and we seem to understand this just fine with other crimes.

WE HAVE ALREADY ACHIEVED HEIGHTENED AWARENESS OF FALSE ACCUSATIONS

You may want to create a world where people who make false accusations are demonized. A world where people have to think hard about the merits of a claim of victimization before they step forward. A world where claims are vigorously pulled apart and scrutinized. But we have already accomplished all of this.

If you think that we live in a world where one can lightly bring forth an accusation, then you have not been paying attention. Legitimate survivors of atrocious behaviors routinely report their fears of reprisal and scrutiny as keeping them from reporting (boys immediately bringing up false accusations is, in itself, evidence that such fears are warranted). And, judging by incidence reports, we have a long way to go before those who initiate sexual activity without consent have a similar fear to make them think twice about acting inappropriately.

INTRODUCTION

1. Michele C. Black, Kathleen C. Basile, Matthew J. Breiding, Sharon G. Smith, Mikel L. Walters, Melissa T. Merrick, Jieru Chen, and Mark R. Stevens, *The National Intimate Partner and Sexual Violence Survey: 2010 Summary Report* (Atlanta, GA: National Center for Injury Prevention and Control, Centers for Disease Control and Prevention, November 2011), https://www.cdc.gov/violenceprevention/pdf/nisvs_report2010-a.pdf.

CHAPTER 1

1. Charlotte Pierce-Baker, *Surviving the Silence: Black Women's Stories of Rape* (New York: W.W. Norton & Company, 1998), 114–115.
2. Sharon G. Smith, Xinjian Zhang, Kathleen C. Basile, Melissa T. Merrick, Jing Wang, Marcie-jo Kresnow, and Jieru Chen, *The National Intimate Partner and Sexual Violence Survey: 2015 Data Brief—Updated Release* (Atlanta, GA: Centers for Disease Control and Prevention, National Center for Injury Prevention and Control, November 2018), https://www.cdc.gov/violenceprevention/pdf/2015data-brief508.pdf. An excellent overview of intimate violence committed against Black women can be found in Dr. Carolyn M., West's "Battered Black and Blue: An Overview of Violence in the Lives of Black Women" in *Violence in the Lives of Black Women: Battered, Black, and Blue* (Philadelphia: Haworth Press, 2002).
3. Christopher P. Krebs, Christine H. Lindquist, Tara D. Warner, Bonnie S. Fisher, and Sandra L. Martin, *The Campus Sexual Assault Study* (Washington, D.C.: National Institute of Justice, Bureau of Justice Statistics, U.S. Department of Justice, October 2007), https://www.ncjrs.gov/App/Publications/abstract.aspx?ID=243011.
4. Rachel E. Morgan and Barbara A. Oudekerk, *Criminal Victimization, 2018* (Washington, D.C.: Bureau of Justice Statistics, U.S. Department of Justice, Office of Justice Programs, September 2019), https://www.ojp.gov/ncjrs/virtual-library/abstracts/criminal-victimization-2018.
5. Patricia Tjaden and Nancy Theonnes, *Full Report of the Prevalence, Incidence, and Consequences of Violence Against Women: Findings from the National Violence*

Against Women Survey (Washington, D.C.: National Institute of Justice, Office of Justice Programs, November 2000), https://nij.ojp.gov/library/publications/full-report-prevalence-incidence-and-consequences-violence-against-women.

6. Callie Marie Rennison and Sarah Welchans, *Bureau of Justice Statistics Special Report: Intimate Partner Violence* (Washington, D.C.: U.S. Department of Justice, Office of Justice Programs, Bureau of Justice Statistics, May 2000), https://bjs.ojp.gov/content/pub/pdf/ipv.pdf.

7. Michael Planty, Lynn Langton, Christopher Krebs, Marcus Berzofsky, and Hope Smiley-McDonald, *Female Victims of Sexual Violence, 1994–2010* (Washington, D.C.: Department of Justice, Office of Justice Programs, Bureau of Justice Statistics, March 2013), https://bjs.ojp.gov/content/pub/pdf/fvsv9410.pdf.

8. Megan R. Greeson, Rebecca Campbell, and Giannina Fehler-Cabral, "'Nobody Deserves This': Adolescent Sexual Assault Victims' Perceptions of Disbelief and Victim Blame from Police," *Journal of Community Psychology* 44, no. 1 (January 2016): 90–110.

9. Black et al., *National Intimate Partner and Sexual Violence Survey: 2010 Summary Report*.

10. Shannon Morrison, Jennifer Hardison, Anita Mathew, and Joyce O'Neil, *An Evidence-Based Review of Sexual Assault Preventive Intervention Programs* (Washington, D.C.: National Institute of Justice, September 2004), https://www.ojp.gov/ncjrs/virtual-library/abstracts/evidence-based-review-sexual-assault-preventive-intervention.

CHAPTER 2

1. Don McPherson, *You Throw Like a Girl: The Blind Spot of Masculinity* (New York: Edge of Sports, 2019), 14.

2. Tony Porter, *Breaking Out of the "Man Box": The Next Generation of Manhood* (New York: Skyhorse Publishing, 2015), Chapter 2 [Kindle].

3. This account is largely based on an article appearing in the July 2, 2003, edition of *Philadelphia Weekly* (http://www.philadelphiaweekly.com/news-and-opinion/cover-story/rap_sheet_concerto-38368719.html).

4. See "Consequences of Masculinity" in *The Tough Standard: The Hard Truths About Masculinity and Violence* by R. F. Levant and S. Pryor (New York: Oxford University Press, 2020), 35–47, for a summary of negative outcomes correlated with men.

5. Smith et al., *National Intimate Partner and Sexual Violence Survey: 2015 Data Brief*.

6. bell hooks, *The Will to Change: Men, Masculinity, and Love* (New York: Washington Square Press, 2004), 72–73.

7. Julia T. Wood and Natalie Fixmer-Oraiz, *Gendered Lives: Communication, Gender, and Culture* (Boston: Cengage Learning, 2015).

CHAPTER 3

1. Martine Hébert, Catherine Moreau, Martin Blais, Francine Lavoie, and Mireille Guerrier, "Child Sexual Abuse as a Risk Factor for Teen Dating Violence: Findings

from a Representative Sample of Quebec Youth," *Journal of Child & Adolescent Trauma* 10, no. 1 (March 2017): 51–62, https://www.ncbi.nlm.nih.gov/pmc/articles/PMC5756079/.

2. Black Women's Blueprint, *When Truth Is Justice and Not Enough: Executive Summary to the Black Women's Truth and Reconciliation Commission Report*, https://www.blackwomensblueprint.org/truth-commission.

3. Bureau of Justice Statistics, U.S. Department of Justice, *Criminal Victimization in the United States, 2002 Statistical Tables: National Crime Victimization Survey*, December 2003.

4. Jay-Z, "Blueprint 2," *The Blueprint 2: The Gift & the Curse*, Roc-A-Fella, 2002.

5. D.J. Jazzy Jeff and The Fresh Prince, "Girls Ain't Nothing but Trouble," *Rock the House*, Jive/RCA, 1987.

6. National Sexual Violence Resource Center, *False Reporting: Overview*, 2012, https://www.nsvrc.org/sites/default/files/2012-03/Publications_NSVRC_Overview_False-Reporting.pdf.

CHAPTER 4

1. "Strauss-Kahn Dismisses Prostitute's Gang Rape Claims as 'Public Lynching Campaign,' " *Asian News International*, May 5, 2012. Accessed June 26, 2012, via Infotrac Newstand.

2. Morgan and Oudekerk, *Criminal Victimization, 2018*.

3. Angela Y. Davis, *Women, Race and Class* (New York: Vintage Books, 1981), 197–198.

4. The best-known test of hidden biases is likely Project Implicit's Implicit Association Test (https://implicit.harvard.edu/implicit/aboutus.html).

CHAPTER 5

1. Davis, *Women, Race, and Class*.

2. "Roasted Alive," *New York World*, December 7, 1899, in Ralph Ginzburg, *100 Years of Lynching* (Baltimore: Black Classic Press, 1988), 29.

3. "She Denies Rapist Was Black," *Atlanta Constitution*, December 2, 1920, in Ginzburg, *100 Years of Lynching*, 68.

4. Leon Litwack, "Hellhounds," in James Allen, Hilton Als, John Lewis, and Leon Litwack, *Without Sanctuary: Lynching Photography in America* (Santa Fe, NM: Twin Palms Publishers, 2003), 8–10.

5. "Sam Holt Burned at Stake," *Kissimmee Valley Gazette*, April 28, 1899, in Ginzburg, *100 Years of Lynching*, 10–11.

6. Ginzburg, *100 Years of Lynching*, 18.

7. "Confederate Veterans Deplore Lynching Except for Rape," *New York Sun*, March 22, 1904, in Ginzburg, *100 Years of Lynching*, 68.

8. Associated Press State & Local Wire, "Bernhard Says Report on Comments Was Misleading," October 2, 2008. Accessed via LexisNexis Academic.

9. "Funniest Jokes." Accessed March 11, 2003, http://rotteneggs.com/r3/show/se/30689.html.

10. Randall Kennedy, *Nigger* (New York: Vintage Books, 2003), 7.

11. "Black/Nigger Jokes." Accessed March 25, 2005, http://www.funfreepages.com/text/black_nigger_jokes.php.

12. Ibid.

13. Kenneth Stern, "Hate and the Internet," *Journal of Hate Studies* 1, no. 1 (2001/2002): 57. Accessed October 3, 2005, via EBSCOhost.

14. *New Nation News—Dark Crime.* Accessed October 3, 2005, http://www.newnation.org/NNN-dark-crime.html.

15. Elmore Leonard, *Out of Sight* (New York: Delacorte Press, 1996), 291.

16. Marina Miller and Jay Hewitt, "Conviction of a Defendant as a Function of Juror-Victim Racial Similarity," *Journal of Social Psychology* 105, no. 1 (June 1978): 159. Accessed October 3, 2005, via EBSCOhost.

17. For a comprehensive review of the effects of racial bias on the criminal justice system, I highly recommend Michelle Alexander, *The New Jim Crow: Mass Incarceration in the Age of Colorblindness* (New York: New Press, 2010).

18. See David Balser, "Dixon Case Bound by Law's Constraints," *Atlanta Journal-Constitution*, March 22, 2004, 11A. Accessed October 25, 2005, via LexisNexis Academic. See Chandler Brown, "Genarlow Wilson: College Next Step to Freed Offender," *Atlanta Journal-Constitution*, January 11, 2008, Main Edition. Accessed July 28, 2008, via LexisNexis Academic.

19. Balser, "Dixon Case Bound by Law's Constraints."

20. Nayaba Arinde, "Supporters Tell City: 'Compensate the Central Park Jogger 5,'" New York *Amsterdam News*, May 25, 2011, http://amsterdamnews.com/news/2011/may/25/supporters-tell-city-compensate-the-central-park/.

21. R. Steinback, "Central Park Jogger Case Is Study in False Confessions," *Miami Herald*, December 18, 2002. Accessed July 28, 2008, via LexisNexis Academic.

22. Tom Weir and Erik Brady, "In Sexual Assault Cases, Athletes Usually Walk," *USA Today*, December 22, 2003, First Edition: Cover Story.

23. Peter Heller, *Bad Intentions: The Mike Tyson Story* (New York: Nal Books, 1989), 98.

24. Ellis Cashmore, *Tyson: Nurture of the Beast* (Malden, MA: Polity Press, 2005), 7.

25. Much of my recounting of Tyson's career is drawn from Heller, *Bad Intentions*.

26. José Torres, *Fire & Fear: The Inside Story of Mike Tyson* (New York: Warner Books, 1989), 107, 132.

27. Christopher D. Maxwell, Amanda L. Robinson, and Lori A. Post, "The Impact of Race on the Adjudication of Sexual Assault and Other Violent Crimes," *Journal of Criminal Justice* 31, no. 6 (2003): 523–538.

28. Nicole Varelas and Linda A. Foley, "Blacks' and Whites' Perceptions of Interracial and Intraracial Date Rape," *Journal of Social Psychology* 138, no. 3 (1998): 392–400.

29. "Internet Pornography Statistics." Accessed January 10, 2012, http://internet-filter-review.toptenreviews.com/internet-pornography-statistics.html.

30. Ibid.

31. Gail Dines, *Pornland: How Porn Has Hijacked Our Sexuality* (Boston: Beacon Press, 2010), 121.

32. Accessed July 25, 2008, http://www.mandingogirl.com/myxxxinterracial.html.

33. Accessed July 25, 2008, http://www.daddysworstnightmare.com .

34. The anti-pornography activists referenced in this section primarily refer to writers such as Dr. Robert Jensen and Dr. Gail Dines, whose works have definitely influenced my thinking on pornography.

35. "5 Old-Timey Prejudices That Still Show Up in Every Movie." Accessed January 6, 2011, http://www.cracked.com/article_19549_5-old-timey-prejudices-that-still-show-up-in-every-movie.html.

CHAPTER 6

1. *Chris Rock: Bring the Pain*, Universal Music, 2002.

2. Terry Spencer, "Girl's Death Sparks Debate over Wrestling's Influence," Associated Press, April 15, 2000, and Jill Barton, "Despite Boy's Release, Harsh Punishments for Juveniles Stand," Associated Press, January 30, 2004.

3. Jenny Dills, Dawn Fowler, and Gayle Payne, *Sexual Violence on Campus: Strategies for Prevention* (Atlanta, GA: National Center for Injury Prevention and Control, Centers for Disease Control and Prevention, 2016).

4. David Banner and Lil' Flip, "Like a Pimp," SRC/Universal Records, 2003.

5. 2Pac, "Keep Ya Head Up," Interscope/Atlantic Records, 1993.

6. Kendrick Lamar, "Keisha's Song (Her Pain)," Top Dawg Entertainment, 2011.

7. R. Kelly, "Your Body's Callin'," Jive, 1993.

8. A. O. Scott, "Blacks Being Themselves, Not Symbols," *New York Times*, January 19, 2003. Accessed April 27, 2005, via Newsbank.

9. Esther Iverem, "Not All of Us Are Oscar Happy." Accessed April 27, 2005, http://www.seeingblack.com/x032802/post_oscars.shtml.

10. *Belly.* Accessed October 23, 2008, http://en.wikipedia.org/wiki/Belly_(film).

11. Centers for Disease Control and Prevention, "The Social-Ecological Model: A Framework for Prevention." Accessed April 16, 2021, https://www.cdc.gov/violenceprevention/about/social-ecologicalmodel.html.

12. The Harvard School of Public Health's website has an excellent summary of the Project. Accessed February 13, 2012, http://www.hsph.harvard.edu/research/chc/harvard-alcohol-project/.

13. Accessed February 12, 2012, http://music.yahoo.com/various-artists/news/--12028807.

CHAPTER 7

1. Angeline Bernabe and Suzanne Yeo, "Arkansas Woman Killed Running: What Women Should Know to Stay Safe on Outdoor Runs," *ABC News*, August 24, 2020. Accessed October 10, 2020, https://abcnews.go.com/GMA/News/arkansas-woman-killed-running-women-stay-safe-outdoor/story?id=72560802.

2. Nas, "Daughters," Def Jam, 2012.

3. Michael E. Miller, "'A Steep Price to Pay for 20 Minutes of Action': Dad Defends Stanford Sex Offender," *Washington Post*, June 6, 2016. Accessed October 12, 2020, https://www.washingtonpost.com/news/morning-mix/wp/2016/06/06/a-steep-price-to-pay-for-20-minutes-of-action-dad-defends-stanford-sex-offender/.

4. Smith et al., *National Intimate Partner and Sexual Violence Survey: 2015 Data Brief.*

5. Centers for Disease Control and Prevention, "NISVS: An Overview of 2010 Findings on Victimization by Sexual Orientation." Accessed April 11, 2021, https://www.cdc.gov/violenceprevention/pdf/cdc_nisvs_victimization_final-a.pdf.

6. Tawandra L. Rowell-Cunsolo, Roderick J. Harrison, and Rahwa Haile, "Exposure to Prison Sexual Assault Among Incarcerated Black Men," *Journal of African American Studies* 18, no. 1 (March 2014): 54–62. Accessed April 17, 2021, via Academic Search Complete.

7. Kaili Calasso, Carly Thomson-Memmer, Aaron J. Kruse-Diehr, and Tavis Glassman, "Sexual Assault and Alcohol Use Among College Students," *American Journal of Health Studies* 34, no. 4 (2019): 162–173. Accessed April 17, 2021, via Academic Search Complete.

8. National Institute of Justice, *The Campus Sexual Assault Study*, October 2007. Accessed October 10, 2020, https://www.ncjrs.gov/App/Publications/abstract.aspx?ID=243011.

9. I rely on some existing compilations as well as individual studies to arrive at this list:

> Antonia Abbey, Angela Jacques-Tiura, and James M. LeBreton, "Risk Factors for Sexual Aggression in Young Men: An Expansion of the Confluence Model," *Aggressive Behavior* 37 (2011): 450–464. Accessed April 11, 2021, via Academic Search Complete.
>
> Joetta L. Carr and Karen M. VanDeusen, "Risk Factors for Male Sexual Aggression on College Campuses," *Journal of Family Violence* 19, no. 5 (October 2004): 279–289.
>
> Centers for Disease Control and Prevention, *Risk and Protective Factors.* Accessed April 11, 2021, https://www.cdc.gov/violenceprevention/sexualviolence/riskprotectivefactors.html.
>
> John D. Foubert, *The Men's Program: A Peer Education Guide to Rape Prevention* (New York: Routledge, 2005), 130–131.
>
> Tina Zawacki, Antonia Abbey, Philip O. Buck, Pamela McAuslan, and A. Monique Clinton-Sherrod, "Perpetrators of Alcohol-Involved Sexual Assaults: How Do They Differ From Other Sexual Assault Perpetrators and Nonperpetrators?" *Aggressive Behavior* 29 (2003): 266–380.

10. John D. Foubert, Johnathan T. Newberry, and Jerry Tatum, "Behavior Differences Seven Months Later: Effects of a Rape Prevention Program on First-Year Men Who Join Fraternities," *Journal of Student Affairs Research and Practice* 44 (2007): 728–749. Accessed April 17, 2021, via Academic Search Complete.

11. Taylor Martinez, Jacquelyn D. Wiersma-Mosley, Kristen N. Jozkowski, and Jennifer Becnel, "'Good Guys Don't Rape': Greek and Non-Greek College Student Perpetrator Rape Myths," *Behavioral Sciences* 8, no. 7 (July 2018): 60.

12. "Daisy Coleman, Subject of Netflix Documentary 'Audrie & Daisy' Dies by Suicide at 23," *NBC News*, August 5, 2020, https://www.nbcnews.com/news/us-news/daisy-coleman-star-netflix-documentary-audrie-daisy-dies-suicide-23-n1235917.

CHAPTER 8

1. Steve Almasy, "Two Teens Found Guilty in Steubenville Rape Case," *CNN*, March 17, 2013. Accessed October 13, 2020, https://www.cnn.com/2013/03/17/justice/ohio-steubenville-case/index.html.
2. Janelle Griffith, "Facebook Video of Sexual Assault Found by Teenage Victim's Mother Leads to 7 Arrests," *NBC News*, September 3, 2020. Accessed October 3, 2020, https://www.nbcnews.com/news/us-news/facebook-video-sexual-assault-found-teenage-victim-s-mother-leads-n1239204.
3. Bibb Latane and John M. Darley, *The Unresponsive Bystander: Why Doesn't He Help?* (New York: Appleton-Century Crofts, 1970).
4. "The 3 Ds of Sexual Assault Prevention," *Campus Safety*, August 25, 2011. Accessed April 11, 2021, https://www.campussafetymagazine.com/university/the-3-ds-of-sexual-assault-prevention/.
5. David Lisak and Paul M. Miller, "Repeat Rape and Multiple Offending Among Undetected Rapists," *Violence and Victims* 17, no. 1 (2002): 73–84.
6. John D. Foubert, *The Men's Program: A Peer Education Guide to Rape Prevention* (New York: Routledge, 2005).

CHAPTER 9

1. Larry Brown, "Serena Williams Puts up Provocative Twitter Picture." Accessed February 21, 2012, http://network.yardbarker.com/tennis/article_external/serena_williams_puts_up_provocative_twitter_picture/4720055.
2. Chris Chase, "Serena Williams' Controversial Twitter Picture: Was It Over the Line?" Accessed February 21, 2012, http://sports.yahoo.com/tennis/blog/busted_racquet/post/Serena-Williams-8217-controversial-Twitter-pic?urn=ten-wp643.
3. The subject ad can be seen at http://feministing.com/2011/12/07/pa-liquor-control-board-to-teens-rape-is-your-fault-and-your-friends-fault/. Accessed February 24, 2012.
4. Accessed November 5, 2005, http://www.virginia.edu/uvatours/rotunda/rotunda-History.html.
5. Tom Weir, "Critics See More Airheads in Clubhouse," *USA Today*, May 7, 2008. Accessed February 25, 2012, via GeneralOneFile.
6. "Intel Apologizes for 'Insulting' Sprinter Ad." Accessed February 23, 2012, http://gizmodo.com/285278/intel-apologizes-for-insulting-sprinter-ad.
7. L. Litman, "'Bros' and 'Hos': Explaining Harvard Men's Participation in the Movement to End Sexual Violence with Theories of Women, Gender and Sexuality," January 2006.
8. Martin Luther King, Jr., *I Have a Dream: Writings and Speeches That Changed the World* (San Francisco: HarperSanFrancisco, 1986), 85.
9. America's Intelligence Wire, "Duke: New Black Panthers Plan Protest in Support of Duke Rape Accuser," 2016. Accessed June 17, 2012, via General OneFile.

10. Susan Taylor Martin, "A Case of Hate: Attack on N.Y. Girl, and Reaction to It, Stirs Racial Tensions," *St. Petersburg Times*, 1998. Accessed November 2, 2008, via LexisNexis Academic.

11. Lori S. Robinson, *I Will Survive: The African-American Guide to Healing from Sexual Assault and Abuse* (New York: Seal Press, 2002), 239–241.

12. Christi Parsons, "Obama Condemns Todd Akin's 'Legitimate Rape' Comments." Accessed August 26, 2012, https://www.latimes.com/politics/la-xpm-2012-aug-20-la-pn-todd-akin-obama-reaction-20120820-story.html.

13. These findings are replicated in numerous studies. For example, a study conducted by Black Women's Blueprint ("When Truth is Justice and Not Enough") concluded that 91% of participating Black survivors "identified the harm doer as Black."

14. Charles Lawrence III, "Cringing at Myths of Black Sexuality," *The Black Scholar* 22, no. 1 & 2 (2001): 65–66.

15. *Glory*, TriStar Pictures, 1989.

16. Emily Simon, "Probing an Unlikely Friendship: Stauffer Takes a Long Look at Brief but Significant Douglass, Lincoln Friendship," *Harvard Gazette*, November 13, 2008. Accessed November 20, 2008, https://news.harvard.edu/gazette/story/2008/11/probing-an-unlikely-friendship/.

For the benefit of digital users, indexed terms that span two pages (e.g., 52–53) may, on occasion, appear on only one of those pages.

Boxes are indicated by *b* following the page number